A BOOB'S LIFE

HOW AMERICA'S OBSESSION SHAPED ME . . . AND YOU

LESLIE LEHR

PEGASUS BOOKS

NEW YORK LONDON

For my girls, and yours.

A BOOB'S LIFE

Pegasus Books, Ltd.
148 West 37th Street, 13th Floor
New York, NY 10018

Copyright © 2021 by Leslie Lehr

First Pegasus Books cloth edition March 2021

Interior design by Sheryl P. Kober

This story is based on memory, journals, scrapbooks, and copious amounts of research. Any factual mistakes are mine and I apologize. Several names have been changed for the sake of privacy. Everyone mentioned has my utmost respect and appreciation. Thank you for understanding.

Library of Congress Cataloging-in-Publication Data is available.

ISBN: 978-1-64313-622-6

10 9 8 7 6 5 4 3 2

Printed in the United States of America
Distributed by Simon & Schuster
www.pegasusbooks.com

The body is not a thing, it's a situation.

—SIMONE DE BEAUVOIR

Some people think having large breasts makes a woman stupid. Actually, it's quite the opposite: a woman having large breasts makes a man stupid.

—RITA RUDNER

CONTENTS

One

OBSESSION
2015

My nipples are cross-eyed. I see it clearly in the bathroom mirror the moment I step out of the shower. As steam clouds the view, I wave my towel and pray it was an optical illusion. No, they're definitely pointing in different directions, as if embarrassed to meet my eyes. Or maybe this is payback. The truth is, my breasts have been loathed and loved, suckled and stuffed, radiated and recon-structed. They have doomed one marriage and inspired another. Yet, every step of the way, they've had the finest treatment in America. By now, they should be perfect.

"Hon?" my husband, John, calls from the bedroom. "What's taking so long?"

Since we married a few years ago, both of his parents passed away, and then I got cancer. This is the first home we've bought together, a condo with an ocean view we'll enjoy for a few years as a reward for all we've been through. The ninety-nine-step climb is like a stairway to heaven, but I didn't have to die to get here.

This is our first night to relax and renew our romance. I try. First, I dab perfume behind my ears and unclip my damp chemo curls. Then I take a deep breath and look again. If I raise up my right shoulder and arch my back just so, my breasts are lush and round and almost even. But there's no ignoring the truth. I pull a cotton nightgown over my head as fast as I can. Then I shove my towel so hard into the plastic hamper that the piece of crap falls over.

My husband tears his eyes from the TV as I stomp into the bedroom. "You OK?"

I snatch my phone from the cardboard moving box by the bed. "I have to call my doctor."

"Now?" he asks, over the swell of applause for *The Late Show*. "Are you in pain?"

Yes, I want to say, *psychic pain.* Then I realize the doctor's answering service won't consider that an emergency. When I shake my head, my husband smiles and pats the bed beside him. I surrender the phone and scooch over. He rubs my leg and glances back at the TV, where the host is mid-monologue. I start to relax. Then the host tells a boob joke about J.Lo.

The TV audience roars.

I turn to my husband who, to his credit, is not laughing. "This guy gets paid millions of dollars and that's the best he can do? She's the producer of a successful TV show."

He shrugs. "Comedians have always made boob jokes."

"Exactly. It's not original. Why are they laughing? There's a neon sign that flashes the word 'laugh'?"

"No, they're really laughing. I bet half the people in that audience are women, and they're laughing, too. Boob jokes are funny."

"But why?" I ask. "Every woman in the world has boobs."

"That's why. They're the first female body part a man sees when a woman walks into a room."

The laughter dies down. The comedian is talking, but I don't care. I hate him. "What makes a boob funny?"

"Boobs just sit there, all round and funny looking."

"Dicks just sit there, too, and they're far more funny looking. Why aren't there more dick jokes?"

"Dick jokes are insulting."

"All jokes are insulting. They make fun of something. Isn't that how humor works? Is it how the word sounds? I mean, no one says 'breast jokes.'"

"Breasts are beautiful, everyone knows that. When you call them boobs, it's funny."

"But 'boob' means stupid. How can an organ that turns blood into milk for babies be stupid?"

"Lighten up, hon." He winces as if I've been shouting.

"I just don't understand why people always laugh at boob jokes. They're not funny."

"Why are you being so sensitive?"

I don't answer, on the grounds that it might incriminate me. I remove his hand from my thigh. He raises his eyebrows. I take a deep breath and try to let it go, but I feel like punching somebody, and he's the only one here. So much for romance.

John changes the channel. We see a young woman vacuum-wrapped in a cocktail dress wave at a weather map of Southern California. Her chest sticks out so far, she's in danger of toppling over.

"There's a boob joke for you. Think she's really a meteorologist?"

"That's just for ratings," he says, which proves my point. Or maybe his.

Now I'm sorry I insulted the woman. The tight dress doesn't make her slutty or stupid. That was my interpretation. How can I laugh when the joke is on me?

My husband clicks to a sports channel. Men on TV shout about games with balls. I want to make a crack about that, but he's just being a guy. He can't possibly understand the frustration of a flat-chested teenager or a nursing mother or a deflated divorcée.

"I don't want my breasts to be funny."

He turns, surprised to see me on the verge of tears. "Hon, your breasts are fucking gorgeous."

"You're just being nice. Look." I pull down my shoulder straps.

He smiles at my bare breasts as if this is a reward. Then his gaze rises to my reddened face, and he realizes this is part of the debate, one he can only lose.

I feel bad, so I let him fondle me.

"You aren't naked very often," he says. "I don't notice the details. It's more fun to see them together with your pretty face."

Now he's pandering, so I pull up my straps. He removes his glasses and rubs his weary eyes.

"When did you get so obsessed?"

"Seriously, hon," I say, looking down. "Do you think I should get them fixed?"

He turns off the TV. "Up to you. I like all breasts. They're like pizza. There's no such thing as bad pizza."

"For men, sure. For women, all pizza is bad." *Especially if we want to stay attractive to men like you*, I think, cursing myself for being caught up in this competition.

My husband slips under the covers. I kiss him goodnight and grab my phone. Then I tiptoe out of the bedroom to let him sleep. Though that's a big fat lie. The truth is I don't want him to hear me call my doctor to complain.

I close the door of the room that will be my office and squeeze between moving boxes to my desk. If only it wasn't so late. I scan my contacts to find someone else to call, maybe a woman who could talk me down. I see my mom's number and wonder what she would say. Or my sister. Each of us has two daughters. That's seven sets of breasts between us. Like most women, we rarely talk about them. They wouldn't want to start now, on the phone in the middle of the night. I call my doctor and leave a message.

On my desk are a few framed photos, the first I've unpacked. The top one shows my bare-chested dad lifting me over his head like a human barbell, the next one shows him teaching me to swim. My favorite is a faded picture of my mother, my baby sister, and me, a skinny three-year-old. We wear matching red bikinis by our apartment pool in Arizona. I remember how important it was to keep those teeny strips of red cotton over our nipples. My sister was oblivious that her top was an inch too high. The sight used to make me laugh so hard my stomach would hurt. Hiding nipples was a rule, like brushing your teeth. Mom's red top has far more fabric, but as she leans down to hold our hands in the picture, her cleavage presses into a perfect line. We all look so happy, holding hands and saying "cheese."

I set the picture down and start unpacking a box of books and magazines. It's a great way to stall in case my doctor calls me back. Maybe I am obsessed, but it's not just me. Everyone is obsessed. Or why would boob jokes be so funny every single time?

I fill the small bookstand, then wonder where to put magazines I didn't read before the move. Flipping through them aggravates me more. How can *Vogue* claim breasts are out of style when they're permanently attached to our ribs? *Elle* shows low-cut Oscar gowns that are either empowering or objectifying, depending on your point of view. It reminds me of Twitter, where #FreetheNipple pictures of topless protestors compete with celebrity nip slips. Censorship is even more arbitrary. *The Walking Dead* TV show can slash a breast into a bloody pulp as long as they don't reveal the areola. Even Picasso paintings get blurred on the news. I shove the magazines back in the box.

Maybe my husband is right, and I'm obsessed. But when you've been every size from AA to DDDD, it's hard not to take the jokes personally. And now I'll never find a bra that will fit.

I give the doctor five more minutes and do some research. I open my laptop and Google "breasts." Within half a second, the screen fills with links to breast cancer, breastfeeding, and chicken recipes. Go figure. I type "boobs" in the search bar and get millions of links to porn. That proves something, but I'm not sure what. I close my laptop.

It's hard to believe the bikini photo was taken over fifty years ago. Born in New Jersey, I grew up in Arizona and Ohio before moving to California. As far back as I can remember, everywhere I've lived, breasts have been the Holy Grail, the quest for female perfection. I'm beginning to think breasts are more than a body part. They might be the whole game.

I have to show my husband.

In the bedroom, he's already snoring. The sliding door is open to the balcony, and the ocean air is chilly. I set the picture on the nightstand, get in bed, and spoon his warm body. My bad boob, the one with the extra scar tissue, is pressed against the mattress. It's uncomfortable. I roll to my good side, facing the picture.

Was I envious of my mother? Was that how my obsession started? She's twenty-five in the photo, a young and beautiful graduate student. And stacked, no doubt about it. I didn't inherit her curves, but I wasn't resentful. I was proud, like my dad.

Goose bumps cover my arms. We aren't just posing for the camera. We're smiling at the person behind it: my dad. This is his perspective, the male gaze. How did it become mine?

My stomach clenches, and I'm six years old again. I'm hanging upside down over the diving pool a million miles below. My father's grip is tight around my ankles as he stands on the high dive. *Don't let go.* All I can hear is the buzz of mosquitoes and the beat of my heart. Far below, past my dark hair and my flailing arms, the water glows an eerie blue. The color is clear to the bottom of the pool, where the drain looks like a mouth waiting to suck me up. I hear my father's voice.

"Fingertips first."

Why America Is Obsessed with Breasts

D id you know that humans are the only mammals with permanent breasts? Blame natural selection—men's eyes are drawn to women's breasts within 200 milliseconds.[1] Not only do they signal fertility, but they are the first visual cue of the opposite sex. We are biologically programmed to like breasts, but in America that appreciation has become obsession.

For most of human evolution, breasts were for babies. In the Victorian era, women's clothing featured the curve rising from a corset, then the Gibson Girl expanded the hourglass shape. After women won the vote, flappers bound their breasts in order to seek the same freedoms young men enjoyed. World War II expanded these freedoms into mandates, as women filled in for the men who were overseas. The United States government opened 3,000 subsidized day care centers for mothers in the workforce.

The golden age of pinup girls also began during World War II. Since bomb casings resembled breasts, "bombshell" became the nickname for busty sex symbols like Jean Harlow. Factory workers wore the new style of "bullet bras," said to protect their breasts from machinery; their biggest benefit was to give shape to their overalls. Alberto Vargas's fantasy girl illustrations in *Esquire*, and then later in *Playboy*, were duplicated as nose art[2] on fighter planes to inspire the troops from World War II through the Korean War. Japanese sex workers began injecting their breasts with silicone to please their Western clientele.

As the war ended, Uncle Sam closed the childcare centers and sent mothers home. Single women were encouraged by the new, powerful advertisers to marry early and start families. From 1946 to 1951, the number of TV sets in American homes grew from 6,000 to 12 million.[3] By 1959, a typical ad for a slide projector featured a well-endowed woman with "the world's finest projection equipment."[4] The Golden

Age of TV blessed domesticity with buxom actresses, the ultimate symbol of abundance.

The *concept* of abundance overruled reality. Men designed "training bras" for girls, push-up bras for teens, plus inflatable bras and artificial augmentation for women. *Playboy* ushered in the sexual revolution with "girls next door." And then, during the postwar baby boom, doctors endorsed newfangled infant formula. That made it official: breasts were no longer for babies.

Thanks to a perfect storm of the baby boom, modern medicine, television, Madison Avenue, and *Playboy*, America became obsessed with breasts.

PART ONE

BREAST ENVY:

Girlhood

Two

DADDY'S GIRL
1965

O n a sticky August evening when I was six, my father taught me to dive off the high board at the public pool. Sunburned families from our middle-class suburb gathered on the cement to watch. I wished everyone would stop whispering and go home, but this was before air-conditioning was common in central Ohio. I was the Friday night feature.

"Hurry," Dad said, so I clutched the chrome handrail and started climbing. When both feet were on the fourth step, I turned back to my dad who, at six-foot-four, was now at eye level. He nodded. My skinny chest throbbed with pride. Dad was an All-American Princeton grad who believed I could accomplish anything if I worked hard enough. I had passed the Red Cross swim test in Arizona at three, then moved to Ohio and raced from Polliwog to Shark. Next was Junior Lifeguards, and it took fifty points to pass. After the swimming test and the struggle to lug a brick up from the floor of the diving pool, all that was left was the dive. I was ten points away from being a Junior Lifeguard with my very own whistle. I could do this.

On the fifth fiberglass step, I hesitated. I didn't dare free a hand from the guardrails, but I couldn't resist a glance down. Big mistake. The fractures on the cement deck looked tiny from here, and the people were shrinking, too. A Beatles song crackled from the public address speakers. *Help*, I hummed along, *I need somebody* . . . Tightening the grip of my left hand, I wiped away tears with the right. Since I was already wet, no one would know. My father's faith never wavered. I could feel the heat of his body behind me as he urged me up, rung by rung.

The music ended abruptly with noisy scratches that drifted across the deck from the office. A teenager's voice said, "The pool is now closed."

A gangly lifeguard climbed down from his chair at the edge of the pool and removed the whistle lanyard from around his neck. I stopped and looked behind me, but my father said nothing. The horn of a station wagon blared from the parking lot between the pool and Hastings Junior High.

As the crowd shifted, my mother's yellow minidress flashed like a caution sign next to the empty lifeguard tower. A flip of brown hair drooped to her shoulders as she hugged Tracy, my three-year-old sister, close. They were a team, the girls' team, and my sister didn't have to do this. As the oldest, I was on my dad's team, so I got to play with a miniature lacrosse stick while he coached at Ohio State.

Except now I wanted off the team.

My mom glanced behind her to the approaching boys in red trunks. These weren't the buff Senior Lifeguards—the boys over eighteen were in Vietnam. These were their younger brothers, too small to help her stop my father.

My mother was not a regular housewife. She was a college professor working on her doctorate in child development. That included nutrition and sex education, but it was in the home ec department, so still a "girl thing." Like most men in postwar America, my dad was still the boss. When my mom looked up, she didn't even look at me. Her eyes flashed with fury at my father.

A few steps higher, and I climbed onto the scratchy board on my knees, moving my hands forward inch by inch without letting go of my grip. The faces were smaller now, like tiddlywinks. In the twilight, the water began to glow. Shaking, I looked back as my dad stepped onto the board and towered above me like Tarzan. One dive, and we could all go home.

"Fingertips first," my dad said, prying my hands from the rail.

Slowly, I stepped to the end. The crowd hushed and the world fell away. My toes clung to the end of the board like a bird holding tight to a branch. I straightened my arms and clasped my thumbs together, aiming my pointer fingers down like a gun. Then I tipped slowly forward.

Boom! A bank of floodlights flashed on, breaking the spell. I startled and straightened up.

"Stop!" my mother shouted.

An iron grip clamped each ankle. Then I was upside down, my arms dangling loose above the water.

"Thumbs!" Dad commanded. "One . . ."

I aimed my hands together and missed. Frantic, I choked back my breath, straightened my arms and found them. I interlocked my thumbs.

"Two!"

The water was crystal clear, with a blue tinge below. It was so still I could see the black drain at the bottom. A sense of calm came over me, suspended between heaven and earth. My dad wouldn't hurt me. I could do this.

"Three!" He let go.

Whoosh. My hands cut through the curtain of water. My nose burned, then I remembered to blow. The liquid peeled away like a second skin, cool and quiet, better than air. When my body slowed, I kicked through the bubbles and broke the surface. I clung to the gutter, expecting applause, but the crowd was breaking up.

My mother cornered my father as he climbed down the ladder. She looked like Lois Lane trying to scold Superman. He was all-powerful and she was merely human; her words bounced off his chest. Tracy cried at the commotion. I felt bad for them, but I wished they would be quiet. I was proud to be on my dad's team now, the winning team, boys against girls. Other parents shepherded their kids across the pool deck as if we had cooties.

When my dad caught my eye, he grinned. My lungs inflated with pride. All was right with the world. I slipped behind him, blocked by his body as my mother yelled. I climbed up the ladder like a monkey, as fast as I could. I wanted to do it by myself. And I did.

The next morning, the instructor whistled for us to line up at the high board. It was time. "Last chance. High dive is worth ten points," he announced, as if I didn't know, as if I hadn't slept in my tank suit— or tried to sleep, while hearing my mother scream at my father through the wall between our bedrooms. Yet, I didn't feel the least bit tired. I was ready. Soon, we would have Junior Lifeguard patches and silver whistles of our own.

The pimpled boys raced to the ladder while the girls complained about the cold water. This was the first year we could try out, and it was only because the pool needed so many new lifeguards. I waited politely and watched. After the boys were finished showing off, the girls climbed the ladder and squealed. Some ran straight off the board and some took forever, but they all smacked the water coming down. They didn't know the secret of pointing their fingers. They didn't have a dad like mine to teach them.

"Who's left?" The instructor sat in a folding chair on the deck and checked names off the list on his clipboard.

I raised my hand. My father cheered me on from outside the chain-link fence, where he glistened with suntan oil in his Speedo. I waved to him and took a deep breath. Then I climbed straight up the ladder to the sky. It felt like the sun was shining just for me. I strutted to the end of the diving board and lined my toes over the edge. Then I clasped my thumbs together, aimed my fingertips down, leaned forward . . . and dove.

When I surfaced, the other students surrounded the instructor. My dad was clapping. I smiled and dove back under, wiggling my hips like a mermaid beneath the water until I erupted with a splash by the ladder. After I climbed out, I pressed through the crowd until I was dripping on the instructor's clipboard.

He looked right past me at a long-haired girl in a flower-power bikini running back from the ladies' room by the office. He blew his silver whistle and shouted, "Walk!" All the kids laughed. She knew better. Plus, we were eager to blow our own whistles and say that.

Bikini Girl climbed the ladder and tiptoed to the end. I waited as the instructor watched. She put her arms out and started leaning. One of the boys called out from the edge of the pool. She stood up, stuck out her tongue, and jumped. The boys clapped and leaned away from her splash. She came up giggling and holding on to her top. The instructor wrote something down.

"Did you see me?" I asked him. "Should I do it again?"

"Good job," he said, glancing up. He waited for Bikini Girl to climb out of the pool, then beckoned us all to gather around. I stood at his side as he handed patches out one by one. Long arms reached over me to claim them. When he called my name, he handed me a certificate.

"Where's my patch?" I asked, dripping on the onion skin paper.

He congratulated the last girl, the one in the bikini who went after me.

"She didn't even dive," I said, but he didn't hear me.

"I didn't want to lose my top, duh," she said to me. She grabbed her patch and crossed her arms over her chest. Her friends giggled.

"You're supposed to wear a tank suit," I said.

"You're supposed to be twelve."

"What's the difference?" I mumbled, scanning the empty fence for my dad.

When Bikini Girl turned to join her friends, her chest smashed me in the face. There was no ignoring the small mounds, hard like Silly Putty, trapped by the flower-print triangles. When she tugged at the fabric tented over the points of her nipples, I wasn't the only one who noticed. I looked back at the instructor, and he quickly looked away. When I looked down, all I could see was my belly button. *That* was the difference.

"You still get the points," the instructor said, as he stood to leave.

I looked at my soggy certificate, then at Bikini Girl, with her nipples sticking straight out. I wasn't stupid. I had the wrong kind of points.

My dad was entering the gate now, and I was afraid to tell him. My eyes burned from the chlorine, my ears ached from the water pressure, and I couldn't find my towel. When he waved at me, I shook my head. He spoke with the lifeguard by the office as I bit my nails and shivered. The big kids were snapping their towels at each other and laughing. My dad would fix this, I told myself, as I sat on edge of the empty diving pool. I kicked the water and watched the waves ripple away. When his reflection loomed, I hopped up and handed him the sodden certificate.

He hugged me against his hard body. "Guess what? You can join the swim team."

I burst into tears. Where was my silver whistle? I had done everything I was supposed to: I swam twenty laps, picked up a ten-pound brick from the bottom of the pool, and dove off the high board. My dad told me that hard work paid off, and I believed him. But he was wrong.

All these years later, my father insists that the end justifies the means, so he was right to drop me off the end of the board. I can't argue. Part of me agrees. After that day, I dove every chance I could. Dad treated me with respect, as if there was no difference between a boy and a girl.

But I would never embody his American dream. No matter how hard I tried, I was destined to disappoint him. And myself. In the end, it was Bikini Girl who truly taught me that the end justifies the means. The means were breasts.

I vowed to get them.

Bra Basics

....

1907 *Vogue* first uses the word "brassiere."

1910 Mary Phelps Jacobs creates a handkerchief bra to replace her corset for a debutante ball.

1911 "Brassiere" is added to the Oxford English Dictionary.

1914 The modern bra is patented by Mary Phelps Jacobs.

1915 Warner Brothers Corset Company pays Jacobs $1,500 for the patent; ultimately earns $12,000,000.

1917 Corset manufacturing is prohibited by the US War Industries Board to save metal for ships.

1920s Bandeau bras flatten chests for the flapper style inspired by boys, who enjoy more freedom.

1922 Full-figured, uplift, and nursing bras are made by Maiden Form (soon to be Maidenform).

1928 500,000 Maidenform bras are sold in department stores.

1932 A, B, C, D cup measurement system is created.

1940s Torpedo and bullet bras are marketed for factory wear and safety.

1947 Padded and push-up bras are created by Frederick Mellinger, founder of Frederick's of Hollywood.

1950s Preteen training bras appear and become standard.

1968 Bras are thrown in trash cans when 400 women protest at the Miss America Pageant.

1977 The "Jockbra" is created from jockstraps by Lisa Lindahl, Polly Smith, and Hinda Miller.

1987	TV commercials for bras show real women wearing them.
1994	The Wonderbra takes the US by storm and increases bra sales by 43%.
2009	Memory foam bras are developed.
2011	95% of women in Western countries wear bras.
2016	New bra companies offer inclusivity of skin tones and body shapes.
2020	Unstructured bras gain popularity at home, shapewear is worn in public, and corsets are elevated to high fashion.

Bra Facts

1. Eighty percent of women do not know their true bra size.
2. The average size has grown from 34B to 36DD over the last fifty years.
3. 4,000,000 new bras are produced each day.
4. The average American woman owns eight bras.
5. There are approximately twenty-three styles of bras; T-shirt bras are the most popular.
6. Proper care is to alternate bras, and hand wash every 4–5 wears.
7. A favorite bra should last 6–8 months.
8. Funeral homes put bras on dead women.

Three

LIVE NUDE WOMEN
1966

The first time I saw a woman's naked breasts, they were in a Polaroid picture of my mother. At age seven, I'd seen plenty of young girls in the swim team locker room. But the older girls, the ones with boobs, showered in their swimsuits before wrapping themselves in towels that magically stayed up. And on television, Playtex Cross Your Heart bras were modeled on plastic torsos.

I knew my mother had breasts. But I had never thought of them in a sexual way. Then one steamy afternoon, I heard the lilting chimes of Scott Joplin's "Ragtime" and everything changed.

I dropped my *Betty & Veronica* comic book on my pink poodle bedspread and kneeled to look out the window. The boxy white ice cream truck was chugging up the street of our new subdivision. After spending twelve cents on cartoons showing two buxom girls battling over a boy, I didn't have enough change for a Popsicle. It was hot, and I was desperate. I ran next door to my parents' room and found the door ajar.

"Mom?" She wasn't there, but I spied the bamboo handle of her purse on the dresser across the room. I tiptoed across the gold shag carpet to scavenge for pennies. When I reached for the purse, my elbow knocked the pile of books and magazines beside it and two *TV Guides* thudded to the floor. I held my breath and glanced at the open door, but no one appeared. I scooped up the small *TV Guides*, careful to not rip the covers with my mom's name printed on them. The article she wrote—something about the strong influence of color TV on kids—paid for our bedspreads from the *Sears Wish Book*. I laid the magazines carefully back on top of her textbooks and plunged my hand into the depths of her purse. Aside from a tube of poppy pink lipstick and a plastic teasing comb, there was nothing loose. As a last resort, I scavenged through the top drawer of her dresser, where I'd found pennies before. Then I reached beneath the pile of silky panties and pulled out a color Polaroid.

My mother was topless. Her breasts were right there, framed by the stiff white border in my hand. I could barely breathe, let alone look below her chin. The face was familiar, with her full pink lips, and the little bow clipping her dark hair back at the temple. This was the smile I waited for each night as I stood by the living room window and watched car headlights dip down the hill on McCoy Road in the distance. But the smile didn't match the pale expanse of skin below. Her breasts were long and full, like capital Us. The sight of my mother's dark nipples made my stomach clench.

I shoved the photograph back in her drawer beneath the panties. Then my fingertips felt the serrated edge of another photo . . . and I couldn't resist snatching it up.

In this one, she wore a white bikini with green trim—I'd never seen anything like it—and sucked in her tummy like a movie star. She leaned on one elbow as she lay on her side, her body swooping down like a roller coaster to her waist before the steep climb back up to her bikini-clad hip. I recognized the wooden legs of our black couch behind her and realized she was posing on the red shag carpet of our living room downstairs.

Shaken, I sat down on the bed. Then I saw I was crushing the hem of a dress laid out for that night's cocktail party, so I jumped up and smoothed it out. The white lace shift would make Mom look like Mary Ann from *Gilligan's Island*, but in the Polaroid, she looked like Ginger.

I shoved the picture back beneath her panties. I had never noticed my mother's body before. Already, she was different from the other moms because she worked, and she was pretty, with her dark hair in a flip like Marlo Thomas in *That Girl*. But was she a "sexpot"? The word came unbidden and scared me. I knew it was bad. But then I thought, *Wow*.

This was the first time I recognized the dichotomy of women, Madonna versus whore, Jackie versus Marilyn. Even the *Archie Comics* cartoonist, Dan DeCarlo,[1] admitted that Betty and Veronica were two sides of the same girl. What I didn't recognize was how this dichotomy was so problematic.

At seven, I was already swept into the tendency to divide women into two parts. It's only now, in looking back at this "opposites" way of thinking, that I realize so much of how women live, how we are treated, and how we are held back comes from this Freudian concept. When most people hear Madonna versus whore, their eyes glaze over. They blow it off as old news. I was the same way, until I explored why mismatched boobs bothered me so much. The problem is deeper than we think, because it starts so early. The human mind naturally divides things into two parts as "either, or," so we tend to categorize everything this way. It's especially easy to do this with women, because the female body is so susceptible to division: the sacred and the profane. Labeling women with two extremes automatically reduces us by removing our complexity. Our entire sex is robbed of individuality. This becomes a curse in the form of a double bind: we are either too good or too bad, damned if we do and damned if we don't.

Breasts define the dichotomy. They exist in the Madonna role to nurture the next generation and in the whore role as a source of sexual pleasure. And yet without that sexual attraction for men, there would be no next generation to nurture. Only now, as I look back fifty years later, can I understand how deep and powerful this contradiction is to our way of thinking about women. At seven, I could only understand that breasts were special, but must be covered. They were good *and* bad. That was the only way to explain why my mother posed for this topless picture . . . and then hid it.

I sifted through her girdles, but I couldn't find that white bikini. Instead, I pulled out a stiff bra and pulled a strap up each arm, then over the shoulders of my striped Danskin top. In the mirror above the dresser, it looked like the cups stood out from my chest for miles. I tried to imagine what it would feel like to fill them.

"Leslie?"

My father's voice boomed through the house as if he could read my thoughts. I shed the brassiere, shoved it in the drawer, and hurried out. Dad had put a deadbolt on their bedroom door for a reason. I understood sex was the reason, but even now, I was trespassing. I ran down the stairs and nearly tripped in my haste to find him. The joke was, when he told my sister and me to jump, we were supposed to ask, "How high?" Sometimes, he snapped his fingers to make us practice. On the count of three, Tracy and I would jump. We only jumped a few inches, and we always did it laughing, but it wasn't really a joke.

In the living room, I heard my name again, so I hurried through the open back door to the screened-in porch. The spicy-orange scent of Bain de Soleil tickled my nose. I ran outside and climbed up the rickety stairs to the wooden sundeck on the porch roof. My parents' bodies glistened with a copper sheen against royal blue blow-up rafts. Foil sun visors shielded their faces.

My mom heard me and pulled up the straps of her bikini, the white one with green trim. My stomach still felt queasy. I knew what she was hiding. My dad's bronzed body glistened in his red Speedo, but that was a normal sight. He spent countless hours with me in the swimming pool and on the grass, lifting me over his head like a barbell. His body meant nothing to me. My mother's body was different. Someday it might be mine.

"Dad?"

"Put the record back on, will you?" my dad asked, squinting at me. "And get the mail."

I nodded and headed down the stairs. He called after me.

"Want to go to the caverns with my geology class tomorrow?"

Mom was already holding her visor back up around her face, so it must have been OK with her. I nodded. I loved being a VIP on the bus with the big kids. Plus, I was working on my rock collection.

Inside, I ran past the black couch to the phonograph side of the entertainment console so fast that I kicked over the albums leaning against it. I put them back carefully to keep the Herb Alpert album with the lady sitting in a pile of whipped cream in front. The name of the album, *Whipped Cream & Other Delights*, simply meant to child-me that she got all the ice cream she wanted. I heard my name again, so I opened the phonograph lid and set the needle down on the black disc. Once the brassy horns played the familiar *Dating Game* theme song, I headed for the front door.

When I went out front to get the mail, my parents' matching Oldsmobiles blocked my view to the street. Both had scarlet and gray Ohio State parking stickers, but Mom's car was blue with a *War is Not Safe for Children and Other Living Things* bumper sticker, while Dad's was silver with a *Save Water, Shower with a Friend* bumper sticker. Mom shook her head at this, but he was a professor of hydrology and visited my second grade class with comic books that showed how much water was wasted by leaky faucets, so it made sense. Mom was getting her PhD now, too. My dad couldn't wait for people to call on the phone for Dr. Lehr so he could ask, "Which one?" They were the youngest, smartest, best-looking parents on the street. All the other moms stayed home and ironed with curlers in their hair. I knew, because when it rained, I knocked on their doors for a ride to school.

I ran across the weedy grass to the curb, where young saplings were wired to sticks like a row of scarecrows. Waves of heat blurred the black pavement on the street, but one thing was clear: the ice cream truck was long gone. I wiped my bangs off my sticky forehead, then opened the mailbox. A thick magazine wrapped in brown paper was jammed inside. I wrestled it out and took it inside to the den.

Tracy's half-naked Barbie was on the rug, so I set the mail on the desk and plucked Barbie up to put her away before my father came in. No matter what my sister did, I would get blamed for it. That was my job as Big Sister.

Barbie was dressed like a singer with long gloves and a strapless black dress. I tugged her gown up over her pointy chest, but the sparkly fabric snapped back. Barbie was born the same year as me, but I didn't know then that she was such a close copy of a German sex toy that the company sued Mattel—and won a settlement. I also didn't know that real women didn't come in these proportions.

When I gave up trying to keep her chest covered, I remembered the magazine in the mail. Nobody was fooled by that brown paper wrapper. *Playboy* was the only magazine that had that. My dad collected them in leather binders on the top shelf above where I was standing in the den. I dropped Barbie. If my parents had time to listen to the record again, I had time to check out the naked pictures. As the kid of two college professors, I knew the importance of research.

I closed the door of the den a few inches, then pulled on the chain to light the lamp hanging over the desk. I didn't dare disturb the wrapper on the plump new issue, so I turned to the wood plank bookshelves

Dad had built against the wall. My Nancy Drew collection shared the bottom shelf with *National Geographic*. The latter had lots of topless women, but that was for science. Most of the native women in those pages were old, with long tubular breasts, but the November issue showed teenagers posed for the camera. I learned later that the editors had darkened the girls' skin to look more like natives, whose nudity was considered acceptable. There were a few black Playboy Playmates—the publisher claimed to be advanced in his exploitation, I mean, celebration of women—but most were white. We took the racism of sexuality for granted so much that years later, comedian Richard Pryor would call *National Geographic* the black man's *Playboy*.[2]

To me, the distinction was confusing on a different level: the native women were caught unaware, but the American women chose to take their clothes off. Breasts were what made *Playboy* special. And the magazine was for men—it said so right on the cover. It wasn't difficult to make the leap of logic: men liked breasts. And breasts needed to be hidden.

I needed to reach the row of leather-bound albums my dad kept on top. I surveyed the shelf below, with five feet of royal-blue-bound Harvard classics. My dad said this was the best collection of stories and articles ever written, by great men in every field of study. I considered using them as a step stool, but the gilded crests on the spines warned me away. The next shelf bowed with the weight of the white *World Book Encyclopedia* set I'd gotten for Christmas. When I was slow to say thank you, my dad insisted that I'd be grateful one day. I pulled out volumes A through D, stacked them on the chair, and stepped up, just tall enough to reach the top shelf. Dad was right: I was already grateful.

When I tugged out the closest binder, it fell to the floor with a thud cushioned by the shag rug. I cocked my head toward the door but didn't hear any footsteps over the music. The binder had fallen open to a splayed centerfold, Miss August. There was nothing revealed below the waist at that time; it was all about breasts. But that was enough for me. I sank to my knees to look. Too embarrassed to unfold Miss August all the way, I read the handwritten notes about her favorite movie. When I finally turned to the front cover, she had clothes on. Miss August had my brown eyes and brown bangs under a white navy cap like my dad's. That could be me. As soon as my dad learned to trim my bangs straight.

I sat in a chair, lugged the album to my lap, and opened the issue again. On the next page was a Columbia Record Club advertisement for the Beatles. Since I had a few of their 45s, plus bubble bath in the shape of Ringo, I felt like a proud member of that club. Next was a full-page ad showing a handsome man above the words, "What Sort of Man Reads *Playboy*?" I raised my hand as if I were in school—the answer was obvious. My dad was that "sort of man."

The leather-bound album on the far left of that lauded shelf was embossed with "1953." My dad had started collecting with the very first issue, displaying Marilyn Monroe on the cover, during his freshman year at Princeton. Since 50 percent of college-educated men at the time reported reading *Playboy*, that "sort of man" was respectable, even admired. The August issue I perused that afternoon in 1966 was one of five million in circulation.

Two years after *Playboy* premiered, the University Library at my father's alma mater subscribed and put one copy in general circulation[3] for borrowing. There was no *Penthouse*, *Oui*, or *Hustler*, let alone Internet porn or cell phone sexting—and women only visited Princeton on weekends. The library provided this centerfold solution for sex-starved young Tigers until 1974.

Playboy publisher Hugh Hefner's parents were direct descendants of the English Puritan Separatists from the *Mayflower*, and never kissed or hugged him at home.[4] When he found out that his fiancé had slept with another man, he married her, but took revenge by becoming the poster child for a new bachelor lifestyle. William H. Masters and

Virginia E. Johnson's pioneering research on sexual response opened the door, but Hefner brought sexual desire into the living room.

Playboy skirted the pornographic style of Bob Guccione's new *Penthouse* magazine by shunning the sexy black costumes of the typical seductress. Hefner claimed the Playmate of the Month was "a young healthy, simple girl—the girl next door . . . naked, well-washed with soap and water, and she is happy."[5] This was sexualized, nonthreatening girlishness, like putting a Shirley Temple face on a Jayne Mansfield body.[6] *Playboy* gained intellectual ground by copying *Esquire*'s lead, with interviews featuring cultural icons ranging from Martin Luther King Jr. to John Lennon to President Jimmy Carter.

Indeed, that afternoon, I flipped through so many pages of printed interviews, I got a paper cut. I sucked on my finger to avoid bleeding on the glossy pages and began to believe what my mom said about my dad collecting *Playboy*s. He saved them for the articles.

A collage called "The Bunnies of Dixie" caught my eye. These girls wore bunny ear headbands resembling the furry pets in the cages of my second-grade classroom. Their candy-colored costumes looked as stiff as the papier-mâché we made in arts and crafts. Three years earlier, an undercover Bunny named Gloria Steinem had written a controversial exposé in *Show Magazine,* but like most households, mine didn't subscribe to that magazine, so I didn't have that in mind. Mostly, as I sat cross-legged in the den, I suspected my mother would look beautiful in a Bunny costume.

The next pictorial featured a young actress named Jane Fonda. I recognized her from the cover of a movie magazine at the drugstore on a rack by the comic books. Fonda was dressed like a cowboy to promote a Western she was in called *Cat Ballou.* Her dad was Henry Fonda, one of my parents' favorite actors and already a screen legend, named "Father of the Year" by the American Father's Day Council. Fonda wasn't a poor model taking her clothes off for money. And she didn't "do *Playboy*" as a career move. But over the next few decades, an increasing number of American women would. At seven, I was already taking this for granted. *You see one boob, you've seen them all*, I thought. Then I noticed the cartoons.

Time to check the hallway again. If anyone saw me, I'd get a spanking for sure. The coast was clear and music was playing, so I figured I was safe for a few more minutes. The first cartoon was a drawing of an old lady, like Granny from *The Beverly Hillbillies*, but naked with bowling pin boobs. She was chasing a bunch of businessmen. It was easy to see why they ran away in such a rush that their ties went askew. Those boobs were ugly. Then I flipped to the end of the magazine and hit the jackpot: a color cartoon that ran for pages. Surely it had been put there for kids. My mother's *McCall's Magazine* did the same thing with a paper doll called Betsy. Every month I cut out the new clothes they printed to cover her undershirt. *McCall's* was written and published by men also, but the glossy pictures showed the happy housewives fully dressed.

Little Annie Fanny was a blond with blue eyes. She had the same curvy figure as Betty and Veronica, with blouses so tight that a taut line stretched across the front. When her buttons burst and her clothes fell off, the men chased her. Annie ran, clutching whatever bit of clothing she could, until she could hide behind a desk. She ran for so many cartoon panels that I could study her closely. And she had the roundest, puffiest breasts I had ever seen.

I read cartoon after cartoon, from one issue to the next, pausing only when I saw a Playmate of the Month with pigtails or another who loved Popsicles. In the back of each issue, whether Little Annie Fanny was hiding under a desk or beneath the robe of a Klu Klux Klan convention-goer, the story was always the same. Annie was never kissing or doing anything dirty. No, she was always quiet and polite. Every time her clothes fell off, her eyes were wide with surprise. Soon, I wasn't surprised at all. But I was just as thrilled as the men chasing her.

Choosing whom to root for gave me a stomachache. I didn't know this was the definition of a double bind, but I understood that my choice felt wrong either way. If I pretended to be Annie, I was afraid of the men chasing me, because I wanted to keep my clothes on. And yet it did make me feel good that I was pretty enough to be chased. If I pretended to be a man, it was fun to chase Annie and see all her prettiness. Yet if I had to chase her to do it, wasn't I bad?

A door slammed from somewhere in the house. The music stopped. I closed the binder and climbed up on the chair. No way could I reach up high enough to slide it back in the empty slot. So, I set it back on the floor, grabbed the closest volume of the *Harvard Classics*, and started reading.

"Leslie?" my dad's voice boomed.

"In the den!"

Moments later, my father peeked in holding Barbie by her impossibly arched feet. Bad enough I forgot to put her away, but then he spied the brown leather binder on the floor. My tush clenched in anticipation of his handprint. It would be days until I could sit comfortably again.

"What are you doing?"

"Reading about Benjamin Franklin." I pointed at the page to prove it.

My father tossed the half-naked Barbie in my lap. "It's healthy to have an interest in the human body," he said.

"I just like the cartoons," I replied, shrugging.

When he scooped the binder up with one hand, I couldn't meet his eyes. I stared at his knees for a moment, then looked up to watch him push the binders into a perfect line. He wasn't hiding them, he was protecting them. I collected rocks; he collected pictures of breasts.

He pointed at the Barbie, so I scurried to the basement to put her away. I tried to stretch her gown over her chest, but it was no use. No matter how hard I tugged, the fabric sprang back to her waist. I finally gave up and put her in the toy box. She was just a doll. She didn't matter.

Later, Tracy told me her friends knew about the *Playboy*s, too. They found them while exploring the crawl space by the basement playroom. Soon after, Dad built the shelves and moved the magazines to the den. My sister's friends were impressed. Their moms were housewives and their dads hid *Playboy* in the garage. All the dads liked seeing topless women, but ours was the only one who acted like it was normal. Those kids figured that our mother allowed it because she was more liberated. The opposite seemed more likely. She lacked the power to say no.

Sometimes my mother read the magazines; sometimes she ripped them up. But she spent most of her time studying for the three-hour interview for her doctorate. There was only one question that took her by surprise: What would she put in a time capsule to represent the period? At the time, she felt that this question from a sociology advisor had nothing to do with child development. Yet it did. The correct answer was *Playboy*.

• • •

Fifty years later, in 2017, I met a female *Playboy* executive at a luncheon, and we bonded over our mutual love of Little Annie Fanny. When I asked if she ever felt she was helping to spread a message of misogyny, the executive was prepared. She said that people were going to read whatever they wanted, so who was she to judge? She enjoyed the business of expanding the brand that had become the third most recognizable logo in the world, after Pepsi and Coke. Other countries compared the Bunny to Hello Kitty. As naked breasts became ubiquitous, magazine sales suffered. The subscription video channel paid the bills. Yet my friend insisted that the journalism was still so good, she was proud to read the magazine in public. Then I learned she was a mother.

"When your daughter is twelve," I asked, "will you still read *Playboy* in front of her?"

There was a long pause before she cleared her throat.

"I won't be working there forever," she said.

Oh, the double bind. She encouraged me to watch Hefner's new Amazon documentary to understand the way he helped women. Hefner produced the footage, so I knew it would be slanted, but in the name of fairness, I agreed. My husband offered to watch it with me. Because, boobs.

During the first few episodes of the documentary, it did seem that Hef helped women climb out of the kitchen of the repressed fifties. A few episodes later, it was clear that he simply ushered them into the bedroom for sexual liberation. As much as the publisher claimed to respect women, his executive secretary, Bobbie Arnstein, was neither paid nor promoted like the men who worked for him. Hef's version of equality extended to his young girlfriends. He could sleep around, but they had to be monogamous. My husband and I watched, incredulous, as the actor playing Hef assured the viewer that Playmates were well cared for. They were strictly forbidden to date customers, except for celebrities. When archival footage showed Bunnies hopping up the stairs into his lair, Hef bragged about the benefits of being a VIP.

"He's a pimp," my husband said.

I was so grateful that he had said more than I dared, that he had justified my discomfort, that I wanted to kiss him. So I did.

After that day when I was seven years old and I found my mother's sexy pinup photo, I never opened her drawers again. But I snuck in the den every chance I got to learn more about the human body. When I heard footsteps approaching, I dropped the magazine and picked up a volume of the *Harvard Classics*. I read *World Book Encyclopedia* from A to Z. Soon I was getting gold stars for spelling and speeding through the rainbow of reading level cards. My mother despaired when I spent my next birthday party in my room with *Eloise* while my guests played Pin the Tail on the Donkey. But I owe my love of reading to Little Annie Fanny.

Losing her was sad, but inevitable. When my dad moved out to enjoy the bachelor life, he took the *Playboy*s with him.

American Women in Playboy

1950s
Tina Louise
Jayne Mansfield
Marilyn Monroe
Kim Novak
Bettie Page

1960s
Jane Fonda
Carol Lynley
Julie Newmar
Elke Sommer
Stella Stevens*
Susan Strasberg
Sharon Tate
Elizabeth Taylor
Mamie Van Doren*

1970s
Barbara Bach*
Jane Birkin
Bebe Buell*
Colleen Camp
Barbara Carrera*
Linda Evans
Farrah Fawcett*
Melanie Griffith
Barbara Hershey
Lainie Kazan
Margot Kidder

Pamela Sue Martin*
Dolly Parton* ◊
Valerie Perrine*
Paula Prentiss
Victoria Principal
Jane Seymour
Dorothy Stratten*
Barbra Streisand* ◊
Raquel Welch*

1980s
Maud Adams
Pamela Anderson*
Kim Basinger*
Christie Brinkley* ◊
Anne Carlisle
Rae Dawn Chong
Joan Collins*
Cindy Crawford*
Bo Derek*
Janice Dickinson
Sally Field* ◊
Jerry Hall
Goldie Hawn* ◊
Mariel Hemingway*
La Toya Jackson*
Grace Jones
Nastassja Kinski*
Madonna*
Donna Mills*

Dana Plato
Tanya Roberts*
Brooke Shields* ◊
Vanity*
Vanna White*

1990s
Paula Barbieri
Drew Barrymore*
Sandra Bernhard*
Jeanie Buss
Naomi Campbell*
Patti Davis*
Shannen Doherty*
Carmen Electra*
Sherilyn Fenn*
Robin Givens*
Margaux Hemingway*
Sally Kirkland
Elle Macpherson*
Jenny McCarthy*
Jaime Pressly*
Lisa Rinna*
Mimi Rogers*
Claudia Schiffer* ◊
Stephanie Seymour
Nancy Sinatra*
Anna Nicole Smith*
Lisa Marie (Smith)
Sharon Stone*

Charlize Theron*
Uma Thurman
Kelly Wearstler
Tahnee Welch*

2000s
Amanda Beard*
Garcelle Beauvais*
Shari Belafonte*
Brooke Burke*
Tia Carrere*
Anna Faris*
Debbie Gibson*

Chelsea Handler* ◊
Daryl Hannah*
Rachel Hunter*
Kim Kardashian*
Holly Madison*
Heidi Montag*
Olivia Munn* ◊
Teri Polo*
Tara Reid*
Denise Richards*
Kristy Swanson*
Tiffany*

2010s
Dree Hemingway
Lindsay Lohan*
Lizzy Jagger*
Kylie Jenner*
Scarlett Johansson
Taryn Manning*
Kate Moss*

* Cover model
◊ Did not bare breasts

Four

HISTORY ACCORDING
TO BREASTS
1967–1970

The problem with history books is that they're mostly written by men. The turmoil of Vietnam, the moon landing, and Woodstock are recorded as a neat timeline of events. For me, raised in the Midwest at the end of the baby boom, the late sixties were chaos. They were formative years, a puberty that shaped sexual identity not just for me, but for the nation. Manifest Destiny, the very notion of progress that emboldened America to expand and conquer, was under attack. Yet one belief still brought us together: bigger was better. It applied to everything. How America viewed breasts defined life for generations of women.

1967

During "the Summer of Love,"[1] 100,000 young people converged in San Francisco and defined a counterculture of peace, love, and psychedelics.

My mom was there, too, but not in bell-bottoms. A newly minted PhD, she represented Ohio State University at the National Council of Family Relations. At eight, I was home playing the bride in a mock wedding ceremony in our driveway. A girl stood in for the boy I adored while he and his friends circled the block on their Stingray bikes. As they pedaled past, I could hear them taunt, "First comes love, then comes marriage, then comes baby in the baby carriage." That seemed like the natural order of events.

A week later, my mom returned from the conference in San Francisco. In Haight-Ashbury, she saw braless, pregnant women working in stores while their bearded boyfriends got high on street corners. When she described this, I didn't understand the connection. A few years later, I dressed up as a pregnant hippie for Halloween. I wore beads and carried a protest sign.

When the summer ended, the September broadcast of the Miss America Pageant was a welcome treat. This was the only show President Richard Nixon let his daughters stay up to watch. That's not why we watched every year. Our mom was a beauty, too, voted Queen Esther, Jewish royalty, at the YMCA when she was in high school. Plus, the previous Miss Ohio lived right across the river and had brought her high school band to play in Atlantic City. She'd won the talent competition singing "This Is My Country," in a red, white, and blue gown. This year, one of Mom's students was the state runner-up. Also, for the first time, Miss America had joined Bob Hope on a USO tour to visit the troops in Vietnam.

We knew all about the war; we took it for granted, like the flowered wallpaper in our kitchen. At dinner, my sister and I drowned liver in ketchup and hid boiled peas under mounds of mashed potatoes to the rat-a-tat-tat of artillery on TV. After Walter Cronkite told my parents the daily body count and closed with "that's the way it is," it was time to clear the table. Watching Miss America be crowned was our patriotic duty.

Minutes before Bert Parks introduced all the contestants, we took turns shaking the wire handle of a Jiffy Pop pan directly over the stove until it exploded into a silver blimp. Then we sat with the kitty on the couch and ate popcorn right out of the package. We thought the judges were nuts to not vote for Miss Ohio. But then Miss Kansas, who would ultimately be crowned the winner, sang "Born Free." I knew the song, so I stood and sang along. That's when I realized I, too, could be Miss America. There was only one problem: the swimsuit competition. I didn't look anything like the curvy contestants when I strutted across the room in my one piece. I wanted to flip a switch and fill it.

Just as I saw the possibilities of breasts, however, they were being defined in a way that trickled down without anyone noticing. With only three TV channels, everyone flocked to the movies. *The Graduate*, released in December, was called "the funniest American comedy of the year."[2] But not for women. This contemporary drama, which ignored the counterculture completely by focusing on a dorky college graduate, made women squirm. Anne Bancroft played the evil seductress with one of the earliest flashes of bare breasts in American cinema. When Dustin Hoffman scared off young Katherine Ross's character by taking her to a strip club, the audience witnessed a jarring close-up of tassel-twirling breasts. My mother identified with Ross and felt just as humiliated. During that work trip to San Francisco, my dad had taken her to a nightclub to see Carol Doda, the first topless dancer.

The Graduate was nominated for six Academy Awards and added to the National Film Registry for being "culturally, historically, or aesthetically significant." Mike Nichols won an Oscar for a film so prescient it defined breasts as a weapon.

1968

I was throwing out my school valentines when "Uncle" Walter Cronkite made a speech against the war. The Tit Offensive, or what sounded like that, was taking forever, with over half-a-million boys fighting overseas. Like many families, we were still listening to the gunfire and running body count during dinner every night.

We had just bought food coloring to dye eggs for our Easter baskets when Martin Luther King Jr. got shot. We heard "I have a dream" over and over on TV. The next day was Friday, and Lillian, our African American housekeeper, was waiting for us after school in her gold sedan. We usually walked the mile home, so it was a surprise to see her there, all dressed up in a black hat with netting draped over her eyes. A large, imperious woman, she told us to get in and didn't say another word as she drove along the Scioto River. We bounced around the back seat past the tall buildings of downtown Columbus. After what seemed like forever, she drove into a neighborhood of checkerboard streets lined with small square houses. She parked behind a line of other cars at the corner by a stucco house. After we climbed out of the car, she told us to mind our manners and wait outside, then she hurried toward the house. The door opened like magic and swallowed her up. We could see the shape of other grownups at the party through the window.

Outside, the air was still, like a ghost town. A handful of dark-skinned girls playing jump rope down the street looked over, then ignored us. My sister and I loved jump rope, but we weren't about to invite ourselves to play. Our pale skin marked us as outsiders, and we knew it. Our housekeeper's daughter was a jazz singer who visited our house when she was in Columbus. We had never been to this side of town, though, so we weren't sure what to do. We sat on the curb, watching ants climb over our Keds. We tried not to look over at the other girls.

After a while, I stood to stretch my legs. The oldest jump-rope girl, who was maybe twelve, saw me and strolled over. I sat back down. As she towered over us, I could see her bra through her cotton blouse. It was bright white, stretching across her chest in high contrast to her dark skin. This was startling. It was against the rules to show your underwear in public. Especially a bra. Of course, I didn't wear a bra yet, but I had seen girls wearing training bras in the locker room. I never imagined seeing one through a girl's shirt in broad daylight. Did she know we could all see it? I tried to ignore it as she scrutinized us.

She asked if I knew any jump rope games. Turns out we both knew Not Last Night, a double-jump counting game. She invited us to play. She really wanted twirlers, but Tracy was too little, so we got to take a turn jumping. The tall girl went first, jumping in as the rest of us chanted, *not last night but the night before, twenty-one robbers came a knocking at the door. As I ran out, they ran in . . .*

The sun began to set, and the windows of the house lit up like pats of butter. People streamed out, hugging each other and wiping tears with handkerchiefs. It was time to say goodbye to our jump rope friends. In the twilight, the girl's shirt turned opaque—I couldn't see the white bra through her shirt anymore. I was glad. I wondered if she felt better, too, but I was afraid to ask.

Senator Robert Kennedy, the beloved little brother of JFK, made a big speech after Reverend King's assassination. Two months later, he got shot, too. The bad news ricocheted past Nixon's nomination, the Yippies, and then the police beating people with clubs at the Democratic convention. I focused on hiding peas in my mashed potatoes until September, when it was time to escape politics once again with our favorite patriotic event: the Miss America Pageant.

My mom, my sister (now a first grader), and I settled in to watch with a bowl of Jiffy Pop. The new Miss Ohio was named Leslynn, a combination of my first name and my sister's middle name, Lynn. That was thrilling, as if she truly represented us. We were sad when she didn't make it to the top ten, but Miss Indiana did, and on the map that was close enough. My favorite part, as usual, was the talent competition. I took gymnastics and that year, Miss Illinois performed on the trampoline. When she won Miss America, I was as proud as if I'd jumped on that trampoline myself. When Bert Parks sang, "Here She Comes, Miss America," I felt closer than ever to winning. As last year's Miss America, the one who sang "Born Free," began her tearful farewell, there was shouting from the TV. The cameras didn't budge, but you could tell from Bert's frown that something was wrong.

On Fridays, we had a current events quiz at school, so I always read the newspaper. An article about the pageant described the protest outside on the Atlantic City Boardwalk. The first stories, from male reporters, described them as bra-burning girls who weren't pretty enough to compete. There was a photo of women in sloppy T-shirts and patched jeans carrying hand-lettered signs. The noise we'd heard during the pageant was a group of women chanting as they unfurled a banner that read "Women's Liberation." This was the first time in history those two words had been put together to define a movement. It reminded me of *Mary Poppins*, when the magical nanny cared for the children while their mother was out getting the vote for women. I didn't realize then that the mother was played as a joke, that she was a bad mom. But I knew every word to "Sister Suffragette."[3]

As a skinny nine-year-old, I was learning what it would take to truly be a girl. Boobs were obvious, but there was something more. I couldn't put it in words, but I could see that the beauty queens wore swimsuits and high heels while everyone else—the host and the judges and the entire audience—was fully dressed. Oh, I agreed with the protesters; I wanted to be equal. I thought I was equal already. I saw that bras had meaning beyond the physical. But I had to wear a bra before I could burn it.

Later, I learned a group called the New York Radical Women had gathered nearly four hundred women to protest that day. Their mission statement included complaints that the USO tour used beauty queens as "military death mascots"[4] and that the pageant was a "mindless boob-girlie symbol."[5] They felt that the patriarchy controlling the war effort also controlled women—and breasts were the most obvious symbol. Protest signs ranged from "Welcome to the Cattle Auction" to "Girls Crowned—Boys Killed."[6] An assortment of bras, girdles, and high-heeled shoes were tossed into a container they called the Freedom Trash Can, along with *Playboy, Cosmopolitan,* and *Ladies' Home Journal.* Since they refused to grant interviews with men—and most reporters were men—the public was not privy to any deeper message. When a lone female reporter compared the act of defiance to draft card burning, the story grew to define women's libbers as bra-burning man-haters. The truth is, no bras were actually burned. The group didn't have a permit for fire on the boardwalk.

When I saw a photo of a sheep dressed like a beauty contestant with a crown on its furry head, it reminded me of the 4-H farm animals at the Ohio State Fair. I knew that sheep moved in a herd, and that they produced milk like women. I still had the desire to be a beauty queen, but I didn't want to be called a sheep. I didn't know yet that Germaine Greer had already called cone-shaped bras an instrument of oppression because they were compared to a sheep's harness. Until that point, I'd only noticed that bras were white and they were uncomfortable. My mom took hers off after work so often I could usually find one under the couch cushions.

Just as I started to identify as a girl, being a girl became a problem. I first noticed it when I played Tiny Tim in the fourth grade Christmas play. Casting a girl in a boy's role was a bold move by our new teacher, a young OSU graduate named Miss Dunlap. She was replacing a teacher who was pregnant, since it was taboo to be "with child" in the classroom. Not only was Miss Dunlap fresh from a run with the conservative Up With People singing group, but she had a Buckeye linebacker boyfriend who visited during recess to autograph footballs. I had no idea why she cast me, but I was thrilled. The wardrobe called for pajamas with pants. While the college kids protested Vietnam and the high school students had sit-ins over the right to wear blue jeans, elementary school girls had to wear skirts. During the winter, knit tights barely kept our knees from knocking on the mile walk to school.

When the boy I'd mock-married complained that I got the part, I was surprised. We were neighbors who had fun riding bikes around the block every summer. Until then, he'd only whined when my bratty sister trailed us on her red tricycle. Naturally, I expected to marry him for real someday. This felt like a betrayal. He didn't want to be in the play. He just didn't like that I was playing a boy.

I looked out the window at the backs of sixth-graders waiting in line to play dodgeball on the playground. Most had hair to their shoulders. If it weren't for the skirts, they all looked the same. This raised an entirely new question.

I shot up my hand to ask. "What's the difference between girls and boys?"

Miss Dunlap squinted at me. "That's something to ask your parents."

A boy sniggered. Then I realized what she meant: penises and vaginas. I had found the Kama Sutra in our den, the one with the line drawings of a man and woman in so many sexual positions that it had gotten boring to look at. I knew about sex. My question was deeper. I raised my hand again. Miss Dunlap avoided my eyes as she passed back our spelling tests.

"I mean the real difference, inside," I pressed, but she pretended not to hear me. Or maybe she didn't know. This was years before Louann Brizendine went to Harvard Medical School, discovered the gap in research, and wrote *The Female Brain*. Every morning after the school bell rang, our class put our hands over our hearts and recited the Pledge of Allegiance. I had assumed "liberty and justice for all" included me. Now I wasn't so sure.

The day of the play, I wore a camisole under my pajama top and shorts under the pants. Then I peeked from the girls' bathroom to be sure no one was looking before running down the hall to the annex stage. I needed to hop under the covers of Tiny Tim's sickbed before anyone saw me in pajamas. Being a girl no longer felt comfortable. But I wasn't sure why.

1969

With draft deferments coming to an end, my father had fewer geology students in his classes at Ohio State. He took me to the campus lab, where he poured water through rocks and encouraged my interest in science. When I told him my plan to be a surgeon, he bought me a dissection kit for my birthday in May. Still stumped by the difference between the sexes, I collected dead birds to cut them open and compare. On the inside, the blackened blood and crushed toothpick bones looked the same between males and females. Now I needed a microscope. I couldn't wait for Santa, so I ordered a kit to sell Christmas cards door to door. The more cards you sold, the better prizes you earned. These were not the sachets and spy cameras offered in the back of comic books in exchange for bubblegum wrappers. These were real prizes. Thirty boxes could earn you a microscope.

I figured I had a chance, because my sister and I knew most of the families in Langport Valley. Our dad was in charge of the Fourth of July celebration, so we passed out flyers and collected money door to door for the block party. All the kids came over to poke crepe paper in chicken wire columns and sneak bottles of Yoo-hoo from the stacks stored in our garage. For the rest of the summer, we all played games at picnic tables in the grassy intersection of yards. Older brothers passed footballs until the mosquitoes outnumbered the fireflies. This year, there were few older boys left, and they didn't join us. They smoked cigarettes by Chief Wyandotte's burial mound in the park by the river. Girls weren't allowed to go there.

When we sold Christmas cards door to door in the sweltering heat, we did well. Either the housewives took pity on sweaty little girls lugging around a massive sample album, or they truly liked the personalized print of Category B. One day, I pulled our rusty wagon to the marble lions guarding the white mansion on the far edge of Langport Valley. Once in a while, a fancy car would be in the circular driveway, but no one from this house had ever answered the door or come to the Fourth of July picnics. We suspected it was haunted. Tracy climbed out of the wagon to walk home.

Desperate for another sale, I pointed to the shady porch. With few trees for shade in our young neighborhood, this was tempting. At seven, Tracy wasn't allowed to cross the street without me, so she moped across the lawn to join me at the double doors. I picked her up from behind until she lifted the brass knocker. When it dropped with a bang, we ran.

Just as we reached the sidewalk, a woman with gray hair who looked ancient—which is to say, forty—opened the door. She waved at us with a handkerchief in her hand, then stuffed it in the sleeve of her baby blue cardigan. The sweater looked oddly out of place until I realized what it meant: air-conditioning. I dragged Tracy back up the driveway. This was not Stranger Danger; this was a woman. When she offered us lemonade, I lugged the sample album inside to an entry hall as big as our bedroom.

In the immaculate kitchen, she sat us down at the table and made a fuss over the greeting cards. She combed through the simple A levels to the B cards with addresses on the envelopes, then to the C cards, with all of those things plus sparkles. She chose the most expensive card, depicting snow-covered pines by a log cabin with smoke curling into the sky. I was thrilled.

My sister was on her second glass of lemonade when the woman asked if we liked toys. It sounded like a trick question, but she was already clipping her check to the order form. So, we followed her down the carpeted stairs to her basement. She showed us shelves piled with games and said her son didn't play with them anymore. We could each choose one to take home.

I had some of the same toys: a tin gas station, a Vacuform set, even Creepy Crawlers. It was fun to see that her son mixed black with the colors to make the snakes even scarier, and impressive that a spider made it out of the mold with all eight legs intact. He even had the Incredible Edibles version, where the goop heated up to make candy that was sweeter than the gumdrops from our Easy Bake Oven.

Finally, she showed us his bucket of G.I. Joes mixed with green plastic soldiers. These were palm-sized, so it seemed polite to take one. After walking us back upstairs, she led us through a narrow hallway lined with photos in matching frames. They were school pictures of her son, starting from Windermere Elementary, where we went. Then he got pimples, then braces, then his hair reached clear to his collar. In the last picture, all his hair was cut off. He wore a uniform and stood in front of the American flag. His eyes were staring straight at us, as if he knew we were there. The lady pulled the handkerchief from her sleeve and wiped her eyes. Her son wasn't coming back.

"Come visit again soon," she said.

We hugged her goodbye, but I knew we wouldn't return until her cards came in, all sparkly with white snow and her name engraved in gold. Then we would leave them on the porch and run. We were right all along; this house was haunted.

Something inside me clicked over, like an arrow on a gas gauge pointing toward full. What seemed like an arbitrary accident of birth now felt like an advantage. The bloody "curse" that girls learned about while the boys played dodgeball at recess suddenly made sense. The future depended on us. I didn't know that there were some female soldiers, or that later, women would fight to be included. What I did know was having breasts meant I didn't have to go to war. I didn't have to die for my country. There was at least one advantage to being a woman. I wanted to feel like one.

When the first man walked on the moon, I figured out how. Neil Armstrong was a Buckeye, which made him family. By mid-July, my sister refused to eat anything for breakfast but Quisp cereal, little spaceship-shaped puffs made by Quaker Oats. I powered up for swim practice with Tang, the juice drink that Buckeye John Glenn supposedly drank while orbiting the earth a few years earlier. When summer camp coincided with Apollo 11, I packed my paisley suitcase full of Pillsbury Space Food Sticks.

Our camp director bent a coat hanger into bunny-ear antennae on a black-and-white TV for everybody to watch the historic event. After a few hours on hard chairs in the open shelter, we had seen so many simulations of the tiny white astronaut walking in slow motion on the pockmarked surface of the moon that the burping tree frogs were more exciting. By ten o'clock, when Neil Armstrong finally uttered his famous words, we had tired of the frogs and started playing Truth or Dare. We sat around the campfire, and I raised my hand to go first.

"Truth or dare?" the cutest boy asked. My stomach fluttered as I basked in his attention. But I was risk averse. For all I knew, he'd dare me to jump in the lake. I chose Truth.

"Do you wear a bra?" he asked.

My face prickled with heat as if the fire was still raging. I said no.

"Thought so," he said and laughed. I looked over to the TV area, but the counselors were folding up the chairs. Man had made a small step, but there was no big step for mankind, or womankind either. I was stuck with this dumb game.

The counselors came over, too excited to go to bed, and joined us around the campfire. We sang "Kumbaya," then played Duck, Duck, Goose. The first boy walked slowly around the circle, touching each girl's back as he passed. Then he grabbed the girl's shirt, snapped her bra strap and called "goose." The giggling girl got up to run around the circle and chase him until he sat down. Then it was her turn to pick the next goose. It was never my turn. I sat there and scratched my mosquito bites until they bled. The message was clear: in order to feel like a girl, I needed attention from boys. To get attention from boys, I needed a bra.

A few weeks after camp, I found out where to get one. My mom dropped my sister and me off at a shopping center carnival while she picked up my father at the airport. Surrounded by the split-level homes of our middle-class suburb, we felt safe. We rode the small Ferris wheel and pointed out Lazarus and Kresge's and Youth Land, where we bought our clothes. As we were ushered off, the sky turned a sickly shade of green. The winds rose, making the dirt swirl up and sting our eyes. A tornado siren sounded, splitting the air. There were no cell phones then, no way to track down our mother. The rides closed and the workers disappeared, so we ran through the parking lot to Youth Land. As hail pinged down, we shouted and banged on the glass doors. Finally, the manager let us in.

We ran through the racks of pinafores and party dresses, down the stairs to the junior department. We had never been there, but we recognized the saleswoman with cat-eye glasses smoking a cigarette by the check-out counter. She chatted with the bald manager while the wind howled outside. Wandering between rows of underwear, we discovered a rack of training bras. I was dying to peek at one close-up, to try one on and train my breasts to grow.

I opened a flat, rectangular Maidenform box and pulled at the white straps connected to circles of pristine lace. They stretched up and down and in and out with unlimited possibility. Tracy giggled, so I shushed her and peered between the racks. The saleswoman, who was leafing through a pile of old magazines, spotted us and came over. She snatched the bra from my hand and steered us toward the camisoles, which were essentially undershirts cut off at the midriff. Then she sat us down with the magazines to wait until the tornado passed.

By the time my mom had picked through the mess of wood and broken glass in the parking lot to find us in front of the store, my sister and I had paged through *Good Housekeeping* issues with articles ranging from "Spring Beauty" to "Sex and Violence on TV." One issue featured Marlo Thomas, the star of *That Girl*, a show we loved about a single girl in New York. Since it was summer, we stayed up on Thursday nights to watch. Marlo Thomas looked just like our mom in dresses with matching jackets and her dark hair in a perfect flip. The article said Thomas had stopped wearing a bra on the show after the Miss America protest. She said, "God created women to bounce. So be it."[7]

I was shocked. Marlo Thomas was a hippie? As soon as my mom showed up, I told her "that girl" didn't wear a bra. Mom said it was because she didn't need one.

I did, I thought, but how could I explain? Mom said to hurry. Dad was waiting in the car.

On the way home, my sister and I were in the back seat and my dad was driving. I was working up the courage to ask when we could go back to the store. It was too embarrassing to say the word "bra" in front of my dad. My mother reached for the radio dial, and my father's hand snaked across the console, grabbed the front of her blouse, and squeezed. Mom called his name sharply and pulled away. She glanced back at me, then turned the radio on. I looked at Tracy, but she was asleep. I didn't know if my dad was wrong to grab her in front of us or wrong to grab her all. He chuckled as if Mom was being silly, but she wasn't smiling.

Up until then, my father could do no wrong. He was tall and handsome and strong and smart. He took me to football games on the back of his motorcycle, gave me money for the candy at his hockey games, and got me a miniature lacrosse stick to play with while he coached the college team. He yelled so loudly at my swim meets that Mom got mad. That day, watching them from the back seat of the car, it occurred to me again that I was more like my mom. There was a chance I had picked the wrong team.

When my dreams came true and my breasts began to bud, the thrill was short-lived. One winter night, I was babysitting for my sister while our parents were out. Our usual babysitter was busy, but I didn't want her big brother to fill in. Last time, he'd pulled the ruffled strap of my filmy blue nightgown down and offered to let me stay up late. He'd been ogling a sexy image of Raquel Welch in her underwear on the cover of my parents' *Time Magazine*, so it was easy to guess what he wanted. He was stupid to think he'd find it with a fourth-grader. Still, I was too embarrassed to tattle. Our families were friends. I told my parents we didn't need a sitter and promised to lock the door. We barricaded ourselves in their bedroom with the new color TV.

Honestly, I have no idea what we were watching. We had so many favorites during those years. It might've been *Petticoat Junction*, with buxom sisters Betty Jo, Bobbie Jo, and Billy Jo living in Hooterville. Maybe it was *Green Acres*, starring the statuesque Eva Gabor as the high-society wife who wore low-cut gowns on a farm, or *The Beverly Hillbillies*, where Ellie May—the spitting image of Little Annie Fanny—played opposite the flat-chested spinster, Jane Hathaway. These shows gave new meaning to the expression "boob tube."

Once a year, *The Wizard of Oz* was on TV and we imagined ourselves as Dorothy. Who knew Judy Garland wore a corset to flatten her chest for the part? Like Dorothy, we longed for the soft embrace of Aunty Em. The Wicked Witch was as hard and flat and skinny as her broom. Breasts were the universal comforter.

Regardless, if only I had stayed upstairs that night to watch. But when Tracy begged for ice cream, I braved the dark stairway to go down to the kitchen. As I filled two bowls with mint chip, the phone rang. I grabbed the yellow handset from the kitchen wall and answered.

A deep voice asked, "Do you have hair on your pussy?"

I nearly dropped the phone. I knew what a pussy was, and that I had one. And I did have a few downy hairs starting to sprout. The entire world faded as if there was a spotlight only on me. I said, "No."

Then he said, in a tone of disgust, "Do you even wear a bra?"

"Yes," I lied. Then I hung up.

I studied the bright, sunflower-patterned wallpaper under the wall phone, but it stood out now, as if I hadn't seen it every day for years. This was a new kind of Stranger Danger. Not the kind where you got kidnapped, but the kind that could happen at home. This man wanted the same thing I did, for me to grow up and have breasts like the ladies on TV. But now it felt like a bad thing. Worse, it was already happening. And it was painful, these pebbles growing beneath my skin. I wore a camisole to protect my nipples from rubbing against my clothes. There was no way to stop growing. And if this man saw me, he would see the bumps.

I looked out the windows, then I sunk to the floor to hide. I was wearing my filmy blue nightgown, but felt absolutely naked. After a few minutes, I crept back upstairs. My sister was on our parent's bed watching TV as if nothing had happened. I closed the curtains and pretended that was true.

After my parents got home, they scolded me for leaving the ice cream on the counter, where it had melted into a mess. I didn't defend myself. I had done something wrong, but I wasn't sure what. And I didn't want to be a woman anymore.

1970

As my body started changing, I watched my mother more closely. At home, I thought I understood how her body worked. In public, it was different, especially when we went to Kahiki. The Polynesian restaurant, with its outrigger-shaped roof and carved doors between towering tiki gods, was the only place like it in the Midwest. Celebrities like Johnny Carson and Cloris Leachman and Zsa Zsa Gabor visited during theater season. It was our father's favorite—mine, too. As soon as our eyes adjusted to the darkly lit village in the lobby, my sister and I crossed the footbridge over the running stream and went to the gift shop. We sniffed the tiny bottles of flower perfume and tried wooden backscratchers through our party dresses. On the night I remember most, Mom lured us out with souvenir tiki necklaces.

The hostess in a flowered sarong led us through the tropical rain-forest side of the restaurant, where thunder boomed and rain poured against the glass wall. We peered through the glass at the squawking parrots until we reached the back where the Beachcomber Trio played luau music. The hula girl seated my dad in an enormous woven cane chair across from the roof-high face of the tiki god. It was the best table in the room, perfect for my dad, who was tall and tan and more hand-some than Elvis. My mother was gorgeous, too, in her form-fitting dress with a circle pin on the sweetheart neck. We scooted into our chairs while Dad ordered two Shirley Temples and a Mystery Drink.

A gong reverberated and the house lights dimmed. The music stopped and a man's voice announced the Mystery Girl. A dark-haired young woman in a strapless bikini top and fringed skirt emerged bare-foot from behind a beaded curtain. Her hands cupped a lava bowl filled with a steaming Mystery Drink. Steel drums pounded as she sashayed toward a twelve-foot tiki god on the dance floor. She bowed her head for a moment, then backed up and danced over to my dad. She kneeled and held out the drink.

My dad sat up like royalty. He was the king and she was the maiden. All around us, middle-aged men in seersucker suits and women pinned with gift shop orchids craned their necks to watch him accept her offering. The Mystery Girl stood, lifted the white flower lei from her neck, and held it up high. Then she bowed so low we could see her breasts bubbling over her bandeau top. When the drumming hit a crescendo, she slipped the fluffy lei over my father's head. The gong sounded again. The room erupted in applause.

Mom took a quiet sip from her water glass.

The marimba music started up. Dad picked up his chopsticks and drummed along, then took a few sips of the steaming drink before getting up to go talk to the band. The other couples turned back to their tables as the waiters returned with heaping pupu platters. My mom spread a napkin on my sister's lap, then pulled the Mystery Drink over to take a sip. When she caught my eye, she smiled, but how she felt was a mystery.

What strikes me now is how the women at the other tables rooted for my father. They were pledged to their husbands. That's what nice wives do. The performance was all in good fun. They didn't see themselves being replaced by the Mystery Girl, perpetuating the cycle of bowing to a man. They were complicit. Fifty years later, when I see Kahiki egg rolls in the grocery store freezer, I remember this night, when I learned women could be their own worst enemies.

Luckily, they could also be your best friend.

On a school night in early May, I came home late from gymnastics dressed in my chalk-splattered red leotard. My dad was in the living room with visitors from Australia. He was leaving his teaching job at Ohio State to run a science organization. He asked me to demonstrate a roundoff back handspring, my most difficult move, for his guests.

My mom came in with a tray of drinks and saw me stalling. She reminded my dad it was bedtime and I was tired. This was the first time she'd spoken up for me and disagreed with my dad. But he explained that the men came all the way from Australia and were leaving in the morning. He asked me directly. After a lifetime of loyalty, I couldn't refuse.

He pulled the sling chairs and the chess table away from the fireplace to clear a longer path. The men squeezed onto the couch at the side of the room. I backed up all the way into the front hall against the stairway. Then I took a deep breath, ran into the living room, and executed a perfect roundoff. My feet snapped to the carpet in perfect unison, but when I pushed off to spring backward, the carpet was mushy and my wrists were weak. I wasn't leaning back enough to get my legs vertical, to let the momentum carry me. I knew it as my feet left the ground, but it was too late. My wrists caved under the weight. Upside down, I crumpled to the carpet.

"I'm sorry," I said through my tears. I had embarrassed my dad in front of his company. The Australian men chuckled and finished their drinks before going to their hotel. I couldn't move my fingers, so my mom called the neighbor, a German doctor, who was not happy to be disturbed so late at night. He examined my swelling hand, said I was fine, and recommended an ice pack. My dad trusted the doctor and called me a baby. I went to bed listening to my parents fight in the next room. They were fighting about me. My mom was on my side.

The next morning, my arm was swollen to my elbow. Mom called her department office at OSU, but no one answered. Her classes had been canceled. She drove me to campus anyway, to go to the emergency room at University Hospital. I cradled my throbbing elbow with my left hand, wincing at every bump on the five-mile ride. Once on campus, we had to go around the Oval, an enormous green crisscrossed by brick paths leading to the oldest university buildings. The last time I'd been there, on the back of my dad's motorcycle, the students were having picnics and flying kites. Now I couldn't see the grass beneath the crowds of shouting students.

I had heard about the riots, but had only seen them on TV. In April, women who reportedly needed a college degree to "out-earn" a man with an eighth-grade education[8] protested the evening dorm curfew. The Commission for Student Rights protested to add Black Studies to the curriculum. Anti-war students marched in protest of Vietnam. By May it was mayhem. Nearly 4,000 students combined forces in a mass protest against the secret bombing of Cambodia.[9] Policemen used clubs and students threw Molotov cocktails. Armored tanks rolled down the street. Four students were killed at our sister school, Kent State.

Today, the campus was on lockdown, and we were in the middle of it. Mom drove slowly past men in the National Guard, who looked like toy soldiers, all lined up in dark helmets with guns at their sides. Protesters waved signs and shouted at the park entrance. It was so noisy I could barely hear my mother's voice when she rolled her window down a crack to plead with the police officer to let us through. He shook his head and backed away from the car.

My mom wasn't much older than the students, and I was pretty sure she agreed with them. She didn't say "far out" or "dig it," but she wore a gold medallion with a sunflower that had the same words as our bumper sticker: *War is Not Healthy for Children and Other Living Things*. Right now, however, she was a teacher in a prim dress and Pappagallo heels. She was also a mother on a mission who was blocked by a wall of hippies going berserk. A guy with a beard flashed a peace sign at me, and I tried to signal back, but my fingers were numb. By the time I let go of my right arm to try it with my left, he was gone. Two people with long hair and tie-dyed T-shirts jumped on the car hood. My mother screamed. We were surrounded, an island in a sea of madness. Then we were rocking. The protesters were rocking our car.

My mom reached past me to pound down the door lock, then the car lurched. Hippies smashed up against my window inches from my face in a wall of long hair and rainbow tie-dye. When the car rocked back, they all looked the same. I noticed the bare belly of a girl. Her top was two long triangles of flowered fabric. As we rocked, the circles of her nipples pressed against the glass like targets aimed right at me.

My mother honked the horn and held it. The rocking slowed. A shrill whistle split the shouts. Mom yanked the steering wheel and shifted into reverse.

When we finally made it to the hospital, X-rays revealed that my fingers were fractured in two places. The doctor plastered a cast all the way up to my elbow. I scribbled with my left hand for the rest of the school year. It stung that my dad hadn't believed that I was hurt, but

I decided he was hoping for the best. The part that bothered me the most was the memory of those nipples pressing against the window of my mom's car. They reminded me of the protest during the Miss America pageant. Not wearing a bra when you needed one meant you were political, that you thought important things. I still wanted to wear a bra, but did that mean I wanted boys to get killed in the war? I didn't want my breasts to be a political statement, but how could I avoid it?

Within weeks, Neil Young's "Ohio" was on the radio. He saw the same tin soldiers I did. The tune was a death knell, too catchy and too close to home. If we weren't safe here, then where? The newspaper reported that Kent State student Sandra Lee Scheuer, the girl in the song,[10] was simply walking between classes when she was shot down. She was minding her own business and got caught in the crossfire. There was no way to separate the personal from the political. Allison Krause, the other girl who got killed, was taking part in the protest. For her, the political was so personal it killed her. The eighteen-year-old honors student was killed by a bullet in "the left side of her chest."[11] Decades later, Neil Young's voice singing "four dead in O-hi-o" still brings tears to my eyes.

Soon after the Kent State Massacre, the documentary *Woodstock*, a four-hour, 70-mm recording of the previous summer's concert, was released in Columbus. During a family vacation in Myrtle Beach, I got a sunflower yellow tank top with the famous dove and guitar logo from a rack of T-shirts on the boardwalk. Despite the cast on my arm, the shirt made me feel like a groovy chick, part of the peace movement. I had no idea that the iconic design was created by a Madison Avenue adman. Or that the original poster was rejected by local merchants because it showed a naked woman surrounded by hearts and arrows. All the symbols of "free love."

Free love was why I was too young to see the concert film. The most iconic photos of the three-day festival show women naked, topless, and having sex. Destined for an Academy Award, the film mythologized an Arcadian utopia. Yet this vision etched in American history by six male photographers was typically one-sided. Most who remember it fondly have a foggy perspective of the marijuana-infused air. Also, the "do your own thing" credo was a lie. Only hippies were welcome—and there was a dress code. Women were not free to wear bras.

When 400,000 "alienated young people"[12] met at Woodstock in 1969, the cost of free love was a price only women paid. Birth control was still illegal for unmarried women and difficult to get without a prescription. There was no law against sexual assault. The closest protection was for harassment, considered a form of employee discrimination under the Civil Rights Act of 1964. And it is impossible to underestimate the peer pressure of so many drug-fueled baby boomers at their testosterone peak.

There are no full accounts from women at Woodstock, which is telling in itself. My mom was busy with family and work, but after hearing men's glorious accounts, she felt sentimental about missing it. Yet for women it was dangerous. The freedom of that topless woman, an image made famous in the film, is misleading. This was long before the public was used to seeing naked breasts in movies. That surely made it even more thrilling for men in real life. Going braless defined women as openly sexual and available, instead of old-fashioned and "uptight." Taking away any sort of covering was a great excuse for drug-fueled young men to see tits everywhere and fuck whomever they wanted. While long hair and sexual freedom represented enlightenment on that farm in upstate New York, this evoked an idyllic past that never existed, like pastoral stories of gods and nymphs.

Despite the rain and crowds and lack of facilities, despite the fact that hundreds of thousands could neither see the stage nor hear the music, concertgoers still describe Woodstock as an epic experience.

Madison Avenue sealed this golden image by seducing baby boomers with television commercials for Pioneer Stereo, Pepsi, even Tampax. And I bought them all. Even now, teenagers see Woodstock commercials for Subaru and Volkswagen that reinforce the myth. Grandparents welcome the opportunity to look cool. When I hear classic rock translated into elevator Muzak and see boho fashion trends, I can't help but feel a Pavlovian longing for this mythical time when women were supposedly as free as our breasts.

I was too young for Woodstock, but somewhere around that time I did get my first bra. I recall a moment of glory, hearing angels sing, but I can't pin down the date. On a Sunday in September of 2016, I called my mother long-distance to ask. She answered the phone, all excited. "Have you seen Miss Ohio?"

"I'm rooting for Miss California," I said, as if I was watching the Miss America pageant. I had forgotten it was airing, but it sounded more fun than the 9/11 memorials airing the same day, and I liked the pretty gowns. I took the phone downstairs to grab a bag of organic popcorn and a bottle of water.

"Did you call your father?" my mother asked. September 11 was his birthday. For a few years after the Twin Towers fell, he celebrated on the following day. I told her I sang to his answering machine that morning, then steered the conversation away.

"Mom, do you remember when I got my first bra?"

"No," she said. "I remember getting you a play bra when you were a toddler. It was cute."

OK, that was weird. But not helpful. I took my snack back to the bedroom and turned on the TV to watch the pageant. Then I got up and closed the door. My husband was fast-forwarding through a football game in the office down the hallway. I was embarrassed for him to hear what I was watching. If he decided to join me, that would be worse. I'd compare myself to the young beauty queens and worry he'd find me lacking.

I settled in and sipped the water. The top ten were probably back-stage, adjusting their cleavage, as the losers smiled through a silly dance.

"How can we still care about Miss America?" I asked my mom. "Remember the protest?"

"The protest was stupid," she said.

I nearly spit out my water. "Mom, you were the only working mother in our neighborhood. Weren't you on the board of Planned Parenthood? I could swear you gave a speech on a program with Betty Friedan."

"It was called 'What Price Women's Lib?'" she said. "I wanted to focus on childcare and nutrition and early education. I still have a copy somewhere. I'll send it to you."

"I thought you agreed with the protestors."

"I did, but I worked my whole life. Even when I was married, I bought my own cars. I didn't have time for the philosophical battle."

"Fine, you were fighting the real one. But you were all for women's liberation. You just got, you know, caught up at home." I meant all her hard work, not the dark days that followed. This was dangerous territory.

"Don't talk to me about your father. My role at work was different than at home. I didn't have role models."

"You were also very pretty. Still are."

"Don't change the subject. One of my students was a runner-up for Miss Ohio. My secretary worked for the pageant in the summer. Miss America is about scholarships."

"Seriously, Mom?" At seventy-nine, maybe she was getting senile.

"The pageant leveled the playing field," she insisted. "These were regular girls-next-door."

"Like Playboy Bunnies?"

She ignored me. "These contestants are not the brains who get academic scholarships or musicians who go to Juilliard. They aren't great actresses who can be a movie stars, or supermodels who marry pro athletes."

I thought of the millions made by the players my husband was watching down the hall. Her thinking was old-fashioned in theory, but it was true that men had more opportunities. "You're saying beauty is the means to an end."

"Isn't it? What are you, living on Mars?" she asked.

"OK, Mom, thanks. I gotta go."

"Of course you do," she said. "Because I'm right."

I hung up to do some research. The nonprofit Miss America Organization's claim to be "the largest provider of scholarship assistance for young women in the U. S."[13] is true. Especially since they include every scholarship and tuition dollar promised at each local, state, and national contest, multiplied by all the contestants in the pool to win.[14] At the height of participation during the 1980s, over 80,000 young women competed at some level.[15] But for every year of the pageant, only one woman wins the crown.

On my TV, the contestants were emerging in evening gowns. Such custom fit and fancy beading had to cost a fortune. What about the contestants who only wore them backstage? This was quite a gamble for someone competing for a scholarship that hadn't kept up with the cost of tuition. It was a deal with the devil.

I called my daughter to ask if she was watching. This was how millions of impressionable girls learned that female power is achieved by how a girl looks in a swimsuit. Only then may she speak for twenty seconds. This has been true since the beginning of the pageant, when suffragettes supported beauty contests as a way to help women get out into public. They wore sashes to show their female form. Women have always had to be pretty to be heard. My twenty-five-year-old daughter thought it was funny that I was watching—as if she was beyond it. She was busy buying makeup for a job interview.

On the TV screen, the last young woman strutted across the stage in her sparkly gown. How wonderful would it feel to be beautiful enough to represent an entire state? This desire to feel pretty is what makes the competition feel personal. A protestor who appeared on *The David Susskind Show* soon after the 1968 protest said, "Every day in a woman's life is a walking Miss America contest."[16] Fifty years later, that still rang true.

As the contestants paraded out in bikinis, I remembered the moment that angels sang.

I was eleven, and already locked in this double bind, the desire to be attractive and to be equal. If I wore a bra, it meant I had breasts big enough to qualify as a beautiful woman. But women all over the country were removing their bras to prove they were equal and deserving of a voice. Naked breasts were a symbol of peace. I was desperately torn. When my broken fingers healed, I retired my Woodstock tank. I got a two-piece swimsuit with a real bra top, and the print was red, white, and blue.

Here I come, Miss America.

Beauty Pageants

1921 First Miss America Pageant is a swimsuit competition rating "construction of body parts," to promote business for the Atlantic City Boardwalk.

1944 Miss America Pageant adds scholarships to prizes awarded.

1947–49 Miss America Pageant supplies two-piece swimsuits to contestants for two years, then bans them due to pressure from Roman Catholic protestors.

1952 First Miss USA Pageant is created by Catalina Swimsuits after Miss America 1950 refuses to pose in a swimsuit. Miss USA, with neither talent requirement nor scholarship opportunity, competes directly with Miss America, but goes on to compete with professional models in Miss Universe.

1968 First Black Miss America Pageant is held the same night as the Miss America Pageant protest.

1979 Miss South Carolina, a motivational speaker, states that the Miss America Pageant has "designated personnel" to be sure the flesh under the swimsuits is all theirs.

1983 Miss California (who lost the Miss Texas Pageant before getting breast implants) wins Miss America.

1984 First black Miss America, Vanessa Williams, is crowned, but is later forced to resign over nude photos.

1986 Miss America Pageant stops printing body measurements in the program following the rise of anorexia and the reduction of body measurements—except for the bust.[1]

1988 Miss San Diego Pageant, a qualifier for the Miss California Pageant, has a "plastic surgery consultant."

1990 Miss USA Pageant allows padded bras to lower the rate of breast augmentations.

1994 Miss America Pageant votes to drop the swimsuit competition. Viewers vote to keep it.

1996 Miss USA, Miss Teen USA, and Miss Universe Pageants are purchased by Donald Trump as part of the Miss Universe Organization. He owns it for 20 years then sells it amid controversy over racial comments in 2015.

1997 Miss America contestants choose their own swimsuits. Two choose bikinis. Miss Hawaii, with the "briefest bikini of all" wins the swimsuit competition. Soon, most wear bikinis again.

1998 Forty of the fifty-one Miss USA contestants have breast implants.

2001 Former Miss USA, Shanna Moakler, is *Playboy*'s December Playmate of the Month.

2009 Miss USA Pageant pays for breast implants for Miss California Carrie Prejean. After a scandal, the pageant sues her for the cost, blaming the discovery of a sex tape.

2017 Plastic surgery is considered the legal "doping" of beauty pageants by insiders.

2018 Miss America Pageant chair Gretchen Carlson eliminates the swimsuit competition, makes evening gowns optional, and adds speaking. Twenty-two states demand her resignation. The word "pageant" is changed to "competition."

2020 The Miss America Competition, whose mission statement focuses on preparing women for the world, is cancelled due to the Covid-19 pandemic. The Miss USA Pageant, whose mission statement focuses on beauty, is pushed to November.

The first black Miss USA, Asya Branch, is crowned.

Five

SMART VS. PRETTY
1972

O ne day, life is a meritocracy: hard work and good grades are all that matter. The next day, your friends start to blossom, and being smart only gets you so far.

From Vietnam to the Pentagon Papers to Watergate in 1972, the drumbeat of injustice brought the nation together in a state of disillusionment. Except when it came to breasts. They were more popular than ever. *Playboy*'s circulation peaked at over seven million copies by the end of my seventh-grade year. *Life* magazine, famous for Pulitzer Prize-winning battle photos, featured a bikini model on the beach for their "Report on Cambodia" issue. Women's Liberation rated a cover, the Beatles break-up another. The cover story on high school pregnancy had no mention of "free love." Jane Fonda, the war protester, was repackaged as a "busy rebel" without a bra, and Ann-Margret was congratulated for her "sex kitten" success.

By the time I was thirteen, the counterculture had been co-opted into a fashion trend. Halter tops and tube tops trickled down to the masses. For me, breasts were not some abstract political issue; they were an intensely personal one.

My father first noticed my breasts the week he moved out to live with his girlfriend. During a final trip to collect boxes of *Playboys*, lacrosse sticks, and bell-bottoms, he strolled through the backyard to say goodbye. My friend Cassie and I were standing waist deep in the cold water of our new backyard pool. By coincidence, we had matching bikinis in the latest style for groovy teenagers: velour triangle tops clipped to plastic rings. The only difference was that hers was purple and mine was orange. OK, there was one other difference. My dad paused on the Astroturf at the edge of pool and looked from Carrie's convex triangles to my flat ones.

"Why doesn't your top fit like Cassie's?" he asked.

Cassie slipped down beneath the water to hide. I wanted to hide, too. How, after all these years of loyalty, had I been reduced to being another specimen in his science lab?

"Maybe because I'm still growing," I said. "I don't have my wisdom teeth yet."

He nodded, accepting the hypothesis. "Great color."

"Thanks," I said. He wasn't apologizing. Orange was the color of his Princeton tigers.

"See you Wednesday," he said.

I nodded. I had no choice. Since he'd stopped teaching at Ohio State, he couldn't take me to football games anymore. I didn't care about football, but it was fun to ride on the back of his Honda motorcycle, drink hot chocolate, and watch the cheerleaders. Now I had to face him over dinner at restaurants on Wednesday nights while he complained about my mother and asked why my sister didn't come.

Cassie looked at me in horror as he carried his cardboard box back through the garage. I adjusted my top and pretended it didn't matter. That night, I wrote in my journal with such heat that, decades later, the anger still rises from the page. But what really stoked my fire that day was that I felt like a failure. My dad had always been my biggest fan, filling me with the confidence that I was smart enough to do anything. Now, I had to be pretty to make the grade.

Pretty was easy to define in a country crazed by football. The common love of sport—a sanctioned aggression—created a sense of community. Weeks after the Kent State Massacre, just as Nixon tried to stop the publication of the Pentagon Papers, even Dennis Hopper, the director of *Easy Rider*, the biggest counterculture motor-cycle movie ever made, was on the cover of *Life* hugging a pigskin. In Ohio, the battle-weary heart of the country, the Buckeyes were the perfect salve. Coach Woody Hayes was the only OSU faculty member who spoke to the students during the riots. And his team—our team—was on a roll, playing in the Rose Bowl every single year. All across Columbus, garages were painted with Buckeye leaves and a big red O. Everybody rooted for OSU. And who led the cheer? Cheerleaders.

Forget Playboy Bunnies and beauty queens, these were the real "girls next door." The first cheerleaders were men at my dad's alma mater of Princeton, and the trend spread quickly. During World War II, women took over at coed schools. When the men returned, fashion favored the "sweater girl" with tight sweaters over pointy bras. This quickly became standard uniform, and female cheerleaders ruled.

During the rebellious sixties, cheerleaders embodied home in a conservative backlash. By now, in 1972, there were cheerleaders in every high school, junior high, and all the way down to my sister cheer-ing for the Pop Warner Pee Wee league. Who could resist a whole-some, happy girl rooting for our boys on the field? Not me. I could no longer identify with the muscular boys, but it sure looked fun to shake a pom-pom. Cheerleading wasn't a sport, but it was a clear path to popularity. Wearing that letter sweater to school every week made you pretty by definition. My dad raised me to do sports, not cheer for them. Still, I knew why the sweater was the most important part of the uniform. Boys wanted to put their hands underneath it.

Do you remember the first time you got felt up? Sure you do. Breast fondling is a rite of passage to womanhood that can leave a lasting impression on your entire love life. At least it did for me. Danny was a classmate who invested hours flattering me on the phone until I agreed to let him "cop a feel." That's what the boys called it, as if feeling a bare breast was a police emergency. Maybe with all those raging hormones, it was. Danny and a friend rode their ten-speeds through the slush on a winter evening to meet me and a friend at Lazarus department store. The elevator alcove in the back of the store was the only warm place we could meet without adult supervision. Shoppers rarely went back there. I'd invited Arlene, a girl with enough carnal knowledge to roll the waistband of her skirt to make it shorter. I chose a clingy sweater with a V-neck that laced up. Then I spent twenty minutes in front of the bathroom mirror tying the laces in a perfect bow. Soon, I would be unwrapped like a gift.

When the elevator closed, leaving the four of us standing alone in the bright hallway by the store offices, the boys unzipped their army jackets. We unbuttoned our wool coats and piled them on the green vinyl couch. After waiting long enough to count the cigarette butts in the standing ashtray, Arlene and her randomly assigned boyfriend got busy. I had the real boyfriend, but now I wished for a darker spot. I was watching the elevator lights, about to chicken out when Danny pulled me to him. He kissed me so tenderly, I forgot about the elevator and felt myself melting like the slush on the carpet. Danny clearly loved me. Then he reached above the waist of my plaid hip-hugger pants. Instinctively, my hand shot out to defend the territory, but my POW bracelet got caught on my leather belt. I extricated my wrist to avoid bending the stamped metal, but by the time it was free, Danny was shoving his hand up my shirt. His fingers were freezing. I flinched. Then I felt the ragged fingernails of his other hand digging beneath the band of my bra. Was I supposed to pretend not to notice? Should I not have worn a bra? What was second-base etiquette?

We kept kissing, but his lips pressed harder as his hand clamped my left breast. He squeezed as if he could get juice out of it. *Ouch.* My eyes flashed open, but his were closed tight. Maybe that's what passion looked like; I wasn't sure. I closed my eyes and tried to enjoy it. Then he pressed his palm against me like a game of patty-cake. All movement stalled for a moment. I waited. One more squeeze, then he pulled his hand from my bra so fast the elastic snapped against my skin. We pulled apart and sat down on the green vinyl coach. His friend was still busy. Arlene had more to feel.

I wanted to rub the sore ridge where the elastic had snapped, but I was embarrassed. The other couple was now playing a vertical game of Twister. We waited. After a few minutes, I couldn't stand it any longer. "Sorry."

He shrugged like it didn't matter, but he didn't look at me or hold my hand. I bit my nails while he inspected the grimy soles of his waffle stompers. Boys of all ages liked breasts. He had expected more. If he was a swimmer, he would have seen me in a nylon racing suit and known better. Unfortunately, he was a landlubber and bras were purposely deceiving. Mine had fiberfill. That made me a liar.

When the elevator dinged, the gropers jumped apart. Time to go. I waved goodbye to Danny, as if there were a chance he would still like me on Monday. Just shy of thirteen, I thought anything was possible.

Arlene pulled me down the hall to the ladies' restroom. She giggled as she lifted up her peasant blouse. The white band of her bra was wedged under her armpits.

"He unhooked it?"

She nodded, turning around for me to fasten it. I could barely hook it together with two hands. The guy was a magician. Apparently, he practiced with his sister's bra on the back of a chair. Arlene was blushing, giddy at the experience. Maybe he'd pinched her nipple and released oxytocin into her bloodstream as well. I read about that in my parents' copy of *The Joy of Sex*. When Danny had pinched my nipple, it hurt. I was dying to know what it felt like to have squishy breasts. But I didn't dare ask Arlene. It wasn't right. Girls didn't talk about our breasts.

Desperate, I ordered a Mark Eden bust developer from the back of a magazine. According to Nora Ephron's essay about breasts in *Esquire*,[1] she had tried it too, but at thirteen I didn't read *Esquire*, so I was alone in my desperation. Aside from my mother and pictures in *Playboy*, I hadn't really seen adult breasts. Neither had most people, except at home.[2] But that was starting to change.

Ten years earlier, film critic Roger Ebert had accused Jayne Mansfield of being "desperate" when she appeared nude in *Promises, Promises*. One year earlier, Jane Fonda showed her breasts in *Klute*, which I knew for a fact because my parents couldn't get a babysitter, so I saw them, too. She was playing a sex worker, so I guessed that justified it, but it was so shocking I hid behind a seat for the rest of film. In another ten years, it would be completely normal. Actresses in almost every role would be expected to show their breasts in movies. Some called it progress.

At thirteen, the only age-appropriate role models I had were the teenagers in the Mark Eden ads. One went from Twiggy to Ann-Margret, from flat to full, in eight weeks, by using the developer. Another was already a *Playboy* pinup. When I got the box in the mail, I hid it under the bed. Late at night, I pressed the hinged sides of the pink plastic clamshell together and chanted, "*We must, we must, we must improve our bust. The bigger, the better, the tighter the sweater, the boys are depending on us.*"

After a few weeks, I tried the pencil test. Ann Landers wrote in her advice column that if you put a pencil beneath your breast and it stayed there, you needed a real bra. I tried the test so often that my shag carpet was littered with the shrapnel of lead points. Years later, entertainment reporter Leeza Gibbons would tell me that she was so eager for breasts as a girl she demanded a schedule for their arrival. Her mother told her not to worry: "What God's forgotten, we'll stuff with cotton."[3] Stuffing was a popular move for girls then, but impossible for someone who dressed in the natatorium locker room before school.

For me, midriff tops came into style just in time. Even without boobs, the angle between a belly and a bra provided sex appeal. When I wore my favorite white midriff top with a jagged edge, my American history teacher, Mr. Conner, always noticed. Usually, I wore it under a white lab coat, since I still planned to be a surgeon, but he noticed anyway. He was a tough teacher, and I was an A-student. When he asked me to edit and hand-copy twenty-nine separate reports, then bind them into a book for the class, I was honored. When he teased me about my shirt, however, it felt good in a different way. A more personal way.

Mr. Conner was also my homeroom teacher, so there was no avoiding him. To be honest, I didn't want to avoid him. On Teacher Appreciation Day, I invited him to be my guest for the girls' required cooking class. I made eggs Benedict, and he choked it down. Every time he told me my shirt was unraveling, I giggled. It was the first praise I felt for being female. I felt pretty.

A few months later, I dissected a fetal pig for the science fair. The gross-out factor made it an easy win for the display category. The day after the fair, I missed homeroom for an early morning dental appointment. I was back for Mr. Conner's history class midmorning, wearing my midriff top with a zigzag edge.

"Who unraveled your shirt?" he asked.

I giggled, right on cue.

By the end of the day, I learned I had missed the lunchtime photo session for science fair winners. I was so hurt I could barely do my homework. I didn't care about not having my picture in the paper as much as the reason why. I was at school well before the photo session, and Mr. Conner knew it. He had noticed me enough to flirt, but not to remember something I'd worked for. Maybe it was a simple mistake, but it made me question my understanding of the world. Wasn't smart worth more than pretty?

The answer plagued me all through high school. Perhaps I was self-conscious because I spent so much time in a leotard or a swimsuit, with only a thin layer of fabric between my body and the world. Gymnastics and swimming were the main sports girls could play in that time before Title IX. Body-conscious sports like ice-skating and tennis were acceptable, too.

At swim practice, there was no way to hide. During the summer, we were half-naked three practices a day. Every time we climbed out of the pool to get a kickboard, hands reached out of the water like octopus tentacles, grabbing at us. The biggest, strongest, fastest boys were the worst, because they had the longest reach. And whatever those boys did was golden. Coach was no help. He was the first to snap towels at the boys, and his favoritism was Darwinian. The boys' showers connected directly to his office, where *Swimmers World* shared space on the desk with the swimsuit issue of *Sports Illustrated*. Whenever girls went into the office to ask what events we were swimming at the next meet, we kept our arms crossed over our clinging suits.

Once our breasts started budding, the pinching hurt. To avoid the boys' reach, we climbed back in the pool from the side, then ducked behind other swimmers to get to our middle lane. That made us slower getting in and put us at the end of the line of swimmers ready to go. We'd have to pass other swimmers or jockey for better spots on the next swim. The slower outside lanes were safe. The boys were nicer, lower on the hierarchy, and more equal to the girls.

When you swam well enough to be in a fast middle lane, there was also trouble in the water on long swims. Without even realizing why, if I saw particular boys resting at the end of the pool when I had a few more laps to go, I often stopped short. It was safer to stand up and turn around than swim to the wall and do a flip turn. Going upside down made you vulnerable to attack. Turning around also offered a second of rest, which made Coach angry. Swimmers who turned short of the wall were lazy cheaters. Or girls.

Ironically, I was a breaststroker, and a good one. Whether it was from the aerodynamics of a chest so modest that I tied the back swimsuit straps together with a shoelace to stop the front from gaping, or from a strong kick, I don't know. After a few years, I worked my way up to consistently medal at State Meet. That gave me the honor of demonstrating during age-group stroke clinics.

Laura, a tall blond, demonstrated backstroke. We'd been summer swim friends since we were in the ten-and-under age group. Four years and two age groups later, my body hadn't changed much, but Laura filled out a swimsuit like a grown woman. Each time she reached her arm over her head, her breasts lolled to one side. I couldn't look away. Neither could the boys, who elbowed each other in the ribs and cackled. Even when my breasts developed, they were small and droopy. I tried to blame it on all the hours spent horizontal in the swimming pool, but Laura proved my theory wrong. She looked like Wonder Woman, played by Lynda Carter on TV. Watching Laura backstroke slowly across the pool was positively painful.

In the locker room one day, Laura complimented my scoop-necked dress, the kind with the choker attached, as if she was jealous. I told her it was from the Limited, the new chain that opened its first store in our local shopping center. Laura's dad was an executive there. She could get the dress in every color, but she was uncomfortable with the low neckline. Who knew boobs caused problems, too?

Soon, we discovered we had something besides insecurity in common: a crush on the same boy. Paul was a prankster, always making people laugh. He had a swimmer's body, with the inverted V-shape that still makes me sigh. Plus, his hunky big brother went to college at Kent State. This connection to the massacre made it all the more romantic. Rumor had it Paul's brother dated Sophie, the sexiest girl in ninth grade. Girls who developed early dated older guys who could drive. But not Laura. She and I spent hours in her bedroom talking about Paul while her big brother blasted Alice Cooper in the bedroom next door. The spring formal was coming up, but after her backstroke demonstrations, I knew my chance with Paul was slim.

Then he called me.

I offered him Laura's phone number. Why would he want me instead of this great girl with boobs? He had seen me dripping wet. He knew what he was getting. Why choose that? And yet he did, and we went steady for years. I had been so sucked into this obsession, so convinced that this kind of pretty was important, that it lowered my sense of self-worth.

Decades later, Laura and I reminisced about those times. Since high school, our breasts waxed and waned, but our friendship remained close despite great distance. The last time she was in California, I reminded her of those backstroke demonstrations. I thought we could laugh about them. Instead, her face lit up. She felt such pride I had to shut the fuck up. She thought her technique earned her that honor, and anything else would've been an insult.

Was I blinded by my own breast obsession? Maybe her hands had sliced neatly into the water pinkies first, but I had been too busy watching the boys—and her boobs—to notice. She confessed that she hated her chest in high school. She was embarrassed when boys looked down instead of up at her face. She was afraid to wear a halter top. And her back always hurt.

Boo-hoo, I thought. *I would've taken those problems any day.* Then I remembered her steady diet of Tab and bubble gum back then. She didn't need to diet. She was trying to shrink. There was no name for body shaming yet, but we had both felt it. Our fragile body images of too much or too little gave us a clear reflection of who we were and who we were not. Like a fun-house mirror, it also gave us a faulty view of everyone else.

• • •

Nixon resigned in 1974, the same year my parents divorced. After being reelected in a landslide two years earlier, Nixon's cheating and lies had finally caught up to him. My father's cheating and lies also caught up with *him*, and these two events changed my sense of him as my idol forever. Like Nixon, who was soon pardoned, my father seemed made of Teflon. Nothing bad stuck to him. He was everything that was wrong with the power of men over women. Yet as my body started to resemble my mother's, my sense of her as my new idol was troubling, as well. Just as I had suspected years earlier, she was on the weaker team. And no matter what she did, she would lose.

No-fault divorce laws were created by Ronald Reagan, then governor of California, who was angry that his first wife, Jane Wyman, accused him of mental cruelty. This type of divorce leveled the playing field, but mostly for men. For wives who hoped for reconciliation, charges of adultery were unwise. The new laws spread rapidly across the country. Once a married man lived out of the house for a year, such as my dad who now lived with his girlfriend and her sons, the divorce could not be contested. Like many women whose identities were defined by their family, my mother was devastated. Not only had she pinned her personal life on my father, but her profession highlighted the importance of family. Heartbroken and hoping for reconciliation, she agreed to share a lawyer. And the lawyer showed such respect for her career that she was ashamed to ask for alimony. When the judge saw she was employed, he gave her a paltry amount of child support. Even her family refused to help: my mother's own father blamed her problems on women's lib.

All at once, my father was rich and my mother was poor. Her income as a woman was lower, while her expenses as a single mother were higher. This phenomenon became known as the "feminization of poverty." Smart had worked against her. Soon, pretty did, too. Neighborhood husbands constantly hit on her; their wives considered her a threat.

For years, I had lain awake at night as my parents shouted at each other in the next room. But during the day, I'd noticed how hard my mom worked to earn my father's praise. I was hurt by his betrayal. When I had dinner with him on Wednesday nights, I fed my fury. I gained enough weight to truly need a bra for the first time, a small consolation. Dad always asked about Mom, but he wasn't apologetic. He was simply a man exercising his right to liberty and the pursuit of happiness.

From his perspective, this was the first time our country—founded by Puritans—had displayed breasts openly. Flush with postwar prosperity and technological advances, ours was the first generation with television sets in every home. Almost overnight, we were bombarded with images of women designed to attract eyeballs. And men's eyeballs are hardwired to scan a woman's breasts within 200 milliseconds. According to the Archives of Sexual Behavior, this is an instinctual attraction to women with estrogen to ensure successful childbearing. But the instinct holds true beyond physical encounters, especially when an idealized version of a woman with generous mammary glands can be seen in the comfort of a man's very own living room.

At the same time, popular psychology grew to favor the pursuit of personal happiness. And what man wouldn't be happier with a nubile, starry-eyed soulmate over a nagging, sagging wife? As the hippie culture of free love went mainstream, the swinging seventies became the defining decade for divorce. With over 900 students in my class at Upper Arlington High School, the number of divorces was statistically small. But of those I knew, the dads left the moms for younger women, whose breasts were purely for sex. If I were a man, I might have been tempted, too.

When I got home from dinner on Wednesday nights, Mom would either grill me about him or hole up in her room in the dark. I learned to pick her lock with a bobby pin to make sure she was still breathing. More than once, I crept across the roof to climb in her window. My job was to keep her alive. I was angry at both of my parents, but Mom's behavior was more frustrating. How could she still want him?

Now that I needed a bra, I rebelled by *not* wearing one. After a long winter, I decided to wear a sundress with spaghetti straps for the first day of spring, despite the slush on the ground. While dissecting a frog in tenth-grade biology class, two uniformed cops came to the door. My mother had been found unconscious at the river. They needed me to identify her coat and her picnic blanket so they could log them into evidence. They put me in the back seat of the patrol car with the roof light still flashing. I heard the word homicide. Didn't that mean murder? I leaned forward to say they were wrong. But who would listen to a silly girl in a sundress?

I sat shivering as we drove, sirens blaring, to the river. How could I explain to these bulky men with silver detective badges that my mom was seriously depressed? That my sister and I had been corking her wine and counting her sleeping pills for some time? That my dad had accused her of being out of her mind for so long, that now sometimes she *was* out of her mind. I saw my reflection in the rearview mirror and redirected my anger. How had I not heard her slip out in the middle of the night?

Just as I was losing hope, the cops confirmed that she was alive. In a coma.

At the park by Griggs Dam, they asked me to identify everything within the yellow-taped perimeter. I nodded at the ant-covered items on our red plaid picnic blanket, then watched a tow truck crank my mother's Toronado into the air. My dad was out of town, and Tracy would be stranded at Brownies after school. I needed that car.

By the time I swiped the keys from the police property department and walked four city blocks to the impound lot, the wind was stirring and rain was starting to fall. The attendant in the hut was a greasy-haired guy with his name sewn above the pocket of his short-sleeved shirt. He offered me a pen to sign for the car and asked for ten dollars. I had no money, no driver's license, and no hope of getting the car out of the chain-linked corral. But I had to. I looked up from his dirty fingernails and saw the wall calendar showing a busty girl in a bikini straddling a Harley Davidson. If ever there was a time to play the pretty card, this was it. I pulled my shoulders back and smiled, sweet and innocent, with the hope that this one time, my breasts would be noticed. I may even have given him a fake phone number. Soon enough, he pulled open that gate.

My sister's school was next to the public pool where my dad had taught me to dive off the high board. The streets were empty, so nobody noticed how I kept ramming my mother's car against the curb. When I got there, Tracy was huddled under the eaves from the rain, the only Brownie left. Dad was out of town who knows where, so we ate Spaghet-tiOs for a few days until my grandfather came to visit. We weren't allowed in the ICU without a grown-up. At the hospital, he slipped me a twenty and told me to take care of my mom. Too little, too late. I had already failed. By summer, when it was clear that Mom needed more time to convalesce, Tracy was shipped off to a camp in Virginia, and I was sent on a kamikaze teen tour of Europe, which ended my true swimming career. I did, however, buy a French bikini made of blue triangles connected by tiny gold chains. No longer swimming six hours a day, I had the right kind of points to fill it.

That fall of 1975, Mom was hired at another university and was voted Favorite Professor within a few weeks. Back to high school as a junior, I studied hard, played sports, produced cable TV shows for the school station, and made out with my high school sweetheart. The bra market expanded, offering bras with front hooks and thin nylon for a natural, nippled look. My favorite outfit was a baby blue, tie-dyed leotard with a denim skirt. Going braless was now less of a rebellion and more of a fashion statement. But the statement was an invitation.

When my dad installed a trampoline in the dining room floor of his new house, he hired my gymnastics coach for lessons. Coach was a twenty-two-year-old Ohio State cheerleader, so impressive that my dad encouraged me to date him the summer I turned seventeen. Dad took us along to do an acrobatic exhibition at a Virginia Beach convention and dropped us off at our very own motel room. That put me in an awkward position. I wasn't a virgin, but sex with Coach didn't feel good in any sense of the word. It physically hurt. When I complained, he scolded me for acting like a baby. I escaped to the beach in my fashionable French bikini, but I didn't understand the sexual politics. I felt shame. For the rest of the summer, I had my own private Woodstock, but in September, I put my bra on and went back to the books. Smart was my safety net.

At the start of senior year, my mother got a new teaching job in Virginia. In order to graduate with my class and complete activities for college transcripts, I needed to stay in Ohio. Mom and I had battled for years over whose side I was on, and my resemblance to my father added to her pain. When he was in town, he followed the girls' high school swim team like a mascot. No matter how many miles I swam, I couldn't escape him.

After a few nights sleeping on the shag rug of our empty home, I moved into the trampoline house with my dad and his new wife, the woman he'd moved in with while still married to my mother. I was a traitor. Worse, I enjoyed the frozen hamburgers the enemy left for me to microwave. She wasn't smart or pretty, but she had big boobs.

The day I got back together with my high school boyfriend, I noticed he had a Farrah Fawcett poster taped in his locker. How could I be jealous? Fawcett's Texas cheerleader beauty was beyond reach. The poster, from an Ohio company called Pro-Arts, was the bestselling poster of all time.[4]

Fawcett starred in the first season of *Charlie's Angels*, which launched "jiggle TV."[5] They answered to a man, but they were smart. As a brunette, I identified with Jaclyn Smith, but Fawcett was the all-American blond next door in a modest one-piece swimsuit. And she didn't have centerfold-sized breasts. What she did have, pressing against that thin red fabric, were nipples. Steve Martin highlighted

the attraction during his opening monologue on *Saturday Night Live.*
He complained that Fawcett ". . . never called me *once*. And after the
hours I've spent holding up *her* poster with one hand! Geez!"[6]

Suddenly, size didn't matter. Nipples did. They were the intersection of the sacred and the profane. The very part that babies needed
for nourishment for a limited time in a woman's life could be suckled
anytime for pleasure. This poster put every boy with a few spare bucks
inches away from heaven.

Fawcett was no dummy. When asked about the success of *Charlie's
Angels*, she said, "When the show was number three, I thought it was
our acting. When we got to be number one, I decided it could only
be because none of us wears a bra."[7] Fawcett would appear in *Playboy*
many times over the years, ultimately baring all in a *Playboy* video.[8]
Along the way, she earned an Emmy nomination for *Burning Bed,* a TV
movie about domestic abuse, and rave reviews for *Extremities*, about
an avenging rape victim. It's hard to avoid the contradiction that her
nipples paved the way for her to stand up for women.

In 1972, the year I became a teenager, the Equal Rights Amendment passed in the Senate and moved forward to be ratified across the
country. It felt like destiny. Five years later, when I turned eighteen,
conservative lawyer Phyllis Schlafly's Stop ERA campaign killed it
three states shy of becoming law. The defeat felt personal. As a female,
I'd have to fend for myself.

That winter, Ohio officially ran out of coal. Governor James Rhodes
closed the schools for a month and we set our thermostats below sixty.
On New Year's Day, we bundled up to watch the Rose Bowl game. As
I shivered under a blanket, my eyes were on the pretty cheerleaders on
the sidelines in Pasadena. I dreamt of those palm trees swaying above
in the bright blue sky.

My father's dream was for me to follow in his footsteps and go to
Princeton. But I was tired of cold weather. I was offended by men-only
eating clubs. I could never wear the school color of orange without

being reminded of that triangle-top bikini that had marked me as a failure. Most of all, I was afraid this choice would seal my betrayal of my mother, and she would never forgive me. Fortunately, my dad had been right about his most fervent ideal: hard work pays off. There was strength in being smart. Now, I had my pick of colleges on both coasts, and I planned to get as far away from Ohio as I could possibly go. I just hadn't told him yet.

On a humid spring day, my father held a luncheon at his house for Princeton prospects from central Ohio. I bided my time in my bedroom, where it was cool. Out the window, I could see him, tan and handsome, surrounded by white-haired men at one of the five round tables on the grass. The other tables were filled with gangly high school seniors in stiff white button-downs and dark pants, like an orchestra. If there were any girls, I couldn't tell.

I rifled through the clothes in my closet, but there was nothing remotely preppy. I didn't fit in; I didn't want to. I was not on my dad's team anymore; I was his natural opponent. I slapped through the hangers faster and faster until I saw a way to make him pay. It was time to claim my power as a woman. First, I curled my bangs into wings like Farrah's famous do. Then I pulled on my fuchsia tank dress and cinched the belt tight. For the finishing touch, I slipped off my bra.

When I made my entrance, my dad looked up. He wasn't the only one. Freshly shaved necks twisted to see my long brown hair, my bright pink dress, my breasts straining against the cotton. But I held my father's gaze. He didn't miss a beat as he gestured to the seat of honor beside him. He introduced me to the alumni and another graduating senior at the table. As their eyes darted down below my chin then back up to my face, I felt embarrassed. After I sat down, the men smiled politely and turned back to their conversations. It was obvious that all they saw was "pretty." I panicked, ready to run back in the house to get my awards and acceptance letters, to show them proof I was their equal. Then an elderly stranger asked about my plans, and it all came rushing back.

"I'm going to California."

My father pursed his lips and nodded, but he never said a word.

That summer before I left for college, I worked as a lifeguard at a private swim club. I sat on the stand in my French bikini and twirled my silver whistle as the children splashed. Now *I* was Bikini Girl, with the kind of points that mattered.

I had no idea that California was a whole different league.

Cheerleaders: Sis Boom Breasts!

1880s First cheerleaders are all men at Princeton University.

1923 Women are allowed to cheer at University of Minnesota.

1940s Men go to war, women fill cheer squads.

1950s "Sweater Girl" fashion (tight knit over cone bra) is adopted by cheerleaders.

1960s Organized cheerleading spreads to all ages, to perform at Pee-Wee, Youth, High School, and Professional football games. All are considered volunteers.

1965 UCLA cheerleaders are said to be the most visible face of the university.

1967 USC Song Girls learn twenty-six routines per year and practice five days per week.

1970 Cheerleaders are 95% female. Bare midriffs replace sweaters in uniforms.

AFL & NFL merger bars cheerleaders from changing teams for better pay.

1980 *Playboy*'s January issue features "NFL's Sexiest Cheerleaders!" Cheerleading competitions begin the tradition of sexy outfits and heavy makeup.

2005 The Playboy Playmate of the Year is an Atlanta Falcons cheerleader.

2006 *Dallas Cowboys Cheerleaders: Making the Team* premieres . . . and is still airing.

2010 School cheerleaders are denied Title IX money due to a court verdict that it is not a competitive sport. The injury rate is ranked the highest of any athletic pursuit.

Playboy features cheerleaders from the Miami Dolphins and Mississippi State.

2014 "Jiggle test" involving jumping jacks prompts five Buffalo Bills cheerleaders to sue.

2015 Minimum wage for game time is required for cheerleaders by California law.

2017 Highest rate of catastrophic injuries for female athletes is in competitive cheerleading.

2018 Five former NFL cheerleaders sue the Houston Texans for being "bullied and body-shamed" for less than $7.25 an hour.[1]

2019 Cheerleading is a billion dollar business with nearly 4 million participants; 1.5 million cheerleaders are competitive. And yet:
- More girls are injured in cheerleading than any other athletics.
- Cheerleading is not considered a sport.
- Average NFL game earnings for a cheerleader is $120; for an NFL football player, $1.2 million.
- Pro cheerleaders help the NFL earn an estimated $8.25 million per game day based on the value of broadcast air time, live entertainment for fans, corporate appearances, and merchandising.
- The Dallas Cowboys Cheerleaders earn $0 for posing in annual swimsuit calendar.
- Cheerleader outfits are among the most popular costumes for Halloween—and porn.

2020 The TV documentary series *Cheer* raises public awareness of the danger of competitive cheerleading, and the exclusion of Title IX protection. Due to the main purpose of supporting other teams, cheerleading is still defined as a school activity, not a sport.

Sexual harassment extends to the NFL executive offices, per the claims of fifteen female employees and several journalists who accused the Washington Redskins organization of workplace misconduct from 2006 to 2019.[2] Fourteen cannot testify due to Non-Disclosure agreements.

Six

CALIFORNIA GIRLS
1978

The Beach Boys' hit spread the image of suntanned girls in bikinis from Brian Wilson's acid-fueled brain to the entire country's subconscious. In 1965, when "California Girls" was number three on the Billboard charts, the "pinup" became a real girl. I puzzled over whether I was a Midwest farmer's daughter or a Northern girl who kept my boyfriend "warm at night." When the chorus sang "I wish they all could be California girls," I jumped at the chance.

It wasn't just me. When David Lee Roth covered the song twenty years later, it bounced back to number three and the bikini-laden video was nominated for four MTV awards. Katy Perry's "California Gurls" topped the others at number one. She embodied the wholesome, sexy power of the California girl, with the kind of breasts most guys dream of. I mean, dream of sucking. At least, that's what my husband says. She doesn't toy with the question of whether its sacred or profane. She isn't encased in a pile of whipped cream like the model on that iconic Herb Alpert album, *Whipped Cream & Other Delights*. She wears cupcakes with cherries for her nipples! She shoots whipped cream from her bikini top! She sprays it like breast milk and sings, "We'll melt your popsicle." It's purely profane.

After years of shivering under winter blankets while watching cheerleaders shimmy under palm trees at the Rose Bowl, my path was clear. College was my excuse to move to the West Coast. UCLA, however, was a rude awakening. Not only did freshman classes over-flow the vast lecture halls, but there weren't enough dorms. I slept on a secondhand mattress on the floor of an apartment three miles off campus, where one of my want-ad roommates had noisy sex all night, every night.

Greek life ruled campus, so I joined a sorority to make friends. I pulled on my peasant skirt, the height of summer fashion in Ohio, and competed with a hundred homecoming queens in designer dresses. There are two reasons why there are so many beautiful women in Los Angeles. First, every beautiful girl with acting aspirations heads to Hollywood. Second, they stay and reproduce. It was painfully obvious that I was not a California girl, at least not yet. Fortunately, I met Diane, a friendly, flat-chested, six-foot-tall transfer student who rowed crew. Together, we were invited to pledge Alpha Phi.

A week later, the entire sorority was summoned. When all fifty girls were assembled and silent, the president turned out the lights and passed a lit candle. A diamond engagement ring circled the wax shaft. When the candle made it back to the row of tittering seniors, the blond in the middle blew out the flame. There were *ooh*s and *aah*s all around. I looked up in horror and caught Diane's eye. This was the goal of college life? Bonded, we soon led the Pledge Class as president and Song Leader. When our leadership skills proved too strong—a dirty song here, a date with a senior's ex there—the sorority held us back from initiation. We quit, moved in together, and tried out for *Playboy*.

You read that right. The *Daily Bruin* advertised an open call for girls of the Pac-10 schools, "no nudity required." Diane learned it was legit from a steakhouse hostess who'd been a Bunny in the Chicago Playboy Club before aging out at twenty-three. She was proud, as if it were an elite sorority of women. And maybe it was, with such notable cotton-tails as Debbie Harry and Lauren Hutton. We didn't need a sorority or an engagement ring to prove our worth. We could personify the California dream in cut-off Bruins football jerseys.

I paired beachy wrap shorts with a bare-shouldered top while Diane knotted a Danskin skirt around a shiny bodysuit. I did her makeup, and she fluffed my perm. Then we drove my little Fiat to a nondescript office building off-campus. Giddy with nerves, we took the elevator upstairs. When the door slid open, I hesitated. This was so opposite our desire to have equal stature to men. Even though we planned to keep our clothes on, we would be judged by our body parts. To assuage our guilt, we decided to use nicknames. I was Lee and she was Dee.

Our new names felt daring, so we held our heads high and knocked on the door of the suite rented for the audition. A clean-cut man in a white button-down looked at us thoughtfully. Since Diane stood a foot taller than me in her platform Candies, we were used to scrutiny. Now we fidgeted. She chattered about nothing while I bit my nails. The man gestured for us to sit on the couch, then asked for photos. We pulled out 3x5s taken of each other at our apartment. He asked if we had body shots, but we did not. I sat up straight, hoping he would ask us to take our shirts off, so we could say no. Instead, he smiled and said, no problem.

Another applicant emerged from the bathroom and thanked him on her way out. She was a polished young woman carrying a flat black portfolio under her arm. Diane shrunk a few inches, then looked at me. She pointed to the glossy 8x10 headshots of models on the coffee table. This was a casting call. That girl didn't look like a college student, but the man didn't care. He kept her photos and gave ours back.

Afterward, we went to Hamburger Hamlet and shared a hot fudge sundae. I read that champagne glasses were inspired by Marie

Antoinette's breasts, but the goblet holding our sundae was more like Dolly Parton. We dug in for comfort. We wanted a public stamp of approval that said "pretty," and there weren't many ways to do that. Just *Playboy*, beauty pageants, and cheerleading. As the real "girls next door," we didn't measure up.

After that rejection, we used brown eye shadow to contour our breasts for dates. Diane cut out pictures of Bond girls and studied them closely. She was a trained dancer, so we fought over my rock 'n' roll-only record player until I let her play disco. She practiced for the city-wide disco dance contest at Dillon's in Westwood—and won. Next she tried out to be a UCLA Song Girl. Since I'd been co-captain of my high school gymnastics team, she talked me into trying out for the cheerleading squad with her. Still ignorant in all things beauty, we ponytailed our hair and wore shorts. Neither of us made the team.

Diane did not give up. A year later, she combined her talent and charisma to win Miss Santa Monica. At the Miss California pageant, she won Miss Congeniality. But personality can only get you so far. She lost to a contestant with cleavage. Then she spotted the January 1980 cover of *Playboy* featuring "NFL's Sexiest Cheerleaders." Lesson learned, she tried out for UCLA Song Girl again. She wore a padded bra, piled on the makeup, and became one of those mythical beauties whose siren call lured me to California. Now she was certified "pretty." When *Playboy* came calling, she laughed.

I spoke to my friend recently about our *Playboy* rejection to confirm my recollection. Did it have to do with boobs? "Of course it did," she said. "Everybody wanted the whole package. Boobs were part of being pretty. You couldn't have one without the other."

From a distance, it's easy to see how the dots connect from beauty queens to cheerleaders to Playboy Playmates. From there it was hardly a leap to drunk coeds flashing their breasts for *Girls Gone Wild* videos in 1997. Those late-night TV commercials were so successful that *Playboy* asked *GGW* to make ads for them. In 2013, the year after

#FreetheNipple took off, *Girls Gone Wild* declared bankruptcy. But they didn't disappear. Four years later, *GGW* had 278 million Twitter followers. To me, this reveals the fallacy of women protesting for the right to bare their chests. Surely, *GGW* fans and Playboy Channel subscribers are all in favor of free nipples. How do we distinguish empowerment from exploitation when the viewer benefits from both?

At a recent dinner held by the Women's Leadership Council of Los Angeles, a mentorship program weighted heavily with law partners and bank executives, members played an icebreaker game over appetizers. The goal was to reveal a personal secret. As a black sheep in the group of executives, I figured what the hell. I confessed my *Playboy* experience and heard a collective gasp. After dessert, a stunning woman at the top of her profession pulled me aside to say she'd been a Bunny at a Key Club. She smiled as if it was a wonderful memory. Yet she told me quietly. Would it have ruined her reputation at the dinner table? Probably not. It may have been a distraction, though, or fuel for any who thought her hard-earned career was helped by good looks. This successful professional was trying to console me that I wasn't alone. But the fact was, she had gotten that public approval. I did not.

After freshman year, I took a fall quarter furlough to enjoy the beach. I moved to San Diego with my handsome Italian boyfriend and my father cut me off. My mother, who had yanked my sister out of high school to follow me to California, called me a college dropout. She called me that for the next twenty years, long after I graduated. Maybe she feared I'd strayed from the safe path. But education hadn't provide safety for her. As a woman, there was no safe path.

My boyfriend and I moved into a Pacific Beach apartment building filled with other couples our age, which is to say, college age. But the guys worked in factories and pizza parlors. The gals taught dancing and served cocktails. This was real life for blue-collar kids who couldn't afford, or had no inclination toward, higher education. For my boyfriend and me, it was playtime. However, being book smart was not a survival skill that paid our rent. When our savings ran out, we ate a lot of leftover pizza. Soon I had to unbutton the top of my favorite sundress to make room for spillage.

As I collected sand dollars on the beach one morning, a man with a fancy camera asked if I was interested in modeling. I was flattered enough to take his business card, but I wasn't stupid. The only modelling I could do would not get me on a New York runway. I'd worked since I was fourteen, teaching gymnastics, cashiering at Wendy's, and lifeguarding. I'd also worked the late shift at a twenty-four-hour mini-market, where men came in to buy *Hustler* and *Penthouse*, magazines far more explicit than *Playboy*. After a few dismal weeks of job hunting, I considered the business card on our banged-up dresser. How many buttons would I unfasten for money? It would be so easy.

A few years later, a Hooters opened on the exact spot where I was "discovered." The "breastaurant" was a fabulous success, despite starting as an April Fools' Day joke in Florida. The owners named it after Steve Martin's *Saturday Night Live* sketch, "What I Believe: . . . that breasts should be called hooters."[1] The first Hooters Girl was the winner of the Jose Cuervo Bikini Contest, but the owners made sure she knew her place. They made her mop the floors before posing in a push-up bra for the billboard.

The Hooters Employee Handbook required the applicant to be the "All-American Cheerleader, Surfer, Girl Next Door." Sound familiar? This was a public access Playboy Club, where employees had to sign a statement acknowledging a work environment where "joking and innuendo based on female sex appeal is commonplace."[2] Their calendar launched "successful modeling careers," including Hugh Hefner's Playmate, Holly Madison.

Still, sexual harassment was so prevalent that even San Diego mayor Bob Filner was barred from four local Hooters in 2013. When the original Hooters was remodeled, the sign called it an "augmentation in process." By 2016, there were 430 franchised Hooters paying minimum wage to the young women who made them famous. Several rose to management positions. I was pleased when the company donated nearly $2 million to breast cancer research after the death of one of the Hooters Girls. Then I read about the $20 million renovation of the Las Vegas Hooters Hotel, and the hundreds of millions made annually by the franchise corporation. The cancer donation was a mere cash tip in the corporate bra.

Would I have applied for a job at Hooters when I was down and out? It's hard to say. I shudder at the thought of my daughters working there. The Hooters bikini contest celebrates the lowest common denominator. *Playboy*, by its very selectivity, seems more elite. Even Hefner refused to show full nudity until *Penthouse* outsold him. In 2017, *Penthouse* claimed to help women by hiring one to take over. Turns out she was a director of pornographic films planning to open a chain of Hooters-style "breastaurants."[3]

Just as I was considering food stamps, I landed a hostess job requiring a shoulder-baring peasant top at a Mexican restaurant. What's the difference between that and a tank top with a push-up bra? Tips. At nineteen, if I wanted to make more money, the path was clear. Learn to balance six plates of burritos or bare my breasts.

After a few months, my boyfriend headed back to UCLA. I missed the deadline for their film school by a day, so I applied to USC. The good news? I got in. The bad news? Tuition. With general education classes to kill, I enrolled at San Diego State. There, I took a philosophy course that revealed classical beliefs that women were handicapped from the start. Aristotle declared that the female has a "certain lack of qualities," a natural "defectiveness." Plato thanked Nature for being created "a man, not a woman." These tracts seemed woefully out of date when even TV commercials claimed we could do it all.

By spring, every coed I knew pantomimed the Enjoli perfume jingle while primping for keg parties. Holding a blow dryer up like a microphone to our lip-glossed mouths, we sang to future husbands,

"We can bring home the bacon, fry it up in a pan, and never let you forget you're a man."[4] We didn't notice that the message was mixed. The commercial starred a beauty who wore a high-buttoned blouse as a businesswoman, a baggy blouse to cook, then a breast-hugging dress for her date. Biology still defined us. We followed Olivia Newton John's lead at the end of *Grease* and dressed sexy for the boys.

With my boyfriend back in LA, I was on my own in San Diego. And it confirmed everything I'd suspected about the pecking order of women. After moving into a coed dorm on a sunny weekend afternoon, I hit the pool. Lana was the first one I noticed in the crowd of sunbathers on the deck. Perusing a poetry book while snacking on cheese and crackers, she was both elegant and amply endowed. She was also an island of calm in a sea of students fighting over bags of potato chips. Boys circled her in awe, then shoved regular girls in the pool. When I spread my towel by hers, she explained that she was an English major dating her professor. Here's the thing with clichés: they're usually true. That's how they become clichés.

The next afternoon, we drove up the coast to La Jolla. We found her professor's apartment and circled the block a few times. On the way back, we stopped at a café and the line of customers parted for her. We were seated immediately and sent complementary cocktails we weren't old enough to drink. I felt golden by association. Excited to show her off, I called my boyfriend 120 miles north to plan a double date. A week later, he brought a friend to meet us halfway in Newport Beach. After a spaghetti dinner, my boyfriend and I walked ahead. A few minutes later, Lana was waiting by my car. Her date had gotten grabby. He was angry that he'd bought her dinner and gotten nothing in return. My boyfriend defended his pal.

When Lana and I drove back down the San Diego Freeway, I averted my eyes from the San Onofre Nuclear Power Plant. The enormous twin domes resembled breasts. Lana never spoke to me again. I thought we were friends, but years later I realized she was more of a trophy. I wanted to apologize, but never found her.

I moved back to the beach in San Diego with two friends from the dorm and another student who answered our ad. I was still in a long-distance romance with my Italian boyfriend, but the other girls were dating. Brenda was the most beautiful, with long legs, long wavy hair, and kohl-smudged eyes. She filled her Danskin bodysuit in a way that stopped the roller skaters zooming past on the Pacific Beach boardwalk. One afternoon she, our roommate Annie, and I were all sunbathing in the sand when a rock star with long hair and a leather jacket wandered up. He looked us all over, then smiled at Brenda. They disappeared into her bedroom. After a few days, she emerged smiling.

Our fourth roommate was a petite student who rented a closet-sized room. She worked full shifts at Denny's to pay off a breast reduction. Insurance companies didn't care about back strain. We were surprised to learn about the surgery, though, because she still had ample breasts. In fact, she had enough to please two steady boyfriends who knew about each other.

A few years later, the American Society of Plastic Surgeons would call small breasts a "disease" that caused body distortion.[5] The FDA approved implants to improve quality of life. As busts got bigger in the movies, most viewers were inclined to agree. I was one of them. I never considered implants, but I taught exercise classes at a local gym wearing a padded bra beneath my high cut leotard.

When I think back, I couldn't have been too "diseased." After hurting my back during summer school in Monterey, I saw a chiropractor who felt me up every week. There was enough for him to palm my breasts on Tuesday afternoons as he stood behind me to adjust my ribs. I stood, staring at his certificates on the wall, wondering if there was a different way to do this. How could I ask him politely to remove his clammy hands from my bare skin? I said it in my head, but he didn't hear me. And soon enough, my rib would pop back in to prove his method right. I was too ashamed to mention it to my boyfriend, whose family had referred me to the chiropractor. They'd either think I was stupid or exaggerating. Right?

In film school, you only needed to *have* breasts to be considered pretty. With so few females enrolled, size did not matter. The instructors didn't expect much of us, nor did they appreciate our perspective. One of my first Super 8 films was called "Common Ground." I borrowed lights and drove for an hour to shoot my sloppy teenaged sister begin her day with cold pizza, a sip of beer, and a birth control pill. I contrasted the footage with my polished mother, now a therapist in Irvine, beginning her day with a beauty routine, a proper breakfast, and her own birth control pill. It was a provocative statement about the reproductive power of two generations of females. My fellow students, all male, yawned, and the professor gave me a C-. A few weeks later, I set classical music to a filmed collage of flowers at Rogers Gardens and he gave me an A.

When our video production class was invited to meet with Sherry Lansing, the first female executive to head a major film studio, I couldn't wait. I was so excited to meet a true role model that I bought a suit on sale at Casual Corner. When we arrived at Fox, however, she wasn't there. As consolation, we were treated to private screening of their brand-new film *Porky's*, about a bunch of boys trying to lose their virginity. The irony was inescapable as I stared up at the screen, where young actors spied into a girls' locker room and ogled their breasts. The boys in the row behind me whispered lewd jokes into my ear. I left in tears, but had to wait in the hallway for it to end. My grade depended on attendance.

Back in my studio apartment, I typed up a complaint to Ms. Lansing. *Porky's* had been made before she got the job, but how could she approve our screening? Frustrated, I rekindled my inspiration by reading *Daily Variety*. An article reported that Christine Hefner, Hugh's daughter, had been appointed president of Playboy Enterprises. Hef was quoted saying he wouldn't mind if she posed in the magazine, but he didn't want her sleeping around. Only he could do that. For me, the message was clear: play like the boys to get ahead. Fearing that my letter to Ms. Lansing could ruin my career, I ripped it up. To this day, I regret it.

Senior year, I was the producer/production manager of a video called "War Games," about a policeman—a Vietnam veteran with PTSD—who shoots an unarmed boy. We hadn't finished casting, so the director, Kevin Tenney, asked me to fill in for a lighting test. I had no acting experience beyond my ninth-grade play, but all I had to do was play wife and console the hero when he awakens from a nightmare. There was no wardrobe, so I pulled a pink cotton nightgown over my bra. Kevin vetoed the bra; he said it was not realistic.

"Neither are those bright lights," I argued. "Besides, Marilyn Monroe wore a bra to bed."

He grinned. "Whatever you say, sweetie."

Clearly, Marilyn needed one more. Mine came off.

By coincidence, Matthew Broderick starred in a feature with the same title that year. Later, he married Sarah Jessica Parker, who always wore bras to bed in *Sex in the City*. She was unusually endowed for such a slender woman, so perhaps she was covering surgery scars. Or perhaps she was shy. Maybe it was easier to claim shyness than to demand respect. To succeed in the film business, women had to play nice. And by the 1980s, playing nice meant baring your breasts.

After seeing the dailies, the crew started calling me Sexy Leslie. A mere hint of breast was enough to merit the nickname. This generic flattery made me uncomfortable. Of course, I wanted to look sexy, but not at school, and definitely not to the guys on our crew. Worse, the footage was usable. My performance wouldn't win any Oscars, but Kevin wanted to save the cash budgeted for a real actress. He wanted to spend it on special effects in the Vietnam scene we were shooting at Camp Pendleton. My real job was to pinch pennies, so it seemed prudent to agree. I had one condition: if anyone called me

Sexy Leslie, he had to shut it down. Kevin laughed and said it was my fault for being a good producer. He meant it as a compliment, but it didn't feel like one. Later, I learned that the Hugh M. Hefner Moving Image Archive stored the student films. Turns out I made it into *Playboy* after all.

Just before graduation, "War Games" won the Student Emmy. The Television Academy held the ceremony in Beverly Hills, and on awards night I was on top of the world, wearing a gold-knit tank dress. This was surely a dress rehearsal for my future Academy Award. It was also a great career opportunity. In 1982, the school had no job placement office or networking events. The school was housed in shacks around a courtyard on the outskirts of campus. The slogan "Reality Ends Here" was graffitied over the entrance. For women, however, reality did not end in that land of make believe. To the contrary, it had just begun.

When it was my turn to take a bow, I smoothed down my sparkly skirt and mentioned seeking a job in production. Laughter filled the room. I felt my face flush and looked around at all the men. Was that impolite? Obvious? Or just unlikely?

I would soon find out.

Bare Breasts in American Film

1960s: *Bonnie and Clyde*, Faye Dunaway; *Easy Rider*, Toni Basil; *The Graduate*, Anne Bancroft*; *Promises! Promises!*, Jayne Mansfield; *Rosemary's Baby*, Mia Farrow; *Valley of the Dolls*, Sharon Tate; *What's New Pussycat*, Romy Schneider

1970s: *10*, Bo Derek; *Animal House*, many; *Caligula*, Helen Mirren; *Carrie*, Sissy Spacek; *Chinatown*, Faye Dunaway; *Coming Home*, Jane Fonda*; *Dirty Harry*, Debralee Scott; *The Evil Dead,* Betsy Baker; *Foxy Brown*, Pam Grier; *The Godfather*, Simonetta Stefanelli; *Hair*, Beverly D'Angelo; *Halloween*, P. J. Soles; *Klute,* Jane Fonda*; *The Last Picture Show*, Kimberly Hyde; *Looking for Mr. Goodbar*, Diane Keaton; *MASH*, Sally Kellerman; *Myra Breckinridge*, Farrah Fawcett; *Pink Flamingos,* Mink Stole; *Pretty Baby*, Susan Sarandon; *Shaft*, Margaret Warncke

1980s: *9½ Weeks*, Kim Basinger; *About Last Night*, Demi Moore; *The Accused*, Jodie Foster*; *The Adventures of Baron Munchausen*, Uma Thurman; *American Gigolo*, many; *Caddyshack*, Cindy Morgan; *Coming to America*, Felicia Taylor; *Dangerous Liaisons*, Uma Thurman; *Die Hard*, Cheryl Baker; *Do the Right Thing*, Rosie Perez; *Earth Girls Are Easy*, Geena Davis; *Fast Times at Ridgemont High*, Phoebe Cates, Jennifer Jason Leigh; *Fatal Attraction*, Glenn Close; *The Last Temptation of Christ*, Barbara Hershey; *Lethal Weapon*, Jackie Swanson; *Porky's*, Kim Cattrall; *Purple Rain*, Apollonia; *Ragtime*, Elizabeth McGovern; *The Return of the Living Dead*, Linnea Quigley; *Revenge of the Nerds*, Julia Montgomery; *Risky Business*, Rebecca De Mornay, Francine Locke; *Romancing the Stone*, Kathleen Turner; *Scarface*, Mary Elizabeth Mastrantonio; *The Shining*, Lia Beldam; *Silkwood*, Meryl Streep; *S.O.B.*, Julie Andrews; *The Terminator*, Linda Hamilton; *Tequila Sunrise*, Michelle Pfeiffer; *Trading Places*, Jamie Lee Curtis; *Witness*, Kelly McGillis; *Working Girl*, Melanie Griffith

1990s: *American Beauty*, Mena Suvari; *American Pie*, Shannon Elizabeth; *As Good as It Gets*, Helen Hunt*; *Austin Powers,* Fabiana Udenio; *Basic Instinct*, Sharon Stone; *The Big Lebowski*, Julianne Moore; *Boogie Nights*, many; *Boys Don't Cry*, Hilary Swank*, Chloe Sevigny; *Boyz n the Hood,* Nia Long; *Braveheart*, Catherine McCormack; *Contact*, Jodie Foster; *Demolition Man,* Brandy Ledford; *Desperado*, Salma Hayek; *The Devil's Advocate,* Charlize Theron; *Dracula*, Monica Bellucci; *Eyes Wide Shut*, Nicole Kidman; *G. I. Jane*, Demi Moore; *The Grifters,* Annette Bening; *Jerry Maguire*, Kelly Preston; *Jungle Fever*, Lonette McKee; *Leaving Las Vegas*, Elisabeth Shue; *Mississippi Masala*, Sarita Choudhury; *Money Train*, Jennifer Lopez; *Mulholland Falls*, Jennifer Connelly; *Nell*, Jodie Foster; *Pretty Woman*, Julia Roberts; *Schindler's List*, Magdalena Komornicka; *Shakespeare in Love*, Gwyneth Paltrow*; *Showgirls*, many; *Striptease*, Demi Moore; *Thelma & Louise*, Susan Sarandon; *Titanic*, Kate Winslet; *Total Recall*, Sharon Stone; *Wild at Heart*, Laura Dern; *Wild Things*, Denise Richards; *Commandments,* Courteney Cox

2000s: *8 Mile*, Gina Lynn; *The 40-Year-Old Virgin*, Catherine Keener; *300*, Lena Headey; *About Schmidt,* Kathy Bates; *Adaptation*, Judy Greer; *Almost Famous*, Kate Hudson; *American Psycho*, many; *Brokeback Mountain*, Anne Hathaway, Michelle Williams; *Closer,* Natalie Portman; *Coyote Ugly*, Piper Perabo; *Frida,* Salma Hayek; *Gangs of New York*, Cameron Diaz; *The Hangover*, Heather Graham; *Harold & Kumar*, Malin Akerman; *In the Cut*, Meg Ryan; *Lucky Number Slevin*, Lucy Liu; *Monster*, Charlize Theron*; *Monster's Ball*, Halle Berry*; *Mulholland Dr.*, Naomi Watts; *The Notebook*, Rachel McAdams; *Rachel Getting Married*, Anne Hathaway; *The Reader*, Kate Winslet*; *Requiem for a Dream*, Aliya Campbell; *Road Trip*, Amy Smart; *Scary Movie*, Anna Faris; *Secretary*, Maggie Gyllenhaal; *Something's Gotta Give*, Diane Keaton; *Swordfish*, Halle Berry; *Taking Lives,* Angelina Jolie; *Unfaithful,* Diane Lane; *V for Vendetta*, Natalie Portman; *Vanilla Sky*, Penelope Cruz, Cameron Diaz; *Wedding Crashers*, Isla Fisher; *The Wrestler*, Marisa Tomei; *The Good Girl*, Jennifer Aniston; *Powder Blue*, Jessica Biel

2010s: *American Hustle*, Amy Adams; *Atomic Blonde*, Charlize Theron; *Before Midnight*, Julie Delpy; *Blue Valentine*, Michelle Williams; *Carol*, Cate Blanchett, Rooney Mara; *Earthquake Bird*, Alicia Vikander; *Ex Machina*, Alicia Vikander; *50 Shades of Gray*, Dakota Johnson; *Gone Girl,* Rosamund Pike; *Hot Tub Time Machine*, Jessica Paré; *Lawless*, Jessica Chastain; *Love & Other Drugs*, Anne Hathaway; *State of Affairs*, Katherine Heigl; *Machete*, Lindsay Lohan; *Melancholia*, Kirsten Dunst; *Mother!*, Jennifer Lawrence; *The Danish Girl*, Alicia Vikander*; *Girl with the Dragon Tattoo*, Rooney Mara; *The Kids Are Alright*, Julianne Moore; *The Rum Diary*, Amber Heard; *The Sessions*, Helen Hunt; *The Wolf of Wall Street*, Margot Robbie; *Wild,* Reese Witherspoon; *Take This Waltz*, Sarah Silverman; *On the Road*, Kristen Stewart; *The Night Clerk*, Ana de Armas . . . and more every year.

*Won Academy Award

Note: Many of these actresses appeared topless in more than one film.

PART TWO

THE BOOBY TRAP:
Adulthood

Seven

FROM MS. TO MOM
1983

Being an adult went beyond discovering who I was—it meant deciding. But soon became clear it wasn't up to me. My identity had far too much to do with my breasts. To be a career woman, I had to hide them. To be a mother, I had to use them. I tried my best to do both.

After film school, I worked freelance as a production assistant and scored two weeks of work on *The Doobie Brothers' Farewell*, a concert video for Showtime. The job paid $200 for a six-day week, but it was on the legendary Paramount lot. During an epic heat wave, I started at dawn running purchase orders from our second-floor sweatbox clear to the executive building. I played along with the flirting—that's what we called sexual harassment back then—and ran back to type memos until midnight. I was living the dream.

When the producer invited me to the shoot, I packed my best sundress, a butter yellow halter, and flew to Berkeley. I ironed my dress on the hotel bed and burnt the bedspread, forfeiting my paycheck. It was worth it. I was working with one of my favorite bands on a real

TV show. The prep meeting was in a cavernous room backstage at the Greek Theatre. Introductions were made, from the band and roadies to the film crew, and finally me. The only one in a dress. Without a bra. I felt slightly self-conscious, until one of the musicians smiled and said they'd been looking forward to meeting me. He pointed to a memo pinned to the bulletin board. When I went to admire my handiwork after the meeting, I saw why. I had typed, *To: The Boobie Brothers*.

I never went to work without a blazer again.

Fortunately, the football-sized shoulder pads Nolan Miller designed for *Dynasty* were trickling down to my price point. Coco Chanel defined "power dressing" in the 1920's, but it wasn't until women entered the boardroom in the late seventies that it meant dressing like men from head to toe. By the eighties, ties morphed into floppy bows that Meg Whitman, CEO of Hewlett Packard, claimed were an "attempt to be feminine but fit [in]."[1] Their resemblance to the ribbons adorning pussy-cats led to the nickname "pussy bows," an irony that is now hard to ignore. I committed to my career by splurging on three.

By now, I'd given my boyfriend the benefit of the doubt when he claimed to get crabs from a toilet seat. I was polite when his mom sent me *The Joy of Cooking* for Christmas. But when he bought me a low-cut leather dress, I exchanged it for a briefcase and broke things off.

I needed a steady job to share rent in Palms, a small neighborhood in the armpit of two major freeways. Despite my production experience, the only jobs available for women required typing. Clearly, that was not my strength. After scanning the classifieds, I applied for a receptionist job at a bicoastal production company. I interviewed alongside a dozen others, but I was the only one wearing a suit. That made me the best man for the job.

With my breasts safely hidden, I did more than man the phones. I estimated budgets, hired crew, and wrapped the jobs for five directors. Promoted to West Coast production manager, I cut my hair short and wore horn-rimmed glasses. I told myself this was to look older and worthy of respect. During my first week, I got to order custom shirts for Bob Hope—famous for boob jokes on USO tours, like calling Jayne Mansfield "the two and only"—on a Texaco spot. During the second week, I got to approve payment for a director's birthday cake, a three-dimensional sculpture of breasts. The third week, my boss invited me out for a drink at the strip club across the street.

To regain a sense of femininity, I wore lace panties under my armor. Victoria's Secret became a household name when the owner of the Limited bought it and opened their headquarters in my hometown of Columbus, Ohio. They were the first to sell lingerie to the masses. They were also the first to use high fashion models to show the world how it should look, so it was a mixed blessing. By the mid-eighties, I could shop at their stores in LA. Newly confident with my lacy undergarments, I bought a new suit with a skirt—in hot pink. A popular new director joined the company and made lewd comments as he followed me upstairs every morning. I complained to my boss, but he told me not to be so sensitive, that the sexy remarks were compliments. When the director skipped the innuendo for a few days, I feared for my job. Sexual harassment laws existed, but complaining was too much of a risk. I wanted this career, not a payout. And somewhere deep inside, I *did* feel flattered.

Despite the workload, my salary stalled at the receptionist level. I asked for a raise, but the big boss in New York said no. My boss, the executive producer, slipped me gas money and said it wasn't personal. Then he invited me to his wife's baby shower, where they served caviar pie. Dressing like a man clearly wasn't enough for me to be paid like one.

One day, I spotted a receipt for piña colada mix in the petty cash and called the prop guy in to explain. Drew, the property assistant, was tall and handsome, always carrying the *Wall Street Journal* under his arm. When I looked up, his blue eyes peered at me through black-rimmed glasses as if my desk wasn't standing between us. I approved the charge. He invited me to a video shoot some of the crew was doing, changing the lyrics of Cyndi Lauper's anthem to "grips just wanna have fun." When I met him at the soundstage, we watched his friend in a Hawaiian shirt lip synch while lounging in a baby pool. The women in bikinis serving him grapes on cue looked far more normal than models we usually cast. Drew described one as "zaftig," and the other "aerodynamic." I was smitten. In a town full of tens, I figured a man who appreciated women of all shapes was an eleven.

He was also a Marine who did two tours of Vietnam and fought a charge of treason when he formally became a Conscientious Objector. The first time he awoke with nightmares from PTSD, I had déjà vu. I'd played the wife of a Vietnam vet who woke up with nightmares in the prize-winning video I produced during film school. Not only did I have a soft spot for war protestors after getting caught in the riots at Ohio State, but being with this man felt like destiny. One night he shoved me against the sink and confessed that he had an emotional black hole from the war. But I was wearing that broad-shouldered power suit. I thought I could handle anything.

Soon after, I went to a wedding in Ohio, where most of my friends were on baby number two. My dad, who had been so proud that I was a career woman, was growing concerned about my prospects. When I returned to California, Drew surprised me with a set of antique furniture, including a vanity where I could look in the mirror and brush my hair. I'd been collecting heart-shaped lockets and opal rings since my first kiss in fifth grade, but furniture? This was serious. Drew was a dozen years older than me and eager to have a family. He thought I would be a wonderful mother. Why he thought that about a woman who took pride in working on holidays, I'll never know. Nevertheless, it was flattering. No one ever wanted my babies before, not even me.

Yet at twenty-five, my hormones were at an all-time high. And here was a man who saw me as a woman. He could be the passionate artist, while I took care of business. I thought I could have it all. When he admitted that his ex-girlfriend, a buxom blond, warned that I'd never marry him, I took it as a dare and proposed. He got down on one knee and proposed back. We wed within the year.

My dream shifted from running a movie studio to making films with Drew. Tired of making commercials, I gave my boss the standard two weeks' notice when my film school friends invited me to make a horror movie called *Witchboard*. My boss was furious. I thought it was because he had spent valuable time training me, and I was grateful. But six months later, I ran into him at a restaurant. He was interviewing the man who would finally replace me—at three times my salary. Those suits hadn't made me equal at all.

Working freelance, I thought it would be easier to get paid on merit. I grew my hair long and wore trendy oversized earrings. Yet the better I got at my job, the more I was hired to prep big budget projects only to have the male producer swoop in for the shoot, then leave me to wrap. I started working my way up the production ladder in movies, but after working with Prince on a concert film and Charles Bukowski on his ode to alcoholism, I cared more about the content. I thought I could do better. I wrote scripts between jobs and collected a folder full of rejection letters.

Finally, I got a bite from a literary agency for a screenplay called "Heartless." The young agent called me in. I borrowed a sleeveless silk top and pants from my mother. I didn't know what writers wore, but I didn't think I needed a jacket. This was about words on the page. During the meeting, the agent asked an older woman to join us. She looked me over for a long minute.

"Did you write this all by yourself?" she asked.

I was speechless. Until now, I hadn't believed the adage that women were like "crabs in a barrel," keeping others down to claim space on top. I thought there was space for all of us. I was crushed to think that I had come so close, only to be pushed down by a woman.

By the time Melanie Griffith played Tess in the Oscar-nominated *Working Girl*, no one could deny that power dressing required hiding your breasts. When she bared her décolletage for date night, she said, "I have a head for work and a bod for sin."[2] At first, I thought she'd nailed the schizophrenic identity of women. But this was a Hollywood sham, and I was working for the dream machine that made it. I was learning the hard way that you couldn't do both.

So, I did the next best thing. I got pregnant.

My Cinderella moment arrived within weeks. My breasts tingled like an early warning system. Sure, they were sore and itchy and destined for stretch marks, but none of that mattered when I looked in the mirror. Instead of drooping from the weakening of ligaments, my breasts puffed up like party balloons. Not only did I lose weight from the initial burn of calories, but for the first time in my life, I had the décolletage of my dreams.

I booked a reservation to celebrate at Ivy at the Shore, a romantic restaurant in Santa Monica that was on my bucket list for when we became rich and famous. We waited weeks to get a table, and after seeing Arnold Schwarzenegger at the valet, I would have been happy to sit by the kitchen. It was one thing to pretend not to notice celebrities on the streets of Los Angeles, but another to dine with them. The pink walls and elephant palms were part Palm Beach, part Rick's in *Casablanca*. The famous soft-shelled crab cost half the price of a baby crib, so I wore a dress I already owned. It was a simple black style made popular a few years earlier by the red-lipped models who pretended to play guitar in Robert Palmer's "Addicted to Love" video. Now that I had cleavage, there was nothing simple about it.

As we strolled inside, a flashbulb popped. The paparazzi mistook us for movie stars. Despite the throng of TV actors waiting at the bamboo bar, we were seated immediately on the porch. We gazed over the heads of tourists on Ocean Avenue to watch the sun, a ball of fire, set over the Pacific. This was everything I'd imagined when I escaped from Ohio.

Drew was pleased about the preferential treatment, but he didn't care nearly as much as I did about my boobs. He was more excited about the baby. Plus, he was an ass-man, or so he had said back when that was my finest feature. Now he had it all. We both did.

Soon, the metaphorical clock struck midnight and my belly caught up to my breasts. All the cleavage in the world couldn't compete with the baby bump. Fashion dictated that my chest be hidden by maternity tops with large bows at the neck, as if I was the infant. More folks wanted to feel my round belly than had ever felt my boobs. Drew joked that it was like sleeping with a party keg.

After eight-and-a-half months, my water broke in the middle of the night. We drove fifteen miles from the Valley to the hospital in Santa Monica, where I paced the maternity ward all the next day and into another night. The nurse who was on duty when I came in went home and was back on duty the next day when I was admitted to the delivery room. She decided that after twenty-one hours of labor, she would not let me surrender to a C-section. She injected my IV with Pitocin to kick-start the contractions and called my doctor. Most of those hours are a blur. But not the nurse.

On my back in a blizzard of pain, I could not keep my foot in the metal stirrup. The nurse grabbed my foot and held it against her soft, padded body. She reminded me of Aunt Beast in *A Wrinkle in Time*. I wanted to curl up with her, to be soothed by her embrace. For the first time, I understood the innate attraction to a woman with pillowy breasts. It wasn't just visual, it was emotional. Perhaps mothers get rounder for a reason.

After delivering the baby and being sewn up with twenty-four stitches between my legs, my body was no longer my own. As my belly deflated, my breasts inflated like dirigibles. Forget sexy, they were baby bottles. Our newborn, Juliette, had jaundice. Nurses stuck Velcro hearts on her temples and attached fabric to shield her eyes from the light therapy. They said it wasn't a big deal, but since she had to stay in the hospital, so did I. She was brought upstairs every few hours for me to nurse. Try to, anyway.

No one tells you that it feels like fire when your milk comes in. The first edition of *What to Expect When You're Expecting* was over three hundred pages, half the behemoth it is today. There was no mention of the excruciating pain of sensitive nipples, nor how shameful it felt to admit that. Perhaps they didn't want to scare anyone. You are essentially liquefying your body, turning blood into milk for tiny cannibals. And yet, you produce so much more than milk: personalized immunity and antibodies and nutrients. Every time you are depleted, your body fills right back up to bursting. I started to understand the nickname "jugs." Despite the Darwinian excuse that men are attracted to women with large breasts to further their line of descendants, the same amount of milk can be produced by mammary glands of all sizes.

Most of my baby weight came off while nursing, but my padded hips served as a thermos full of emergency liquid. Add the body fatigue of a long-distance runner to the lack of sleep, and you are almost grateful for the mind-numbing tasks of taking care of an infant. But baby brain only lasts so long. Then you get punchy. Nipples work like a shower head, spraying tiny streams into the sucking mouth. When there is an issue of aim and you spray milk across your hungry baby's face, it is hard not to laugh at her bewilderment. When your sore nipple cracks and a milk duct on your other nipple gets infected and the baby starts screaming, your mother visits and gives her a bottle. Then it's your turn to scream.

"Mom, she may never want me again."

"I was trying to be helpful."

"Helpful would be laundry." I was serious. My week-old baby had enjoyed a full meal without me. I was failing her.

Desperate, I called the La Leche League. The woman who answered was militant in her instruction. She made me feel embarrassed, as if it was my fault that civilization had progressed to the point where I was confused about the very organs that identified my sex. I joked about needing a wet nurse, something royals used on TV. Twenty years later, wet nursing would come back, known as "cross-nursing," in small towns across America. But the woman ignored the joke and ordered me to apply salve on my breasts, rub the baby's gums with milky fingers, and switch sides to try again.

I vowed to succeed at my biological destiny. My baby deserved custom-made antibodies and immunity-boosting enzymes. I needed to be a milking machine, like the dairy cows mocked at that Miss America protest long ago. I also needed to justify the fog of baby brain, the lack of focus on getting my next job, and a brief absence of ambition.

One blessed night, while watching infomercials at three AM, a miracle happened. The milk flowed at the exact time the baby was sucking.

The oxytocin rushed through my body and filled me with a secret. I knew now this child would be only and always mine. No one else could possibly understand. She was my everything. I would keep doing this and never have sex again, especially down where the stiches were healing. Even that was worth it now. This was my baby and, oh, this was bliss, and I was in love. Nothing would ever be the same.

Later, of course, I had to nurse her again. And again and again and again and again. Soon, I hated everyone who had neglected to mention how this was so freaking messy, how I would leak everywhere I went. Bad enough no one had mentioned the bloody horror show of childbirth—this was supposed to be the easy part.

Finally, I got the nursing down to a routine, one that changed as the baby grew, nearly every freaking day. Some days, I was able to get showered and neatly dressed, with the baby napped, fed, and swaddled. Then I'd get to the diaper department of Toys "R" Us only to hear a random child cry. Immediately, my milk let down, soaking through the nursing pads and ugly bra until wet circles formed on my only clean blouse. After moving up through four sizes of maternity bras, I also needed to buy a larger swimsuit in case—and this was dreaming—the baby's schedule allowed for playtime in the pool. By the way, next time you shop for a bathing suit, be sure to smell for breast milk.

After a few weeks, an old friend of my folks who was practically my godfather was in town. He invited me, which now meant us, to lunch. I was excited to leave the house. When we stopped at the light across from the mall, I looked up at a Victoria's Secret billboard, where a model spilled out of her push-up bra. I wondered how mothers explained it to their sons. I didn't ask what Uncle Ronnie thought.

The three of us went to the new Cheesecake Factory and sat in a booth. The baby slept through to the dessert course. Craving chocolate, I ordered a slice of cake for Uncle Ronnie and I to share. When it arrived, it was enormous, six layers of cake with thick frosting and whipped cream. Ronnie's eyes widened at the decadence of it, but he didn't object. Then Juliette woke up fretting, ramping up for a cry. I assured her that she'd be getting a taste soon, but she refused to wait.

I'd worn a plaid shawl to accessorize my wardrobe of extra-large sweaters from Target, so I draped it over my shoulder. I lifted up my sweater just enough to unsnap the flap of my bra and aimed Juliette's mouth at my enormous nipple. Then I caught Uncle Ronnie's eye. He had the same expression from the cake: shocked, but not objecting. He hadn't said a word about the Victoria's Secret billboard, but now he stopped talking mid-sentence and studied the plaster ceiling. We were hidden in a booth to avoid trouble from the restaurant, but I couldn't hide from this man buying me lunch. I didn't want him to be uncomfortable, or worse, to regret naming his daughter after me. But with a hungry newborn and no bottle in my bag, there was no way to spare him.

Uncle Ronnie's eyes narrowed at the first flash of my breast, as if recognizing my sexuality, the attraction of bare flesh that led to the plundering and production of this child. After the baby latched on, I lowered the shawl to cover her face. Then I continued our conversation about the enormous slice of cake and pretended not to notice how his shoulders relaxed. Whether he felt more comfortable with sacrament of motherhood or was simply calmed by the sight of her tiny hand curled around a strand of my hair, I don't know. But he couldn't pretend this wasn't happening.

He put his hands in his lap and smiled. "I remember when you were a little girl in Arizona, and you used to play with my dog outside by the apartment pool in your swimsuit bottoms. One day when I came over, you wore the bottoms like usual, but you were inside. You got very upset. You were three, but you wouldn't let me in until you put a shirt on."

I laughed. "I guess covering my chest was important."

He sat back and took a bite of the cake. He moaned in pleasure, nothing sexual, but the real deal. That's how I felt, too. He laughed and glanced from my face down to the baby's body hammocked in my left arm. I forked the cake with my right hand. She startled and her sock fell off. Uncle Ronnie reached across and retrieved it just as she shifted, revealing an inch of my underboob. He blushed.

I went ahead and took a bite of the cake that looked so sinful, so obscenely large and rich even though it was only milk and eggs and sugar. I felt sinful, too, the same as the cake. My body made breakfast, lunch, and dinner. It also made dessert.

When the baby had her fill, I lifted her across the tabletop for him to hold. I fastened my bra and pulled my shirt down while he laid her over his shoulder and burped her. This was more familiar. Now we were a team. But I was no longer that little girl he knew.

"I've never seen anyone nurse before," he said. "Not in public."

"I appreciate your patience," I said, and I did. It would be thirty years until it was legal in all fifty states (and a nip slip could still bring a charge of public indecency), but I was too tired to make a political thing of it. I took a quick bite of cake and reached for the baby.

"A girl's gotta eat," he said, smiling.

Mouth full, I nodded. Nursing breasts gave me a sense of power. Even when my baby wasn't with me, I could feel the proof of motherhood. This new identity began to take over how I saw myself in the world. It also began to influence how others saw me.

It wasn't always good.

When my baby was four weeks old, my dad called to ask when I was returning to work. The very idea of work required a chess game of childcare. I lacked the brainpower even to begin. During World War II, Uncle Sam had provided childcare so women could take over soldier's jobs, but as soon as the war ended, the centers were closed. Advertisers had helped by showing buxom women back in the kitchen. When I was born, doctors were pushing newfangled infant formula. When my daughter was born in 1989, the Military Child Care Act initiated affordable daycare for military families. But helping civilians, according to Uncle Sam, was akin to Communism. By 2020, the United States would rank thirty-fourth on the list of family-friendly countries.[3] I couldn't afford to stay home. Yet I couldn't afford not to.

"But what do you do all day?" my father asked.

I tugged on my dirty ponytail, scanned the disaster area around me in the kitchen, and fought for words to describe the exhausting cycle of infant sustenance without crying. My father would go stark raving mad with the job of new motherhood, all the detail work of feeding and foraging, dishes and diapers, the boredom and repetition. I could explain that the baby had colic, the technical term for "refuses to sleep." Or how his phone call would rob me of precious time to do laundry and lay down. But I couldn't complain, lest he regret paying my college tuition. For now, the only topic of conversation that might interest my dad was my husband's job. Not mine.

Oh, how far I'd fallen.

My father had been so upset when I quit my steady staff job that I got him work as an extra on every film. That meant he spent more on airfare than he earned. When I was pregnant, a producer from my last film hired my husband as art director on his new film, *Great Balls of Fire*, and invited my father back. By the time Juliette was born, they needed a baby for a still shot at the end. So, when she was ten days old, I took her to a set in Los Angeles, nursed her to a state of bliss, then handed her over to Wynona Ryder. Soon my father could see his name, his granddaughter's name, and his son-in-law's name in every movie theater. Everyone's name but mine, the one that had gotten them there.

The night of the premiere, I sprinkled glitter across my chest like the models in *Vogue,* then stuffed my golden globes into a low-cut velvet bustier. I tightened a belt around my waist and donned a shimmery full skirt. An hour later, Drew escorted me down the red carpet leading into the club on Hollywood Boulevard. I felt glamorous, like that night at the Ivy when I was pregnant for the first time. Except tonight, a dozen flashbulbs popped as an entire crowd of photographers vied for shots of us.

"Who are you?" they cried, with catcalls and whistles. "Look over here!" I turned my head as another reporter shouted, "Are you somebody?"

"Nobody," I said. Sure, I was the art director's wife, the baby actress's mother, and the extra's daughter. But it was my boobs that made me special. I was nobody without them.

We went inside to the party, but the magic was gone. The producer gave me a big hug. He hadn't seen me since we'd worked together. He nodded at my curvaceous figure.

"Motherhood looks good on you."

He was a dad, so I knew he meant it in the nicest way. His wife had been an accomplished career woman, then stayed home to be a mom and make pottery. I hadn't thought that would ever happen to me, but here I was.

As my boobs started to leak, I couldn't help but feel hurt. Then the toasts began. I lifted my glass of water as a person with no credit, on screen or off. I wanted to leave, to feel my baby at my breast and be connected to creation. It felt important. At home, I had purpose.

My nursing plan came to an abrupt halt a week later. I was sick with an intestinal bug and too depleted to recover. After several weeks,

I was in pain day and night with barely enough milk for the baby. My doctor prescribed antibiotics, but if I took them, I couldn't nurse. The pediatrician said the magic of my liquid gold tapered off exponentially each week. Still, five weeks didn't feel right. Lactation experts suggested I pump to maintain my milk supply while taking medication. Then I could start again.

The first wave of plastic pumps was acceptable on the go, but for round-the-clock nursing, I needed something stronger. I rented a Medela machine, a desk-sized contraption that reminded me of an iron lung. It was an electric udder, and I was the cow. First, I pulled a chair close enough to press the funnel around my breast and adjust the suction. After a few clanks and wheezes, it groaned and squeezed tightly until my milk squirted into a small plastic bag. Four times a day, I milked myself and threw the drug-tainted milk down the sink. Then I fed the baby with formula.

After six weeks of scrimping to pay for the machine while being sucked dry by it, I was clearly not recovering. When you leak even a few drops of liquid, the mammary gland refills it. I was nursing more, not less. Meanwhile, thanks to coupons and canned formula, three-month-old Juliette was thriving. Time to surrender.

As painful as it was when the first milk came in, making it stop was worse. Doctors prescribed medication to rush it. It reminded me of childbirth, how we remember it in metaphors, like sitting on a hot stove as the burner heats up. If we remembered what pushing a baby from our bodies actually felt like, the human race may have ended long ago.

The physical pain of stopping was not nearly as intense as the emotional pain. That very year, 1989, the American Association of Family Physicians recommended breastfeeding exclusively for the first six months for both medical and psychological benefits.[4] The truth is nobody really knows all the benefits: the antibodies, the hormones, the nutrients, the fuel. There is more research in the Library of Congress about tomatoes than there is about the custom concoction we make for our young. There is also far more information about erectile dysfunction, but I digress.[5] What I did know was I had failed in my first job as a mother. Who knew what suffering Juliette might endure? For now, the one suffering was me.

When a freelance producer called one night needing an emergency replacement on a commercial, I was thrilled. I wasn't nursing anymore and my husband was in town. This was ideal: only a week or two of work, and for the first time, I'd earn the producer's rate. I researched childcare options and found a nanny. I packed my briefcase and pressed my blazer.

Drew watched from the bed and asked what I would do if the job went overtime. Every job did. I called around and booked a second shift nanny. But what if she had to leave and I was fifty miles away? What if something happened to the baby, and I was stuck in LA traffic? I stared at the popcorn ceiling for a long, painful night and imagined all the ways our baby could die. If something happened, Drew would blame me. And I would have no one to blame but myself. I was grateful to have a husband who cared so much about his family. I was blinded not only by hormones, but by confusion about my new role. I was no longer just a woman. I was a mom.

By dawn, I was a wreck. I called the producer and canceled at the worst possible time, burning that bridge forever. This was the end of life as I knew it. I was unable to say that I mattered as much as the baby; I was no longer sure it was true. I had been objectified for as long as I could remember, hiding my breasts in a blazer to work like a man, displaying them to be an object of desire, and using them to be a mom. Had Drew ordered me to stay home, I would have laughed and gone on my merry way. This was far more powerful. Valued by society for one purpose at a time, it felt like the natural order of things.

My film school friend Kevin visited with his wife and new baby one day to compare notes. I spent most of the evening in the kitchen, where he found me.

"Why do you let him talk to you like that?" Kevin asked. I had no idea what he meant. I was just making dinner.

Soon after, I saw *Presumed Innocent*, the film version of Scott Turow's bestseller, and the stereotypes were comforting. Carolyn, the sexy attorney with whom leading man Rusty has an affair, gets murdered. It's no accident that her downfall begins when she unbuttons her silk blouse. Her full breasts were an invitation to evil, the tool of a home-*wrecker*. I identified with the home*maker*, the wife, who hid her cleavage in baggy blouses. A former professional, she was insecure about reentering the job market. She was a mother first. And—spoiler alert—mothers are above the law. I could work with that.

Torn between the burning love for my baby and the brain-numbing tasks of motherhood, I vented with short pithy essays. My mother suggested I string them together into a book. By coincidence, my old UCLA roommate was planning to visit. She'd pretty us up as Madonna and child. We went to a mall photo studio where the walls were covered with glamour shots of girls with sparkly cleavage. There would be no sparkles for me—no cleavage either. First, Diane chose a white lace camisole, an ironic symbol of purity for a woman so obviously fucked that she had a baby. Next, she positioned a long lock of hair over my demure décolletage. Then she made faces until my baby smiled for the camera. I mailed the photo with the manuscript, *Welcome to Club Mom: The End of Life as You Know It*, to a publisher. They loved it, except for the subtitle. Too negative, they said. I changed it to *The Adventure Begins* . . . and it did.

When I got pregnant again, I looked forward to a few months of glamour. My breasts popped immediately. Unfortunately, so did my stomach. On the bright side, I could balance my toddler on my baby bump. I also had most of the bras I needed. I went up two band widths and four cup sizes by the time I was six months pregnant.

When Demi Moore posed naked while seven months pregnant on the cover of *Vanity Fair*, there was a public outcry over whether this was sexy or obscene, powerful or pandering. And yet, while Moore's bare belly was heralded as a breakthrough, her breasts were too much of a tease. She covered her nipples with her hand, coining the term "hand-bra." Why? Moore wasn't shy. She had appeared naked in *Oui* ten years earlier. Apparently, the public wasn't ready for the reality of distended nipples or enlarged areolas or any other details of pregnancy. The pregnant woman was not allowed to be sexual. She was a baby carrier.

Even photographer Annie Leibovitz dismissed the shot as merely a magazine cover. She said, "If it was a great portrait, she wouldn't be covering the breasts."[6] I'd seen Moore while interning on *Fridays*, back when she was married to a drummer. I had also bumped into her in a bar when she was dating Bruce Willis, the father of this baby bump. Emboldened, I copied her pose for a personal photo. I wore a lace bra to be respectable, though I wasn't sure why it felt that way.

After my second child was born, I went all in. With one child, I'd bartered for time with a neighbor mom three mornings a week. With an infant plus a toddler, that didn't work. My mother lived in a different city, and there was no cheap childcare. I'd published one book, but writing was a gamble that would have to wait. If I could nurse this baby, I'd devote an entire year to being the best mother possible: full time.

The birth was so fast after my water broke that my baby was in fetal distress. She had inhaled meconium in the amniotic fluid. As soon as the cord was cut in the delivery room, she was whisked up to a brightly lit table, where an emergency team of doctors went to work. At eight pounds, Chloe was larger than expected. She ruptured my insides in a way that required surgical repair. I couldn't see much past the doctors' shoulders from where I lay, but they stuck a tube down her tiny trachea to vacuum out particles that could lodge in her lungs. As a result, she had a chafed throat and refused to suck on a pacifier. Except for Mommy.

Have breasts, will travel. She clung to me for comfort, then stuck around for meals. Some mothers were adamantly against "binkies," but I was desperate for one to work. Every time I managed to slip a soft rubber nipple into Chloe's mouth, she spit it halfway across the room. She wanted *me*. I wanted her, too, but I also had a toddler at my knee. As a result, I learned to cook, clean, and do laundry with the baby on my hip. Dinner consisted of the baby food chain: Drew fed me while I fed one girl with an airplane-shaped spoon, and the other with my breast. When big sister started preschool and asked for the name Running Deer as her Native American alias for Thanksgiving, we gave the baby a nickname, too: Wants to Be Carried.

At the local park, while I chased my toddler with an infant in my arms, other mothers smiled like I had finally found my purpose. Drew was proud to be out in the big bad world, working to put pork chops on the table. My father decided it was wonderful that I could stop working for a year to take this kind of "vacation."

The daily routine with a growing baby changed so often it was impossible to predict. My breasts were always filling and topping off, just in case. I didn't understand why breastfeeding was called "nursing" when the baby was not sick. My baby was the opposite of sick. She was thriving.

When we could scrape enough money together to afford a maid for deep cleaning, I was so grateful that I had coffee ready for her when she arrived. I didn't know her entire circumstance, only that she spoke more languages than I did. And if I was very lucky, I could put both children down for five minutes while my whole body throbbed from exhaustion.

One summer day, our maid arrived with her husband, who was dressed in a button-down shirt. My husband, relaxing in in the backyard, saw the man at the window with a rag in his hand and called me outside. He wanted the man to leave. He refused to pay a man to do housework.

I was confused. "You would rather deprive them of the money?" I asked. "This is honest work."

"You want me to fire them both?" Drew asked.

"No! She needs this job. But why is it OK for the wife and not the husband? Breasts make her lesser?"

When he rolled his eyes, I knew I was right. Up on the pedestal or down in the maid's quarters; there was no middle ground. Why did the ability to feed human beings make us uniquely qualified to clean up after them? My mother was right. Women's lib had udderly—ahem, *utterly*—failed me.

The more immediate question was how had I married a man so old-fashioned? Did he really believe women should do work that he deemed "demeaning" to men? When we met, I was a professional with a job. Now I was home putting my breasts to work, and powerless. In so many respects he seemed so modern, so passionate, an artist. Yet once he fulfilled his biological destiny, he was part of the white American patriarchy that kept my hands tied. My ability to feed the baby was not equal to his ability to feed me.

I cried as I explained the problem to my precious housekeeper. By the tilt of her head, it was clear she felt sorry for me. She was earning money alongside her husband, equal partners who would rise together.

The philosopher Friedrich Nietzsche said that the master who is comfortable in the role as the master therefore has less self-awareness than the followers that he treats and views as inferior. I was the follower; I had traded indentured servitude for the roof over my head. I had neither the cash reserves to leave, nor the courage to fight. As furious as I was with Drew, I was also ashamed of myself. How had the breasts I'd longed for all of my life put me in a prison?

After nine months, I was tired of milk-stained shirts. I was hungry all the time. I still had an extra ten pounds on my hips, and I was weary of pumping each breast just to grocery shop. Whoever says breast milk is free forgets the amount of time and physical energy it takes to create it. My sweet girl had mastered a sippy cup. She no longer needed me. Bottom line? I wanted my boobs back. And yet I was ashamed at the thought.

In 2005, when Florence Williams opened a new debate with her *New York Times* piece about environmental toxins and food additives that affect breast milk,[7] mothers had a new reason not to breastfeed. A few years later, *Forbes* featured another article on toxic breast milk. The good news was that breastfeeding was presented as an egalitarian issue that affects us all. Yet, that same year, 2012, when *Time* ran a cover story about the debate over breastfeeding called "Are You Mom Enough?"[8] there was an uproar over the photo of a fully dressed woman breastfeeding her toddler son. Americans can discuss the nutritional benefits of nursing, but how dare we show the bare-breasted act?

In 2015, as *Forbes* warned of toxins in breast milk yet again,[9] the mayor of San Diego proclaimed the first International Day to Normalize Breastfeeding.[10] The mom who created the group proclaimed 2016 the year of the "brelfie," celebrating women who take nursing selfies. By 2017, breastfeeding was a status symbol for upper-class millennials. It's been defined as the moral high ground, the supreme sacrificial act of a woman. Now, as ever, women are shamed when nursing is not their priority. Outside the Pump Station, a celebrated store in Santa Monica dedicated to breastfeeding, a sign read, "Where Nurturing Begins," as if nurturing is exclusive to breastfeeding. And that's not fair.

The American Medical Association and the American Academy of Pediatrics still recommend breastfeeding exclusively for six months, then combined with solid food for twelve. But most American women don't breastfeed that long.[11] While 75 percent breastfeed at birth,[12] the number dwindles to less than 50 percent by six months. These statistics are attributed to many things, from the fact that for many women it's physically challenging to the fact that for many working women it's impossible. Without hospital, workplace, and governmental support, the debate over how to raise healthy American children is moot. It's no secret it's dangerous to be born here. Our infant mortality ranks thirty-third in the world.[13] My children were lucky, being born white and having access to health care. In the United States, only Asian babies have a lower mortality rate. Non-Hispanic Blacks have double the odds of infant deaths. Babies born in rural areas, where there are fewer hospitals, are at a higher risk in every group.[14] Helping all children thrive, no matter the race or ethnicity, needs to be a national priority. Our cultural discomfort with the sight of nipples, especially the sight of nipples being used for their basic function, is a ridiculous barrier.

After nursing Chloe for ten months, I caught a terrible cold. I called the doctor, who assured me that an antihistamine would not hurt my daughter. He neglected to say that it would dry up my breast milk. Within days, it did. Hallelujah, I had an excuse. I was sad to no longer have that special connection, but now I could give equal time to my three-year-old. In truth, I missed nursing far more than Chloe did.

Breastfeeding had worked as natural birth control for me, curbing the hormones that triggered ovulation. Now, my doctor prescribed the Pill and suggested I begin with my next period, due after Christmas. I counted the days dutifully through a stormy holiday with my husband, Drew, who was struggling with sobriety, PTSD, and a herniated disk. Then we had make-up sex.

Sure enough, my early warning system was on high alert. My breasts were tingling within days. My husband was not ready for another child, so I called my doctor to ask about terminating a potential pregnancy. This was before the "morning after" pill. I didn't know I could get the same effect by taking several birth control pills at once. Just as doctors didn't trust women to drink moderately or to enjoy sex during pregnancy, they didn't volunteer basic biological information. It was far too early for my pregnancy test to show positive, and I was too polite to press. But I knew. Being pregnant is an out of body experience, like hiding a big secret, and I felt it with every breath. Plus, my boobs hurt.

I had two small children, no job, and an underemployed, extra-large man who meant well but scared the daylights out of me when he was angry. I was pro-choice, but since I was married, the choice to get an abortion made me uneasy. I thought marriage would protect me from everything. At least, that was the idea.

We had always been wary of having children due to Drew's exposure to Agent Orange in Vietnam. So far, we'd been lucky. Now, it felt like that luck had run out. Another child, even a healthy one, was too much pressure. My husband did not want another and I was afraid. My doctor located a private hospital that required cash up front, which was tough since we lived paycheck to paycheck. Still, it was too soon. The fertilized egg wasn't big enough to find, let alone remove. My husband was so ashamed he swore me to secrecy. If I so much as said the word "abortion," he lashed out in fury. He acted as if it was happening to him.

I moved through the weeks with our little girls as if walking underwater. At Mommy & Me exercise class, a friend announced her pregnancy. I smiled and congratulated her, wondering how they could not see the swollen breasts straining against my leotard.

Finally, the day came, and Drew dropped me off at the hospital. He didn't know how I sobbed to the nurse. How I lay in the recovery room with five other women, listening to one wail for her mama. How my mother picked me up with the girls and took us to dinner at Red Lobster and gave me a photo in a frame labeled "Mommy" in faux kiddie font. How I was back to full-time mothering as I bled the next day. He didn't want to know and refused to ever talk about it. Several days after the procedure, he left town for work on a Visa commercial in Nashville. Then the Northridge earthquake struck.

When the pounding began in the middle of the night, I ran out of the bedroom past the crashing furniture and down the swaying hall to the nursery. I scooped up both girls and went to wait in the main doorway. The baby nursed at one dry breast while my toddler cuddled against the other. There was no light, no sound, and no movement for endless hours until dawn. I remember thinking so clearly that I had done the right thing: two breasts, two hands, two children.

In the light of day, there was no electricity and no phone service. Dogs howled before every aftershock. Sirens wailed in the distance. I lay in bed and bit my lip so the girls wouldn't hear my teeth chatter in fear. We foraged for shoes to climb over the rubble and ate melted ice cream from the freezer. The next night, we lay fully clothed on the big bed, listening, waiting until the roads were safe. Then we fled past the fires and down the deserted freeway. It took a year to rebuild the house, but the cracks in our foundation remained.

Breastfeeding Basics

Only 40% of Americans believe that breastfeeding should be permitted in public.

Who Breastfeeds?

- American Academy of Pediatrics recommends infants be breastfed for 6 months.

- Four in five mothers try breastfeeding.

- 49% of babies breastfeed for six months, 27% breastfeed for twelve months.

- 82% of white babies and 64% of black babies are breastfed for a time.

- Barriers to breastfeeding:
  Jobs with limited maternity leave.
  Difficulty with breastfeeding.
  Low access to support at hospitals or at home.
  Fear of toxic breast milk.

Legal Battles

- 2018: US opposes the United Nations Health Assembly resolution to support breastfeeding.

- 2019: Breastfeeding in public is legal in the US, but a nip slip can draw charges of public indecency.

Support

- International board-certified lactation consultants and trained La Leche League volunteers.

- Kellymom.org, an evidence-based, educational support community run by a certified lactation consultant, has 368,000 likes on Facebook.

Key Facts

- Breastfeeding burns 500 calories a day.

- Breast milk provides customized immunity protection as well as nutrients for the baby.

- Benefits of breast milk far outweigh threat of toxic chemicals.

- Breastfeeding has nutritional, psychological, economic, and environmental benefits.

Eight

BIRTHDAY BABE
1997

Y ou're deformed," my mother said.

We were in the plush pink dressing room of Victoria's Secret for our first mother-daughter shopping trip since I'd had children of my own. So far, none of the strapless bras I'd tried on worked under the dress she'd bought me for my thirty-eighth birthday celebration. Since my mother lived several hours away and still worked full-time, we didn't get together often. Still, "deformed" was harsh. I snatched my camisole from beneath the rejects on the bench and held it up to block her view.

She pointed at the mirror across from her padded bench. "I'm not criticizing. It's a fact."

I looked up, but only to admire the raw silk of the fuchsia dress hanging on the door in the plastic garment bag. Then I met her eyes, perfectly made up to go with her blond bob and navy pantsuit. I'd barely brushed my teeth that day.

"What does your husband think?" she asked.

"He's an ass man." Or so he said. I'd heard him call a car "Tits" as tribute. "This is how they're supposed to look."

She sighed and pulled a lacey set of lingerie from a doll-sized hanger. "Try this. You need some pretty underwear."

"I really don't," I said. It wouldn't make a difference. Drew hadn't seen me naked in months. Thank heaven camisoles were back in style.

When she shook her head, I understood she wasn't talking about sex appeal. She was like the mom in every myth who wanted her daughter to have security. Except the wish was even stronger for her. She'd suffered so much from her own divorce that she'd been suicidal. In a strange contradiction, she was now an ally to Drew, the dominant male. The fact was, I was dependent. She wanted me to succeed where she had "failed"—in keeping a man. Boobs were job security.

I whispered, trying to downplay those dark days neither of us would ever forget, "Don't worry, Mom. He loves me like I am. He thinks I'm a babe."

After a moment, she looked up to my eyes in the mirror. "Do you?"

Annoyed, I turned to look directly at her. She had skipped up to a higher level on Maslow's hierarchy of needs, from shelter and security to self-esteem. I wasn't falling for it. She could save the psychological voodoo for her therapy clients. "I'm almost forty. I don't need to be sexy anymore."

I did need to be nicer, though, since she'd paid for that dress. I snatched the brassiere, a wispy little thing with rosebuds blooming across gossamer cups, far too pretty to be called a bra, from her outstretched hand. After hooking the strap in front, I tugged it around, then leaned over to pull the straps up as the salesgirl had instructed. For a moment, we both stared at the gaping space between the fabric and my chest.

"Must be from your father's side," my mother said. "His mother was flat-chested."

"No, Mom. It's from breastfeeding. You didn't breastfeed!"

"Thank goodness," she said, and unhooked me.

I reached for the next brassiere, with eyelet cups edged by satin ribbon. It was exquisite, a work of art, a monument to all that is female. How could you not feel beautiful with that beneath your clothes? If just looking at it gave me goose bumps, I could only imagine how heavenly it would feel to fill it out. After putting it on, I turned to admire it in the mirror. The effect was more sad than sexy.

My mother shuddered. "When I was a mother, breastfeeding was considered—"

"Barbaric, I know." I leaned back to be unhooked.

"Then again, so was childbirth," she said, ignoring me. "I didn't even know you were born until I woke up and asked the nurse."

I fumbled to unhook the bra myself. Clearly, we weren't meant to bond at her breast. Perhaps we weren't meant to bond over shopping expeditions either. Ready to roll, I scanned the bench for my white T-shirt. She was still talking.

"My pediatrician said formula was better for the baby. It was scientific. Jackie Kennedy redecorated the White House, NASA built rockets to the moon, and formula came in a concentrate."

I realized she was apologizing, not for calling me deformed, but for following her doctor's orders. She was barely twenty-two when I was born. Her bustline wasn't merely genetics, it was the result of perfect cultural timing. She had avoided both breastfeeding *and* burning her bra.

"It's OK, Mom," I said, and meant it. She didn't have to buy me things to make up for it, but I knew it gave her pleasure. And if I could, I would do the same for my girls one day.

She hung up the bra, then caught my eyes in the mirror. "You could get a lift."

"And lift what?"

The salesgirl, a chirpy young thing with a measuring tape around her neck, knocked and poked her blond head in.

"Pretty dress," she said, pouting at the fuchsia silk. "I could never wear spaghetti straps or empire waists."

Was I supposed to feel sorry for her? Was it sad that her boobs needed support, that they filled out these beautiful brassieres, that she could rock a triangle bikini? I wanted to punch this gal, but she'd never feel it. Her puffy chest would absorb the blow.

"So, how are we doing in here?" she asked.

I wanted to go home and climb in my bed where, unlike her, I could sleep on my stomach. Instead I asked, "Do you carry this in a 32AA?"

She shook her head, then lassoed me with measuring tape. Five years since my last measurement, maybe I'd be rewarded with an extra inch. Women with A cups were petite, but perky. Not sexy, but saucy. They wore open blouses in Ralph Lauren ads. It was a chic, young look. My stomach lurched. Was I too old for Victoria's Secret?

The salesgirl studied the numbers on the tape. When she didn't meet my eyes, I knew I would have to settle for camouflage. Shelf bras didn't cover droopy nipples. Band-Aids were my best option. My breasts were like wounds.

"We could add foam inserts," she said.

I glanced at the confection in my hand. "That would hide the lace."

"We have a push-up Miracle bra. It's similar to the—"

"Wonderbra, I know. I stood in line for two hours at Macy's to try one on the day it came out. All it did was asphyxiate me."

My mother and the salesgirl gathered the rest of the rejects, variations of dainty embroidery and delicate French lace. Maybe France was the answer, where they'd had lingerie since the beginning of time, where a woman could feel beautiful forever.

"Let's go to Nordstrom," my mother said. "They have more sizes. And prosthetics."

"No thanks. I'll get the strapless with pads." I snatched my T-shirt from the bench.

When the salesgirl was gone, my mother stood up. "Have you ever considered implants?"

"No," I said, insulted.

A few weeks earlier, I'd run into a porn star at a family barbecue across town. The other parents and I were discussing elementary school Career Night, when a voluptuous woman in an elegant sleeveless turtleneck joined us. Mistaking her for an actress, I asked about her work and was surprised to learn she had a website that streamed her live. Not only live, but without the turtleneck. Her six-year-old daughter climbed on her lap and I couldn't resist asking what she would do for Career Night. Everyone backed away, and we had to leave. The host accused me of being bourgeois, meaning a hick from Ohio. I apologized for sounding rude, but I was curious. Deep down, I felt superior. For nearly a decade, my post-nursing chest had worked as a shield. I hid behind it to justify my existence. Now I wielded it like a weapon.

"I'm not a bimbo," I said to my mother.

She picked up the hanger with my birthday dress. "They might give you more confidence, that's all."

I shook my head, too old for this fuss. "I'm going to be thirty-eight."

"I remember," she said. "I was there."

"You were asleep."

"Thirty-eight is nothing. You're not dead. You could even have more children."

No, I thought. The last time Drew threw a plate at the wall, I had imagined a life with a new man and a new baby. But I knew in my heart I had nursed my last one. And if my biological destiny was complete, then I didn't need breasts anymore. After zipping my khaki skirt, now an essential part of my uniform, I looked in the mirror and brushed my dyed brown hair. There was a respectable woman of average height, weight, and style. That was the real milestone of being almost forty. It was the start of my life as a "mature" adult who no longer needed to compete. I vowed to make the best of it.

I grabbed my backpack purse and found my mother waiting for her turn at the register. I reached for the bra to put it back. "Forget it. I can get a cheap one at Target."

My mom stepped out of my reach. "No. You deserve a good bra. When your girls are older, you can buy them good bras, too. Pretty ones."

I sighed and looked up at the wall, where images of half-dressed young women wearing angel wings smiled down at us. What would my girls think of these freaks of nature? Works of art, Drew would say. At least they didn't have enormous breasts. Oh hell, the entire enterprise was a shrine to breasts. I picked up a catalog from the stack on the counter. The cover girl had a come-hither pose. I chuckled and my mom looked up.

"My friend said she found one of these under her son's bed," I said. "She had to wash the stiff sheets."

My mother winced. "Did you see the Super Bowl commercial?"

"No, but I read that the fashion show had two million views on the web."

She handed her credit card to the salesgirl. "I saw a magazine picture of that model named Heidi in a bra worth ten million dollars. It was made of diamonds."

"Wow," I said. "I wonder what that would feel like."

"Heavy, I'll bet," Mom said, and we laughed.

I took the pretty pink shopping bag in case one of the girls wanted it. Later, I would regret saving it. This was a sly indoctrination to a world where women were seduced into needing the kind of breasts worthy of being crowned with diamonds. The company masqueraded as the savior of women, but really it was the enemy. I feared trouble ahead for my girls. Only one thing was certain: I'd never call them "deformed."

All week, I prepared for my big day. I dieted, went to the gym, and got my hair done. On that Friday, I got up early to make pancakes in the shape of hearts. Then I drove my girls to school, parked the car, and pressed my lips to their cheeks. Next, I went home and polished my toenails to match my pink dress.

That afternoon, I waited my turn for the shower with a towel wrapped around me. The door opened and my extra-large husband stepped out into the small bathroom. I dropped my towel and squeezed past, shouting over the streaming water. "My mother thinks I should get a boob job. What do you think?"

Drew paused long enough for water to drip on the vinyl floor. "I love you just the way you are."

I smiled and pulled the door shut.

"But if you wanted to," I heard him call, "I wouldn't mind."

I cranked the water to hot. Drew just meant it was up to me, I told myself. It was my body, after all. Besides, I shouldn't have put him on the spot.

An hour later, my skin was anointed with baby oil and my lashes bore three coats of mascara. My bra was padded just enough to prevent my nipples from showing, hallelujah. My daughters hovered like tiny birds helping Cinderella before the ball. Except I was never sure if fairy tale princesses lived happily ever after, since we never heard from them again. Eight-year-old Juliette zipped my dress until it caught on my hair. Five-year-old Chloe sprayed perfume until I coughed. Together, they adorned me with pearly earrings and silver sandals.

When it was time to go, Drew turned off the baseball game without a second request. He even opened the car door for me. I looked up at the sky and gave thanks for everything. I knew I was born lucky, just being white and middle class and American. The rest was gravy: my education, my healthy children, and a handsome husband who was taking me to a fancy restaurant for dinner. I loved my life, my dress, everything. This was my night.

On the way to dinner in Malibu, we exited the freeway to drive over the Santa Monica mountains. A hand-stenciled sign taped to a light post read "Heartless." I had forgotten! Years after that agent had asked if I wrote my screenplay "all by myself," I had sold it all by myself—to another woman. Judith Vogelsang was a TV series director daring to make the leap to feature director. That night, the crew was reshooting a night scene.

The story was a romantic thriller about a shy librarian who gets a heart transplant from a glamorous socialite and becomes the next target for murder. It was low budget, under $2 million, but the story, and every word of the screenplay, was mine. I made sure of it by doing all the rewrites for free. The producer was planning to pay a man the same $10,000 fee I got for the whole script to dumb down the character arc and ramp up the violence. I couldn't let that happen. Since the film was nonunion, there was no guarantee my name would stay on the project. I needed the credit to get in the union and get more, better-paying work that I could do from home. As it turned out, the film would be in rotation on the USA Network for three years before screening in theaters across Europe for nine more. *Heartless* financed the next five films for the producer, who never called me again.

The main shoot had wrapped months ago, but the last scene with the star, Mädchen Amick from *Twin Peaks*, got rained out. And here they were. Everything I had dreamt of while growing up in Ohio had come true.

I pointed to the sign. "Let's stop by."

Drew glanced at the clock. "Don't we have a reservation?"

I knew we did. I was the one who'd made it, to request an ocean view table at sunset. It would be fun to check out the shoot, but I'd been on sets before. Tonight, it was my turn to be the star. At a restaurant in *Malibu*. I got excited all over again.

"You're right, let's go," I said. Seeing that sign was icing on my birthday cake.

When we arrived at the restaurant on the Pacific coast, it was golden hour, the time of day when the light is soft and the air feels warm. Drew looked distinguished, with streaks of gray in his hair against his dark jacket. As he pulled into the valet area, the sun made the raw silk of my deep pink dress shine. A charming young man opened my door and welcomed us. Sure, it was his job to be friendly, but he seemed happy to see such a handsome couple. I took his hand to step out.

Inside the wood-beamed entrance, the young hostess complimented my dress, then led us toward the windows overlooking the ocean. As I stepped down into the seating area, a woman's voice cried out: "You look *gorgeous!*"

I looked over to see who'd shouted and spotted an older woman with a silver chignon beaming at me from a table by the window. She was a complete stranger, clapping her hands together as if she was thrilled to see me. The white-haired gentleman sitting beside her tapped his cane in agreement.

"Thank you!" I called. "It's my birthday!"

"Happy birthday!" she cried.

Other diners held their cocktails up toward me in a good-humored toast. Could my day get any better?

Drew and I sat down and ordered two glasses of champagne. We raised them up and clinked the crystal. The bubbles burst on my tongue like fireworks.

Drew looked past me over my shoulder. I held up the menus to show him we already had them, but he didn't notice. I turned to follow his gaze behind me. A young woman sat at the table directly across from him with a nondescript date. She was pretty, but not gorgeous, I thought, in a dress of cheap stretch fabric. Her cleavage, however, was remarkable, her breasts squeezed together like a butt crack.

Drew smiled and took another sip of champagne. I moved over a bit to block his view and pointed out my favorite appetizer, crab cocktail. Every few minutes, his gaze drifted past me. At first, I thought he might know the bimbo. When I finally asked him, he said no.

"But you gotta admit . . ."

"She's very pretty," I said politely. Like my dad had said long ago, it was healthy to appreciate the human body. Like my husband said, women are the true works of art. And, clearly, he liked breasts more than he'd admitted. I finished my champagne and played my best card. "I bet she doesn't have kids."

I looked over to see the woman who had shouted my praise. She was gone, vanished as if she had never been there. The table was set with clean napkins and fresh silverware. The clock had struck midnight; my Cinderella moment was over. And I didn't feel gorgeous anymore. I felt old. Time to face it: even when I felt as beautiful and as proud as I possibly could, it wasn't enough for my husband.

Better Boob Jokes

I was so flat, I used to put Xs on my chest and write, "You are here." I wore angora sweaters just so the guys would have something to pet.

—JOAN RIVERS

I made so many jokes over the years about how small my chest was that I started to think that maybe my boobs overheard me and were just like, "You know what? We're sick of this. Let's kill her."

—TIG NOTARO

I was the first woman to burn my bra—it took the fire department four days to put it out.

—DOLLY PARTON

My breasts have a career of their own. Theirs is going better.

—JENNIFER LOVE HEWITT

Girls have got balls. They're just a little higher up.

—JOAN JETT

Just slung my bra off and threw it to the other side of the couch where there are already 2 other bras. If my math is right, it's Wednesday.

—@JESSOBSESS

One of the main functions of a push-up bra is to lower the number of mothers who seem like mothers.

—MOKOKOMA MOKHONOANA

Scientists now believe that the primary biological function of breasts is to make males stupid.

—DAVE BARRY

Nine

DIVORCE: THE "A" WORD
2004

The size of my breasts had nothing to do with my divorce. The fact that I had them did.

If marriage is like a dance, then Drew was Fred Astaire and I was Ginger Rogers dancing backward in high heels. With every step back, I dug my heels deeper into the quicksand of denial. Even now, I don't want to look close enough to see the footwork. It's too painful, too embarrassing. I feel my heart flail, and my skin prickles in shame. How did I not see this happening? I was smart and confident and liberated. I'm battling a panic attack trying to write this down. That's why I'm compelled to explain. If there is ever a time in our lives when breasts make us vulnerable, it's marriage.

Drew used "divorce" like a swear word every time we argued. With my family history, it was a slap in the face. For eighteen years, I refused to utter the "D" word aloud. No way would I allow our children to endure one. I didn't realize there was another word far worse. My husband only hit me once, I told myself, and it was an accident. The bruises were gone in a week. What I didn't realize was the bruises that build up on the inside last far longer. The worst word is "abuse."

• • •

Marriage was a blast at the beginning. But once my breasts bloomed with pregnancy, our relationship shifted. My body was the most obvious change, but psychologically I was weakening.

Six months pregnant, I was working on location in Rancho Cucamonga when Drew called from his own shoot in New York. I mentioned having a few Braxton Hicks contractions, and he got angry. How could I risk the health of our baby for a pizza commercial? I figured this was the sign of a good father. Of course, I wanted the best for my baby.

We made a deal. We couldn't both be working the long hours of film production, let alone living out of suitcases on location. Since I made the milk, and he made more money, it was a no-brainer. I would stay home until the baby was settled. But the baby was never quite settled enough. When I had the opportunity to jump into a producing gig for the full pay rate, he threatened that if anything happened to the baby when I was across town, he would never forgive me. Overwhelmed with hormones and blissed out by love for this baby girl, I agreed to extend our deal. Now I managed the food, the finances, the house, the husband, and the baby. I wrote late at night to keep from going crazy.

With our second child, the job got too big for me. I complained, but our deal remained the same. If I wasn't earning money, I needed to go all in at home. I turned off the computer and devoted an entire year to motherhood. But I had not been trained for this. Plus, I hated to cook. Every time I washed a load of laundry, I thought of that funny T-shirt, "For this I went to college?" But it wasn't funny.

One night, a friend of Drew's rode up on his new motorcycle and bragged that he'd had a homemade lasagna dinner and a Cuban cigar, and as soon as his wife finished cleaning up and putting the kids to bed, he was headed home for his blowjob. He waved at me through the window, where I paid bills at a desk in the bedroom. Drew came in and told me his friend called him stupid for marrying a smart woman. The guy was an asshole, but he made me feel lucky to have someone like Drew.

Every time I gave myself a new goal to justify my existence, I achieved it. But it was never enough to change the deal. I adored my little girls. Drew loved taking pictures of the three of us baking. He thought I looked the sexiest in a flannel nightgown. When he wanted us to dress up and visit the set so he could show off his family, I understood. We'd met when I was an executive with my own office, my breasts hidden beneath a suit, but now they were proof of my position. Still, I took a wedding vow, not in sickness and health, but "til there is no more." There was always more. I couldn't get out of the deal.

•••

Then came the money trap.

Once my breasts had found their biological purpose, I needed to make money to avoid being defined by them. My pregnancies were planned, but I often wished I'd waited. I was financially dependent. I wasn't high up enough on the career ladder to pay for a housekeeper or enough of the bills to make a difference. By the time the girls were in school, I had been out of the workforce too long to fit back in. Drew constantly complained of financial pressure, but he took great pride in the fact that he paid the mortgage. My work was a hobby in comparison. Late one night when I was writing, my husband stood by my desk, calculated the lousy few pennies I was earning per hour, and laughed at my efforts. Paychecks defined his power. That meant he owned my work. He took credit for every sentence I wrote, and it was impossible to disagree. To show my appreciation, I added his surname to mine. Not only did this sacrifice the alliteration that I loved, but it cut short my credits on professional listings. Soon, I existed only in relation to him.

Since I worked at home, I also wrote for the PTA newsletter, volunteered in the girls' classrooms, and chauffeured them across the city for playdates and ice-skating, softball and violin. This was all good and fun and worthwhile. I wanted my girls to enjoy everything I had missed when my own mother was working. Yet everything my mother complained about during the second wave of feminism was true. We needed childcare and parental leave to share the burden. I showed Drew financial charts of what my caregiving time would be worth in dollars, but it didn't make any difference. Without money, I had no power. And none of his respect. When my first novel won a prize and I got a free trip to New Orleans to accept it, he was too busy to come. When I was on CNN, he didn't wake the girls to watch. In public, he was proud of me; in private, he expected dinner on the table at six. I didn't have the right to complain. I needed to keep him happy.

• • •

You know that expression, "Sticks and stones may break your bones, but words can never hurt you"? It's bullshit.

The criticisms started small. I couldn't fold a pair of socks or back the car out of the driveway without being corrected. When he got home in time for dinner, the first thing he said was, "What's burning?" He pointed out the cellulite on my thighs, "just to be helpful." He was painfully honest about my discount clothes, made fun of the music I loved and the TV shows I watched. Sometimes, he called me a "fucking civilian," the lowest of insults from a Marine. It was my patriotic duty to please him.

As the girls got older, they recognized the sound of his car in the driveway. They hid in their rooms until we knew which way the wind would blow. It's just Daddy, we said to excuse him. I bought him a heavy bag and hung it in the garage. I hoped he would take out his anger with boxing gloves. He never used it. I was an easier target.

When he started in on the girls, it was different. Juliette was a wiggle worm who tended to fall off her chair at dinner. When he yelled at her for "fooling around" at yet another meat and potatoes meal, she countered by becoming a vegetarian. When he was in town for Chloe's softball games, he yelled at the girls' errors until the coach asked him to leave.

I started leaving Post-its on the bathroom mirror that read, "Be Nice." Sometimes I wrote, "Please be nice." Then I'd worry about his reaction and pull them down. I could handle the insults; it was my normal. But I wanted to protect the girls. Now, I dropped my name altogether and used only his. I was a wife and mother, a daughter and sister, a bad cook and stupid driver. My name didn't matter. When I looked in the mirror, I no longer saw me.

Drew convinced me I had no friends. I lay in the backyard hammock, listened to James Taylor, and cried. Soon, I lived in baggy, nondescript clothes—it didn't matter what I looked like. I was wearing Drew's extra-large denim shirt with a hole in it while waiting outside of Juliette's Brownie meeting at a church, when the security guard tried to kick me off the property. He thought I was homeless. Then one morning, I dropped the girls off at school and someone said hello. I looked around, surprised. At least one person in the world actually liked me. I started going to therapy. Drew made fun of therapy, and the money it cost.

As I got stronger, the attacks escalated. He told my brother-in-law I was a "cunt." It's no coincidence that men describe women in terms of our female body parts. Just like breasts and boobs, we are one extreme or the other. Pussy describes weakness. Cunt is more powerful— that makes it evil. Cunt became his favorite word, later repeated on voice mails so often I was torn between saving them as evidence for a restraining order or erasing them to avoid the toxic energy.

My husband told my mother I was a bitch. She immediately called to lecture that if I wanted to be loved, I needed to be lovable. She didn't want me to end up divorced and alone, so I assured her I was trying my best. When I asked him to please keep my mother out of it, he denied talking to her. He said she was lying. He said I was crazy to believe her. When I was frustrated, he said I was being overly sensitive, like a typical woman. I was the love of his life!

"Gaslighting" is an expression coined by a British play that was adapted into a creepy film that won an Oscar in 1944. In *Gaslight*, a man drives his wife crazy with lies and intimidation. According to Merriam-Webster, gaslighting means "to attempt to make (someone) believe that he or she is going insane." My father had done that to my mother forty years earlier. He told her she was crazy to think he was unfaithful, that she was being paranoid. The technique was so powerful, she still didn't recognize it was happening to me a generation later.

Why did I put up with this? I loved him, as far as I knew what that meant. He gave me two beautiful girls who deserved a father. I told myself he had a good heart, that his intentions were good. Sometimes he sat in the backyard holding an antique rifle in a death grip. He was troubled, exhausted, depressed, drinking. But I was not a quitter. There would be no "D" word for me.

Besides, more often than not, he was out of town. Life was so peaceful then it was easy to forget all the bad parts. The girls and I developed a smooth routine in a home free of hostility. When he got home weeks or months later, I was exhausted from being a single, working mom with two active daughters and a revolving door of pets, but I went out of my way to welcome him. He didn't want to help me or pick up the slack. He wanted to take the throne as king of the castle. He needed to rest and take charge and then stress over the next job to fulfill his part of the deal. Our deal was killing me, and it was killing him, too. So, we fought. And secretly, I counted down the days until he would leave again.

● ● ●

Drew started bringing home friends for me to entertain. He was a huge John Wayne fan and loved to play the hero, taking younger people under his wing. One night, he brought a young woman over for dinner. After putting the girls to bed, we sat in the yard and she started telling me about her boyfriend problems. My husband left and went to bed. I was supposed to share my wisdom, because, hell, I was a woman and that was my job. I was flattered, but um . . .

Another time, after rising at dawn to go to the farmers market and make cupcakes in time for a team party, I had ten minutes to spare before four more activities. I slipped into our small, kidney shaped pool and lay, throbbing with exhaustion, on a blow-up raft. Drew arrived home with a work associate and his wife. They stood there, waiting for me to dry off and play hostess. But I couldn't move. With five minutes left, I made a decision not to get up. We never socialized with the couple after that and it was all my fault. I didn't get in trouble for it—what an incriminating sentence—but I knew I had behaved horribly. I didn't keep up my side of the deal, as wife.

This moment seems small, but the guilt is still palpable. Guilt may be the greatest female weakness, our original sin. Guilt is an attack on ourselves for letting others down. Perhaps this is why men get away with blaming others for their failures, while women tend to blame themselves. That's how men and women are, we say. We take it for granted. How many women say "I'm sorry" just to express concern?

Once we bear children, we are biologically programmed to feel extreme responsibility for them. This feeling grows to include others we care about. We feel responsible for their happiness. When something goes wrong for them, we feel guilty about it.

I had changed the course of my life when I agreed to the original deal. Now I needed to justify that decision by being the perfect mother, the perfect partner, the perfect woman. I'd bought into the myth of doing it all, but the reality was impossible. Forget outside ambition. Between the children, the housework, and keeping my husband happy, there wasn't enough time to do even one thing well. I was doomed to fail. And feel guilty because of it.

•••

Booze was a problem early in our marriage, but I was determined to ride it out. I went to Al-Anon, a program for families and friends of alcoholics, and ran away screaming. Those stories of losing homes and children and marriages were not about us. Shania Twain's new hit, "You're Still the One," was playing nonstop on the radio. The CD cover showed her standing in dark water, covering her naked breasts. I sang along as I folded laundry, "Just look at us holding on."

I didn't know when he started drinking again. He denied imbibing beyond the few beers he "deserved" after work. When it became obvious, he blamed me for driving him to it. I didn't know any better. The only time I saw him with hard liquor was when we went out to dinner on special occasions. If I uttered any concern, he went ballistic. On those rare nights out, there was always a scene. He would complain about every little thing until the waiters avoided us, and it was always my fault.

On our last anniversary, he walked out before the main course was served. After twenty minutes, I realized he wasn't coming back. The next time it happened, I didn't wait so long. I paid the bill and left.

•••

One day when Drew was home resting, I agreed to make dinner at six. After I finished the taxes, children's school forms, and student work from a class I taught at UCLA, I got caught up with a writing assignment of my own. I'd ghostwritten a coffee table book to pay tuition for an MFA, handy credentials to be a full-time teacher and take the pressure off my husband. I lost track of the time.

At 6:15, Drew started shouting. I ran to the kitchen and found him opening the dishwasher full of clean plates. I assured him I would empty it now and make dinner. He slammed the dishwasher shut and whipped around. A foot above me, his eyes were narrowed with fury. I didn't see his hand until it hit my face.

Then I was on the floor.

I lay there, stunned. The girls ran in. They said they heard me scream.

The two of them helped me up as their father explained how Mommy was standing too close when he turned around. I clutched my face and asked the girls to give me a few minutes. I wasn't sure what to do next. About dinner or anything else.

"It was an accident," he said. "If I meant to hit you, you'd still be out cold."

Moving in slow motion, I got ice from the freezer. Wary, he stayed out of my way. He outweighed me by at least eighty pounds, so what he'd said was probably true. But it didn't feel like an accident. He blamed me for not making dinner on time, for being selfish, for being in his way—but this time I wasn't buying it. I wasn't the one who'd lost control. I went down the hall to the bedroom and climbed under the covers. Now, what?

After a while, the girls came in to check on me. They were hungry. I got up, powdered my face, and took the girls out to dinner. We went to a little hole-in-the-wall Thai restaurant, where I smiled at their chatter and pretended all was fine.

Drew saw a therapist at the VA. He came home and thanked me for not putting him in "the system." I hadn't even considered calling the police. That would cost money for bail and a court date and, if I kicked him out, a hotel. He'd eventually come home even angrier.

My lip swelled, and half my face turned black-and-blue. On the bright side, I had an entire week to write while I hid. And I went right back to the justifications. Drew wasn't a wife beater. I was not a battered woman, or a victim of domestic violence.

But then, why was I too ashamed to tell anyone?

We went on as if nothing happened. I prayed our daughters would forget. I didn't want them to think this was OK. I wanted them to be treated better.

A few months later, it was time for my writer's residency at Antioch University. It was less than an hour's drive, but with my husband's unpredictable schedule, I couldn't count on him to cover for me. Sure enough, he booked a job. My mother was undergoing medical tests for cancer over a hundred miles away, and in no shape to help. My father and his third wife wanted to visit, so I suggested that week. The timing was perfect.

Drew hated my father. He thought the pain my father caused my mother and the drama of my childhood was the root of our relationship problems. In his mind, he was defending me. Yet his anger was used against me. This twisted logic put me in the position of defending my father in order to defend myself.

As luck would have it, Drew's job was cut short. He was in the bedroom resting when my father's booming voice announced his arrival. He and his wife went through the house to sit on the back porch. Drew slammed out of the bedroom and demanded that my father leave. He looked like the Tasmanian Devil, a spinning, whirling mass of fury coming down the hallway. I put my hands up to slow him and he slammed me against the wall. The door of Juliette's bedroom clicked shut beside us. I ran down the hall ahead of Drew to close the porch door. Hawaiian music was playing, so my father and his wife didn't hear the shouting. Drew paused in the kitchen, where he grabbed a beer and eyed the food I was prepping for a barbecue. His T-shirt was stained with red, and I thought he was bleeding, but it was wine. I promised him my father would get a hotel after dinner, but it wasn't enough. Drew, a former Marine who bragged about knowing seven ways to kill a man with his bare hands, stormed past me. He headed outside to beat up my father.

My father, an Ironman triathlete in his seventies, saw him and leaned back on the rattan couch. I screamed and got between them to referee the madness. I grabbed my husband's shirt and ducked as he swung at me to let go. My father looked on in horror. I saw motion through the French doors to the living room, then Juliette emerged.

"Go back to your room," I shouted.

Drew saw her, too. He swore at both my father and me, grabbed his car keys, and left. I was relieved, but also nervous about him driving. As soon as Juliette went inside, I burst into tears.

I started preparing dinner with an eye on the clock to pick up Chloe from softball. My dad came in to get a soda. I had my explanation handy. Drew was having a rough time, I would say. He had a lot of rough times.

The phone rang before I could say anything. It was Drew, demanding that my father leave before he returned. I hung up.

"You don't have to live like this," my father said.

I looked at him. It felt like he was speaking a different language. This was just how it was. That day was a little worse than usual because my dad was there. But I had grown used to the shouting, the scenes, the walking on eggshells. Marriage was supposed to be hard, right?

We had dinner, but I barely remember it. I kept thinking my dad was the one who taught me to never give up. "You can't fail until you quit," he said. And I was not a quitter. But he had never seen me as a woman. In this particular situation, that was a good thing. He saw me as a person. A person who didn't have to put up with this kind of behavior. My dad changed their flight to leave earlier, but his words stayed with me.

With my father gone, I had to skip a seminar so I could take Chloe to softball practice. On the way home, I bought Drew's favorite cut of pork chops, a meal the rest of us hated. I didn't know what else to do. I needed to get organized. When I got home, Juliette was waiting quietly in the kitchen. She helped me unpack the meat without any of her usual comments about animal cruelty. As I folded the bags she said, "Daddy told me to tell you he moved out."

I was more upset by the fact that she was bearing this news than the news itself. Just as I'd been in the middle with my parents, he had put her in the middle of us. I wasn't having it. When she added that I was supposed to call him, I laughed.

After picking up her sister, we got ice cream and drove around the neighborhood. We looked through lit windows where fathers were eating dinner with their families. They were used to Daddy being gone for work trips, but this time, he was gone for good. We were a family of girls, like my mother and sister and me long ago. I had failed. We climbed into the big bed together and cried ourselves to sleep. Our hearts were broken.

In the morning, I dropped Chloe at her coach's house a few hours before the game. She was always so busy that she was the most surprised by our split, but she was happiest in a group of friends. I hugged her until she pushed me away, then I promised I'd be at her game by the second inning. Juliette came with me to a graduate school seminar on Edgar Allan Poe, whose dark themes felt appropriate. It was so hot I wore what my daughter called a wife beater tank top with bellbottom jeans. I felt an invisible sign on my forehead that read, "My husband left me." My classmates raved about Juliette, who was not only precocious, but familiar with Poe, and wished us a fabulous summer. We locked our arms together, climbed back in the car, and pretended that we would.

After stopping to pick up a case of Gatorade for the team snack on the way to Chloe's softball field, my phone rang. It was Drew. Juliette got in the car while I paced the parking lot.

"I'm ready to come home," he said.

I stopped short on the steaming pavement and looked at the phone in disbelief. After all he had put us through over the last twenty-four hours, now he wanted to come home? Perspiration beaded on my fore-head and beneath my tank top as I stood, melting in the hot sun. I couldn't bear to go through this again. I pulled the damp cotton away from my flat chest. I had sacrificed so much: my best years, my whole body. More than anything, I wanted to be a good mother.

I looked at my innocent daughter, sweating in passenger seat. She would be dating soon, and her sister was next. I didn't ever want them to feel trapped or dominated or afraid or lied to or criticized or humili-ated or attacked or diminished or disrespected or guilt-ridden or made crazy or black-and-blue. I didn't want any man ever treating them the way their father treated me.

On the other end of the phone, Drew was still silent. That's how I realized it was a question. I felt a shift of power. Did I want him to come home?

I said no.

The following weekend, my fully packed car was stolen from the grocery store on the way to the desert to help my mother through chemotherapy. Life was in session. After eighteen months of counsel-ing attempts, custody issues, a restraining order, a false deposition, and more physical threats, drunken scenes, and broken promises, I took my name back. The very maternal instinct that lured me into this trap had now helped me out.

I'm not proud of how long it took me to escape. But I make this confession as a cautionary tale. With more women as the breadwinners, logic suggests that we will be free from traditional gender restraints. But studies show this not to be true. Women still carry the burden. We have the freedom to leave the house, but only after the beds have been made. Until we have adequate parental leave, affordable childcare, and equal pay, our breasts—our very femaleness—will keep women vulnerable. Emotional abuse, economic abuse, and physical abuse are a dangerous triad.

If it could happen to me, it could happen to anyone.

Emotional Abuse

A covert form of domestic violence.[1]
This abuse can be more unbearable than physical violence and often leads to suicidality.[2]

Warning Signs

You:

Fear your partner.

Feel a lack of privacy.

Experience unusual feelings of depression and anxiety.

Lack self-worth.

Have friends who notice a change in you.

Feel pressure to do things you don't like.

Your Partner:

Is controlling of your behavior and household decisions.

Is extremely jealous.

Isolates you from friends, discourages activities.

Turns you against family.

Displays extreme anger.

Constantly criticizes.

Holds financial control.

Makes false accusations.

Calls your reactions "too sensitive."

Gaslights—lies to you and others, calls you crazy.

Belittles your opinion and taste.

Blames you for his cheating.

Exhibits Jekyll and Hyde behavior.

Shames you about your past.

Calls you names.

Humiliates you in front of others.

Makes silly demands.

Treats you like a child.

Stonewalls—ignores or disappears without warning.

Occasionally makes grand gestures and/or gifts.

Makes threats of physical violence.

Statistics

- 48.4% of women in the United States have experienced psychological abuse.[3]

- 43% of dating college students experience abuse, often beginning with lack of digital privacy.

- 1 in 3 teens in relationships experience abuse, raising the risk of substance abuse, depression, and more abuse; most do not report violence.[4]

- 28% of women in the US experience at least one episode of physical abuse.

National Domestic Violence Hotline:

1-800-799-7233

or thehotline.org.

Ten

BOOB JOB
2005

During my divorce, I shed fifteen pounds purely from stress. My hip bones stuck out farther than my breasts. I got sick so often my doctor ordered full body scans. This was the immune system's reaction to grief, not for what I had lost, but for the dream that hadn't come true. And just before my forty-fifth birthday in May, as I was cleaning up another dinner I'd barely touched, my mother called. Her cancer was in remission now and she was in good spirits.

"I'll pay for breast implants," she said, on a long-distance phone call. "You deserve it."

As a reward? I thought. *A birthday present?*

"As a divorce gift," she said. "You only live once."

"I'm not a bimbo!" I said, then glanced at my daughters on the couch. Fortunately, they were too entranced by *Josie and the Pussycats* to hear me. I took the phone down the hallway.

"Neither is your sister. She has implants, you know, and a master's degree."

"I know, Mom, but she competes with beauty queens reading news off teleprompters to feed her family. It's practically a business accessory."

What Mom didn't know was that Tracy decided to do it after reading a manuscript I wrote called *Gilding the Lily*, about a young woman who was asked to get a boob job to replace a sick actress. While it was cathartic for me, Tracy was interviewing a plastic surgeon at the time, who offered her a deal. But now I could hear the hurt in my mother's voice.

"I meant, no, thank you," I said. "You already bought me a birthday dress." This year's dress was stunning, a tight beaded shift she insisted on, knowing an attorney I'd lunched with twenty years earlier had asked me to dinner.

"Men like breasts," my mother said.

I sat down at my desk and turned on my computer. Sure enough, my dinner date's name popped up in my email. When I'd met him for a drink, he'd admitted he had an on-again, off-again girlfriend, a model. Then he'd appraised my black blazer and jeans, my long hair and red lipstick, and broke a wine glass in his bare hand. As the bartender scrambled to clean up the shattered glass, the lawyer lamented that we hadn't married when we first met. He was upset at our bad timing. For me, the timing was perfect. His flattery gave me confidence.

"Not all men," I said in response to my mother. The lawyer seemed perfectly happy with the way I looked.

"I just don't want you to be lonely," she said.

"I'm not, I promise. I'm too busy. But thanks for your concern."

I hung up and considered which file on my desk to attack. The first was stuffed with manuscripts to review for my writing students. The second held my ex's Veterans Administration application for disability, which required a letter describing how PTSD had destroyed our marriage. The third held a Japanese poem about happiness I had to translate to finish my graduate degree. I pushed the files away and went online to explore another path to happiness: breasts.

The number of augmentations per year in the United States had increased more than 55 percent since my mother had first suggested it over ten years earlier. Back then, the only person I knew who had implants was the erotic film actress who played the murdered socialite in my movie *Heartless*. Judy (the director) and I joked about her "Tupperware" breasts. I didn't want anyone joking about me. But now there were safer, softer implants and 5 percent of American women had them. Most got them after childbearing. Yet, with full custody of two teenagers and a home I was struggling to keep, I could never pay for such a frivolous procedure, let alone find the time for post-op recovery. As much as I wished my mother would help with the mortgage instead, that was my job. This was a gift.

Bottom line? I wasn't getting any younger. But it was clear from that dinner date it wasn't too late. I emailed the lawyer back, mentioning the breast implant idea.

He emailed within seconds. *Why?*

I sat back in my plastic desk chair. His question was freeing: he didn't see the need. Ironically, that strengthened my temptation to check it out. This wasn't a desperate act, it was a desire for something extra. Icing on the cake. A flag popped up with another email from him. If I did have the procedure, he wanted to see the results. Ha! That was not going to happen. But if ever I was going to check this out, now was the time.

A week later, my high heels clicked across the marble waiting room of a board-certified surgeon's office in Beverly Hills. When I checked in for the consultation, the receptionist handed me a pound of paperwork and a bottle of spa water. She was startlingly beautiful, with gleaming skin and lustrous hair. So was the office worker on the phone next to her, and the woman on the computer. These women were various ethnicities, each polished and tasteful in silk blouses and tailored dresses. The medical staff scanning the wall of records behind them wore lab coats and ponytails. They all had one thing in common: high heels. I almost laughed, but I'd dressed up, too.

It was comforting to know that the doctor of this elegant office with a view of the Hollywood Hills had majored in molecular biology. The packet of paper said his primary office was in Irvine, where he'd begun in reconstructive surgery. He had patents, gave lectures around the world, and his partner was on TV. *Sometimes you get what you pay for*, I thought.

After sinking into the white leather couch, I started filling out forms on the glass coffee table. My "reason for consultation" was the aftereffects of breastfeeding. This was true, but it was beginning to sound like an excuse even to me. Why did I have to justify my desire for breasts? I was ashamed of being caught in this competition. When a woman entered in dark glasses with a bandage over her nose, the receptionist immediately called a nurse who emerged from the inner sanctum and ushered the patient inside. Privacy was ensured. That didn't make me feel better. The truth was, I didn't care about what anyone else thought. I wasn't sure what *I* thought. Then I turned to the medical history page and sat up in alarm. From now on, every time I went to a new doctor, would I have to write down height, weight, and breast augmentation? This was a mistake. I stood to leave. Then I heard my name.

A physician's assistant wearing a lab coat, sneakers, and absolutely no makeup on her porcelain skin waved the clipboard at me. Her name was Orla. She looked so normal, so natural, that I turned and trailed her like a puppy into the nearest exam room. If someone like her worked in this house of plastic enhancements, it couldn't be that bad. Soon, I met Dr. Calvert, who looked so much like Christian Bale in *Batman Begins* that it was difficult to hold his gaze. I was grateful that we met when I was fully clothed. But then, of course, I was asked to disrobe. They never say "undress," it's always "disrobe." It sounds more medical.

When he returned, he sat on a stool and pushed the paper robe off my shoulders. He stared straight ahead at my chest. "Up here,"

I wanted to say, but he was working. Even my years of dressing in a locker room hadn't prepared me for such scrutiny.

"You're an ideal candidate for surgery," he said.

At first, I was insulted. "Do you tell everyone that?"

"No," he said. "May I touch you?"

What nice manners, I thought. No male had ever asked permission before. Once I said yes, he started chatting as if his hand on my chest was the most natural thing in the world. That was more like what I was used to, when you pretend it isn't happening.

He dictated notes about ptosis and a lot of other medical terms that I was relieved to hear. He said my skin was quite thin, and the drooping had stretched further due to gravity over the twelve years since I had last nursed. He made it sound as if I was late getting here, as if this was a medical necessity. He covered me up and sat back.

"What are your goals?" he asked.

I told him I wanted to be a full B cup, no more. "I'm a writer," I said, wishing I were wearing my glasses to prove it. By now I equated intellectuals with people who didn't prioritize beauty. The brain was the thing.

He looked at me and shrugged. Implants are measured by volume, in cubic centimeters. Since women have unique rib cages and torsos of various lengths, the same size will look different on two bodies. You can't just order a cup size—that's a fashion category. He suggested I look at pictures, then return to try on a sample bra with assorted implants. There was no rush. They booked six months in advance.

"Sounds good," I said. "I just want to look natural. But do you think I'd have a little cleavage?"

He laughed. With the right bra I would definitely have cleavage. He offered to lift my nipples, but it required cutting them off and sewing them back on. What was the point of pretty breasts if they were scarred? He said the critical thing was to use whatever amount of volume filled up my empty sacks. Otherwise, I'd have excess skin hanging down. He'd fit my body, not my dreams.

"My dreams are small," I reminded him. "Subtle."

He prescribed 350 cc implants. Orla wrote down the size and I panicked. This was getting too real. I countered with a request for 300s. The doctor said every patient wishes she had gone larger.

"Don't you mean their husbands?" I asked. I'd come across an episode of *The Howard Stern Show* where Donald Trump said that if his wife Melania was in a car accident, his first response would be, "How are the breasts?" Plus, Hefner's Bunnies now had a hit reality TV show, *The Girls Next Door.* It was hard to stop my daughters from watching it.

Dr. Calvert promised to keep a few sizes available in the operating room. He normally did anyway, since one side might differ from the other. Due to my thin skin, he would insert them under the muscle to avoid seeing the outline. I had researched saline and silicone, and was wary of leakage and immune issues. Fortunately, my lumpy breast tissue qualified for the new "gummy bear" texture of silicone, a stronger gel that felt more lifelike and had less chance of rupture. He said that if I didn't like them, they could be taken out.

Next, his assistant took topless pictures with a digital camera. *This is the furthest thing from* Playboy, I thought, as I stood facing her and then turned sideways. These were mug shots, as if my breasts had done wrong.

When I got home, I looked at before and after photos online. These included true deformities, enlargements, and reductions. The women were of many skin colors and bikini tans. Some women had perfectly fine breasts that morphed into orbs. I felt protective of those women, careful to approve their right to control their own bodies. The image I saw of my chest on the camera was among the ugliest. Why did I feel so anxious? I congratulated myself on checking it out. Now I could let it go.

The doctor's office called a few days later, offering me an earlier surgery slot that had opened up due to a cancellation. I'd just completed a full physical for my birthday, and there was just enough time to do blood screens to complete the pre-op. The opening was in ten days. I had twenty-four hours to decide.

I stayed up all night researching safety. A year earlier, Olivia Gold-smith, author of one of my favorite books, *The First Wives Club*, had gone in for a face-lift, fell into a coma, and died. She'd been taking other medication, but there was no word yet on the cause. This was an elective surgery, and I was scared. But I was also curious. I was healthy and strong. After a long and difficult divorce, I took far better care of myself. I hiked, bought myself flowers, even splurged on the occasional facial. I read that women who had breast augmentations during a rela-tionship were destined to be single. It was a sign that something was not working, that whoever prompted it wanted more. I was relieved that I hadn't done this during my marriage. I was doing it for me. And if I didn't do it now, I never would.

The biggest challenge was telling my daughters. I didn't want them to copy me or to overvalue large breasts. I also didn't want them to feel responsible, so I had to stop blaming breastfeeding. The girls knew I adored them. In the two years since the separation, I'd done everything humanly possible for them—working, driving, shopping, cheering, and tucking them into bed when they let me. Just this once, I could be selfish. My mother volunteered to help. When Juliette was invited to Vegas with a friend's family, the timing was ideal. Though I hoped she wouldn't see Elton John's show Red Piano. The stage design featured enormous, inflatable breasts.

• • •

After the surgery, my chest was on fire. And it felt wrong to be laid up, bound like a mummy for vanity's sake. *Sorry, kid, Mommy can't make dinner because she got a boob job.* It took my mom plus a babysitter to cover my basic schedule.

One night, the girls climbed in my bed to watch our favorite chick flick: *Legally Blonde*. When Warner breaks up with Elle to marry a Jackie instead of a Marilyn and she protests, "What, my boobs are too big?" we cracked up. It made me feel better. Boobs had nothing to do with brains. Self-confidence did. Why not have it all?

When the bandage was unwrapped, my worst fears came true. My breasts were like beach balls floating up to my collarbone. I was instructed to massage them, then bind them from the top to force them down. I had no patience. What if this was permanent? It was a horrible mistake. I couldn't sleep on my stomach or shave my armpits, and they added a pound and a half to my weight. Every day I looked in the mirror and moaned.

I also called Dr. Calvert. I left messages and waited by the phone. When he returned my calls at the end of the day, I apologized and he talked me down. He said they would take six months to settle. And I was the only one who ever complained they were too big.

Too soon, it was time for my final graduate school residency. I prepared a three-hour seminar on literary novels versus bestsellers, complete with an exercise asking students to revise the first page of *The Da Vinci Code* in the style of Pulitzer Prize winner *Gilead* and vice versa. I wore a black T-shirt and an arm full of bangle bracelets. My mentors scored it highly, but one student evaluation stuck. It referred to me as a Valley Girl. True, I lived in the Valley. But I feared what she really meant was *bimbo*. I regretted not using Ray Bradbury's *Fahrenheit 451* in my seminar. Originally serialized in *Playboy*, it was a better example of a commercial crossover. Books and boobs—like me.

When the girls and I met my father and his third wife for a weekend in Chicago, I was still wearing a compression bra. I hugged his wife, who was only a few years older than me, and felt the hard balls of her old-school implants. We spent the weekend going to museums and seeing shows. Either he didn't notice my enhanced figure, or he didn't care. Still, hugging his wife goodbye made me wonder. One way or the other, all his women were well-endowed. Was this where my insecurity started? I hoped the answer was no.

When it was time to take off the tight sports bra, I went straight to Victoria's Secret. I used to be too small to shop there. Now I was too large. I was still a 32 band, but their largest in that size was a B cup, and that cut across my newly full flesh. I looked like the sisters in *Pride and Prejudice,* displaying my assets to attract a suitor. The saleswoman claimed a 34B was the same as a 32C. It wasn't.

I called the doctor to suggest he go into the bra business and fill a gap in the market. With 329,000 breast augmentations that year, how could there be so few bras to fit them?[1] I recalled what my mother said and went to Nordstrom.

As I waited in the dressing room, a lingerie specialist named Nancy explained that Victoria's Secret sold "fashion" bras. Nordstrom sold *foundation* bras, in every size and price. Embarrassed, I gave her my whole excuse about nursing boobs, but she didn't give a hoot. It was my body, my right. Then she helped me into an exquisite brassiere.

Angels sang.

My chest looked beautiful, with a gentle swell rising above delicate lace. My mother was right. When I looked at the size, I nearly fainted: 32D. No one could tell when I was dressed that I was more than a full B. Apparently, my small back made the cup size bigger. Why had I felt so ashamed of my desire to have a boob job? Moreover, why did I still?

I applied for a Nordstrom credit card and returned week after week to Nancy. Now I needed T-shirts that wouldn't pull and blouses that wouldn't gap. My sweaters clung, too, and sheath dresses were history. Bikinis fit so well it was embarrassing. I had no intention of competing with my teenage daughters, so I switched to one-piece swimsuits. The only problem was paying for them.

Inspired, I worked furiously to reboot my career. I was teaching and running workshops, but I had no idea whether I could afford to revise my thesis to sell it or if I should go back to film production. I borrowed money for a business consultant. He taught me to network with people as if I was going to a party. Show up with no expectations and have a good time. Be polite, he said. You never know who you might meet. It was six degrees of separation to everything you wanted.

I started calling two former business associates each week. I offered to buy them coffee to thank them for past help, to ask for advice, or just to catch up. I splurged on a trip to New York to thank the literary agents who'd rejected my thesis for their time. I wore my black blazer, good heels, and carried a leather briefcase. I didn't show my boobs, but I wore a beautiful bra beneath my blouse. My confidence soared. I didn't know why exactly, but there was no doubt my fragile ego was boosted, in part, by the size of my breasts.

Everyone I spoke with became a potential contact. Some became friends. I made eye contact at the grocery store and invited yoga mates to hike. One day, I woke up with a new story in mind about a woman who goes through a difficult divorce, but, with the help of other women going through the same thing, lives happ*ier* ever after. At the end, she flies to Paris. That was my dream, too.

With nothing to lose, I kept trying. I didn't have the money to go to charity benefits or hobnob in Hollywood, but I met a producer through the guy on the next Lifecycle at the gym. I reached out to new agents. Within a year, I sold my book project from the outline and a TV movie from the pitch. Would I have done this flat-chested? Maybe. But I would have hid behind my glasses, doubting myself for lacking a bestseller or an Academy Award. Call me shallow, but now I had a new weapon. Two.

Once my confidence was back on all burners, I made eye contact with everyone who looked interesting. When I smiled, men flirted with me at Starbucks, ushered me to good tables at lunch, and offered to buy me flowers at the grocery store. I felt like a sex object at forty-five. And I loved it.

I was ready to date.

Breast Augmentation by the Numbers

"Small breasts are 'a disease' that leads to 'a total lack of well-being.'"
—AMERICAN ASSOCIATION OF PLASTIC SURGEONS, 1982

- Breast augmentation has been the most popular cosmetic surgery in the U.S. since 2006.[1]

- The US has the highest number of breast augmentation surgeries in the world.

- Nearly 5% of American women have breast augmentation surgery.

- 299,715 breast augmentations were reported by board-certified plastic surgeons in 2019.* Additionally, there were 113,118 breast lifts in 2019 (reshaping and nipple placement, no implant).

- 107,238 breast reconstruction surgeries were reported by board-certified plastic surgeons.*

- Average age of recipients: 37% are 30–39; 29% are 40–54; 29% are 20–29; 3% are 13–19; and 2% are 55+.

- For gender confirmation, transfeminine top surgery uses implants for "a more feminine appearance."[2]

- Silicone implants are used in 85% of cosmetic surgery and 94% of reconstruction.

- Average size implants in the US are 300–400 cubic centimeters.

- Texas, California, and Florida average the largest sizes (up to 425 cc).

- Price of augmentation surgery typically ranges from $4,000 to $10,000, with over $1,183,000,000 spent annually.

- Race of women receiving breast augmentation: Caucasian 70%, Hispanic 11%, African American 9%, Asian-Pacific 7%.

- 33,764 breast implant removals a year, either to replace or remove for good.

- 46,340 breast reductions (unrelated to implants) per year.

- Biggest complaint about implants is loss of sensitivity—looking sexy feels less sexy.

- Mental health evaluation is recommended for all procedures.

- First mentioned in *Playboy* magazine in 1965.

*American Society of Plastic Surgeons, 2019 report.

Eleven

PEEK-A-BOOB: DATING
2006

After hearing nightmares from single friends, I vowed to give myself a year before joining an online dating service. I had no interest in marrying again—every wedding ring resembled a little gold handcuff. I'd conquered dining out alone. Now I wanted to dress up and go out with interesting company. Considering I had spent years in baggy sweaters and T-shirts from Target, this required date clothes. I'd bought a blazer, blouses, and heels for business meetings, so all I needed was a cute top. The question was cleavage. I liked having it, but I didn't want to show it. How much was too much, or not enough? I settled on a square necked top that tied in the back. That way, I could offer an hourglass figure, but without showing much skin. Now I just needed some men.

After my divorce, I lost several married friends who were either threatened by the specter of divorce or only had time to socialize with couples. I turned to Cathy, a trustworthy friend from back when her triplets were in nursery school with Chloe. I mentioned my interest in dating, but it wasn't until I grabbed her by the shoulders, looked her in the eye, and asked her to think of every single man she knew that she came up with names. Within weeks, I had dates with her husband's accountant, her neighbor's brother, and her Bunco friend's cousin. She warned them I was a newbie. And she knew where they lived.

You would think men would view a new divorcée as ripe for the picking, but two out of my three coffee dates offered dating advice. The other guy was sweet, but he had two young boys in need of a mother, and I was not interested in the job. Still, the next Sunday, he called to ask if I wanted to meet him at the movies in an hour. I was at my desk and both girls were safe in their rooms doing homework. What the hell. I brushed my hair, picked up my car keys, and met him at the theater. We each paid our own way and sat in the back row for *Wedding Crashers*.

Right from the start, we were laughing. *What a great idea*, I thought, *having a man as a movie buddy*. Then the con men on screen, played by Owen Wilson and Vince Vaughn, started scoring with the pretty wedding guests. I wasn't alarmed that women would fall into bed with a sweet-talking lawyer at a wedding reception. That was their business. However, the montage of topless young women falling back on beds— boom, boom, boom—caught me by surprise. I felt self-conscious. We were both still laughing, but was I rooting for the men making the conquest or the bare-breasted women tricked into hooking up? Was it funny when Jane Seymour, playing the mom, asked Wilson to check out her silicone breasts? Apparently, yes. We ended the "date" still laughing, and I gave him a hug goodbye. But we didn't go out again.

Several years had passed since I'd had sex, so I wasn't opposed to the idea. Baring my breasts was the problem. I decided on a two-date rule. In an era of easy hookups, I figured it wasn't much different than when I dated in my twenties: sex was expected on the third date. I didn't want to be a tease, but I did want to be a good role model for my daughters. So, unless I could picture myself naked with the man, the second date was the last. No man except my ex-husband had seen me naked in over twenty years. No man had ever seen my new boobs.

After dating three men, I spent more time on the phone than meeting people in person. After years of loneliness during my marriage, I loved the attention. I turned down an ocean cruise from an older man, and a mountain cruise from a Harley Davidson biker. Sure, I accepted a discount from a young salesman at Banana Republic, but when we met for coffee, he talked about his mother. Then I wasted a salon blowout on a hot producer who was perfect on paper, but bitched about his ex until his coffee was cold. Meanwhile, two-and-a-half years had passed since my ex and I had separated but there was still post-divorce drama. After serving him with a restraining order that was lifted when he lied in court, I hit pause in my personal life. Now that I'd sold a novel and a screenplay pitch, it was time to start writing them.

Years had passed since I'd written a script, so I pulled out the coffee-stained, crayon-scribbled spiral notebook from a seminar I'd taken twenty-five years earlier. Everything I had sold was written according to the structure steps in these notes. I taught the techniques myself in classes and private workshops. Grateful, and still in networking mode, I decided to send the instructor, John, a thank-you email.

Chances were good John would never receive it, so I mentioned the time he'd come to my Santa Monica apartment for dinner. The evening was memorable for being so awkward. I was a newlywed with a possessive husband and John didn't bring a date. He was a nice guy who I hoped to have as a friend, but Drew made that impossible. In the decades since, I'd been in touch, like any student, to announce the premiere of the film I'd written and again for the publication of my first novel. One night when I was in the kitchen making spaghetti, a baby on my hip and a toddler at my knee, he'd called to say congratulations. Even while drowning in the sea of domesticity, I'd been thrilled. By now, twenty-five years later, he was surely married with three kids. This was simply business. I emailed that I owed him a cup of coffee.

He emailed back and offered to pay. Big spender.

For most business meetings, I wore designer jeans with a black blazer and heels. This was a sweltering summer day, so I also wore a black sundress. It had a scoop neck just high enough to be professional and just low enough to be friendly. What the hell, right? John showed up in shorts and leather flip-flops so, clearly, he didn't think of this as a date, either. The pressure was off. His hair was now white, but I recognized the Coke-bottle glasses and the dimples when he smiled.

Our coffee lasted three hours. He'd never married. That was so strange to a softball mom like me that I wondered if he was gay. Then he admitted he didn't remember me but had checked out the picture on my website. I wasn't sure if I should be insulted or flattered, but when he invited me to dinner, I said yes.

Then I remembered Cathy had set me up on two blind dates for the following week. Not even coffee. Dinners. Both men sounded intriguing on the phone, but this was too much for me. What if it was too much for John? After a restless night, I canceled the other dates. John had never married, but he seemed sincere. Best of all, I could picture myself naked with him.

For our first date, I bought a fancy lace top. It seemed fine in the store, but when I got home, it looked far more revealing. My fashionista daughter insisted this was modest by modern standards, but I was incredibly self-conscious. This was the first time I was aware of using cleavage as a lure. I spent most of the dinner tugging the neckline up. Good or bad, my date was all smiles. John had no fashion sense of his own, which was disappointing, but also comforting. He wasn't a player who needed to look slick. He was stealthy in his approach, a man with a history of relationships with sophisticated women. As our dates continued, it became clear he was a connoisseur who savored every detail. He noticed my earrings and my shoes and everything in between. It was fun to dress up and be appreciated. I had never felt so calm and confident, as if all I had to do was show up.

Two weeks later, my father was due to fly in from Ohio for a short visit, so I planned a small dinner party with my sister's family for his seventieth birthday. Since both men had graduated from Princeton, I took a deep breath and invited John. Tracy gave my new date the third degree, initiating a game of True or False to learn if he had seen the scar on my upper thigh. He had not. My father, however, was thrilled to meet a fellow alumnus. Dad was still larger than life, the kind of man whose energy fills a room. He was especially pleased that John recognized him as the man who unicycled in the annual reunion P-rade. Then my father lit into his usual tirade about what a shame it was that I hadn't gone to Princeton, especially now that the three of us could've shared the Tiger glory. When he was done, he looked at John for agreement.

John shook his head and shut him down. He was grateful I hadn't gone, because I would have been there too late for him. He said I would have met and married a nice Princeton man and he'd never have had a chance to meet me.

Tracy and I tried not to laugh as my father failed to think of a comeback. The theory could have just been a compliment, but John was not one to waste words. And he was no longer just a date I invited to dinner. Now I'd come full circle with two red-blooded white men educated in the cradle of the American elite. They had taken different routes to the Ivy League: At sixteen, my father had gone to a men's school that required a suit and tie, kept *Playboy* in the library, and invited women only on weekends; John had gone on scholarship, joined the first coed eating club, and, as captain of the squash team, dated the captain of the women's team. My father had married three times, while John was a lifelong bachelor. My father was a Republican while John was a Democrat. Yet both men prized breasts.

And neither knew my secret.

When John invited me to Santa Barbara for a long weekend, the end of innocence was near. We were two months past my two-date rule. I was out of my mind with anxiety. This was an obvious invitation to intimacy, and there was no way to avoid it. I insisted John have a full physical, including the new HPV test. Once he told me he passed, I couldn't procrastinate much longer. Sure, I wanted to be swept off my feet on a romantic weekend, but what about my breasts? I wanted to blurt out my secret to get it over with.

That Saturday, after a full day of shuttling the girls around town, I settled in my bedroom to do paperwork while watching *Seinfeld* reruns. The first episode showed Seinfeld dating Sidra, played by Teri Hatcher. Now she was on *Desperate Housewives* and I was hooked, so I put my work down and watched Elaine tell Jerry that Sidra's perfect breasts probably weren't real. Jerry was freaked out. He didn't want to date someone with fake breasts. Later, Elaine accidently groped Sidra and confirmed to Jerry that they were real. Relieved, he started dating Sidra again. When Sidra realized he knew Elaine, she suspected the grope was intentional and broke up with Jerry. She tortured him further by saying, "They're real, and they're spectacular."[1]

I turned off the TV. The rerun was over ten years old, but it still rang true. What if my new boyfriend agreed with Jerry, that breasts had to be real to be spectacular? This could change everything he believed about me. I was a liar by omission. Was it too late to tell him that the breasts he'd fondled were fake? Could he already tell? The scars were hidden underneath my breasts, but what if I raised my arms and he saw them? He had complimented that low-cut lace blouse I'd worn on our first date. Would he accuse me of pulling a bait and switch?

I surveyed my friends for a solution, but the suggestions varied. I could keep the lights off and not tell him. I could make a joke and say, "Yes, they're mine, I paid for them." Except, my mother had. How embarrassing. After a few sleepless nights, I decided to break up with him.

The past few months had been great, but I had no intention of marrying. I didn't need a boyfriend. One of my students offered to set me up with her older brother, who sounded pretty nice. I would keep dating until I found someone I didn't care so much about. Then I could have sex and not care what anyone thought.

Still, Santa Barbara sounded fun. I hadn't been on a vacation in years. My Filofax was so full of obligations, I could barely read my schedule for the next day. I needed the break.

On Monday morning, after dropping the girls off at their schools, I went back to Nordstrom to find Nancy, my personal shopper in the lingerie department. She said my nerves were normal, I looked beautiful, and I shouldn't worry. She brought me a black lace bra with a bamboo pattern and a matching thong. I added a garter belt and stockings, the kind I'd worn when I was younger. Nancy made it feel like an investment. If I was happy, he'd be happy, too, she said.

I looked in the mirror. This was as sexy as I would ever get. I was forty-six and, in my eyes, fading fast. I really liked this guy. He was nice to me all the time. Who knew "nice" was such a turn-on? Who knew it was even *possible*? I thought of my "Be Nice" Post-its, meant for Drew. With John, I could relax. I didn't have to worry about what I was thinking or saying or doing or how to keep the girls happy and out of harm's way. I wasn't a mom or a daughter or a sister or a divorcée or anyone else besides me. I could just breathe. I felt happy. If he didn't, well, I guess he could search for happiness elsewhere.

Now the question was: When? I didn't want to confess on the way there. I didn't want to be trapped in the car with him after that, or ruin my chance to even get to Santa Barbara. I'd been there before, but rarely without my daughters and never just for fun. Plus, I'd already spent a fortune on lingerie. I put off making the decision.

I spent two hours typing up a schedule and an emergency list for the girls. I'd also screened several babysitters about staying overnight, which was embarrassing since it was so obvious that I was abandoning my children to go have sex with my new boyfriend. At least he was officially my boyfriend now. And my teenage girls were eager to have me absent for an entire weekend; the babysitter was up for the extra pay.

I could barely speak on the drive up. I watched his hand on my knee, was shy about choosing music, and too embarrassed to ask to stop at a restroom. When we got to the bed and breakfast, I chatted to the proprietor nervously as John checked out the antique-filled rooms to be sure we had the nicest one. We borrowed bikes and rode to the pier. When we got off the bikes and strolled along the beach, I thought about telling him then. But he was holding my hand and saying how happy he was to be there with me. He was so sweet it sounded phony, as if he was making it up for a laugh. But instead of laughing, he started humming. The guy was serious. The seagulls were swooping, and the waves were crashing, and the sun was setting, like a real-life romance novel. I couldn't wreck it just yet. He had carefully researched local restaurants and made dinner reservations, and I was hungry. I decided to wait until later.

He didn't even rush me while I dressed in the bathroom. I took forever, not only out of nerves, but because adjusting my bra straps and garter clasps were feats of engineering. He just read a book until I emerged, fully dressed in a black chiffon dress I got on sale at Banana Republic. He wore a jacket with shoulder pads so big that some girl-friend must have picked it out in the eighties. The tweedy look was perfect for him, though, and his smile was like sunshine. The restaurant was so romantic, with a vase of red roses on the white tablecloth, that it felt tacky to bring up my boobs. My dress had a sheer black netting to my collarbone, just covering my bamboo bra. I could feel his eyes dart across my décolletage as I sat bathed in the candlelight. His eyes were shining, and he was saying more sweet things, so I just nodded along. When the waiter poured me a glass of wine, I sipped from the crystal goblet and finally relaxed. This was fun. This was exactly what I wanted, nothing more.

I told him, very clearly, that I would never marry again. To me, marriage felt like jail. Not only was that true, but I figured it would offer relief to such a committed bachelor. It would also allow leeway if he hated my boobs.

"To fun," he said, raising his glass.

An hour later, the lights were off, and we were kissing on the soft couch of our hotel room. John had brought candles and a music player from home, which would have felt calculating if it wasn't so smart. My dress was already puddled on the floor by the time he pulled down the strap of my bamboo brassiere. He started kissing my neck, then my collarbone. Oh my God, it felt so good. But when his head dipped below my chin, my heart started beating like a kick drum. I wedged my fingers in front of his forehead and shoved him away. He blinked at me like a startled puppy.

"There's something I have to tell you," I said, covering my chest with both hands. He waited. Now I had to say the words. "I have breast implants."

He nodded and kissed me again.

"Did you hear me?" I asked.

He pulled back to look at my face. "Yes," he said. "I don't care." He lifted my hands away. "Beautiful. You're beautiful."

He kissed me on the lips, and I thought, *OK*. Then I thought: *He is a really good kisser*. By the end of the weekend, he had proved how much it didn't matter. He said he had figured my boobs were fake due to my build. All that worrying and he already knew! And he didn't care. He loved them, and he loved me. We had such a good time that weekend, he joked that the hotel was going to put a plaque on the door commemorating the historic event.

As we dressed on the last morning, I had one last concern. "Would you like me if I was flat-chested?"

"Of course," he said.

"No, I mean, would you have been attracted to me in the first place? If I didn't have, you know." I thought back to our first coffee date. The photo on my website that promoted his reply was a headshot. But that day in the coffee shop . . .

"That's a moot point," I remember him saying. "You do."

Resigned to the fact that I'd never know, I packed my lingerie back in my suitcase to leave Santa Barbara. And I decided on two things. First, I'd send a thank-you note to Nancy at Nordstrom. Second, I would never show him my before pictures. My boob job wasn't a secret, but why scare him? This was a man who had never married, nor had children. He was naïve in that way. And he didn't need a steady girlfriend, so why not have one with breasts? I was happy he had balls, but it wasn't the same thing. I was happier that he was smart and funny and cute.

As we put our suitcases in the trunk of his car for the drive back to Los Angeles, I asked one more question: "Would you have been attracted to me if I was stupid?"

He laughed. "No. You're the whole package."

So are you, I thought. Win-win.

A few years later, comedian Joan Rivers published a book called *Men Are Stupid . . . And They Like Big Boobs*. Beyond the jokes— so funny from a woman's point of view—it was a guide for how to choose a doctor if you decided to explore plastic surgery. The question was, did women like boobs, too, or did they like boobs because men did? Thanks to the biological laws of attraction, this was another moot question.

Later, when I asked John about that fateful weekend, I explained how worried I had been about telling him. He said that when he was on a holiday "in a nice room in Santa Barbara with a beautiful girl wearing incredible lingerie who tells him she had work done," he thought, *Hmm. What do I want to do here?* It was a no-brainer. He also claims that when I asked if he would have been attracted to me without full breasts, he answered, "Yes. You have a face that could 'launch a thousand ships.'" No wonder I don't remember that; it sounds ridiculous. But sweet.

Clearly, John was not one of the stupid men that Joan Rivers joked about. He confessed knowing that a thin woman was unlikely to have large breasts. Since he had dated women of different sizes, he was already used to the fact that we were all different. Smaller breasts were perkier, larger breasts drooped more. Some men had preferences, but he did not. Like pizza—he dragged out that old cliché—they were all good. He claimed that when men look at a woman, they simply see a person with breasts, a magical, visual, tactile element that men don't have. In any form, they were mesmerizing.

The problem is that when breasts of all sizes are celebrated as sexual, they can overpower everything else. When *Wedding Crashers* was censored for TV, the girls falling back on the bed were no longer topless. They wore sexy bras. Obviously, the director shot the scene both ways, knowing that bare breasts were too risqué for TV. The censors were comfortable with boys and girls in the TV audience rooting for men to crash parties and lie to young women in order to have sex. They were not comfortable showing that young women have breasts.

In real life, even one inch of breast is dangerous. Within a year of our weekend away, Senator Hillary Clinton wore a pink blazer over a black V-neck on the Senate floor as she gave a talk about the financial burden of higher education on students. Her talk was broadcast on C-SPAN, a cable channel nobody watched. But the inch of skin below her clavicle was too much. The *Washington Post* dedicated 746 words to bashing her for "sexual provocation."[2] They said cleavage was OK for confident sexual women, but not for one who usually covered up. Soon it was called Cleavage-gate, in reference to the illegal break-in that led to President Nixon's resignation. One inch of female flesh was equated with a federal crime. You could dress like a normal woman to be pretty, but not to be smart.

Fortunately, I had found a man who appreciated that women could be both.

Years later, I learned that when John got home from our weekend in Santa Barbara, he clipped a newspaper article entitled, "How to buy a diamond ring." The clipping yellowed in his file cabinet for four years until I changed my mind about marriage.

Breast Censorship

Nipples: The Intersection of the Sacred and Profane

1930s   Nudity in film is prohibited by the Hays Code; promiscuous characters die young.

1958   Cartoon cows require skirts drawn over udders to pass censors.

1963   Jayne Mansfield's breasts are banned in Cleveland for 60-second shot in *Promises! Promises!*

1972   George Carlin's "Seven Words You Can Never Say on Television" includes "tits."

1977   Bare breasts are shown on TV for first time in the *Roots* miniseries—those of the African American slaves.

1999   Bare breasts are censored in *Eyes Wide Shut* via CGI to avoid an NC-17 rating.

2000   *American Psycho*, a slasher film, cuts 18 seconds of sex workers in a threesome to avoid an NC-17 rating.

2004   Animated puppet breasts are censored in a *Team America* sex scene.

2004   Nipple-gate—CBS fines Janet Jackson $550,000 for a "wardrobe malfunction" during the Super Bowl halftime show.

2004   Two-second breast shot of elderly cancer patients is cut by NBC's *ER* to avoid fines.

2006   According to the documentary *This Film Is Not Yet Rated*, "lesbian boobs" merit an NC-17 rating, while "straight boobs" often get an R.

2013 Nude scenes are trimmed in *The Wolf of Wall Street* to avoid an NC-17 rating.

2014 Nipples are banned on Instagram, prompting the #FreeTheNipple campaign.

2015 Master artworks by Pablo Picasso and Amedeo Modigliani have nipples blurred on TV news.

2015 On *The Colbert Report*, Stephen Colbert draws a dot in the middle of two circles; Comedy Central censors blur it.

2016 #ManBoobs4Boobs—"man boobs" are shown in breast cancer PSA since female breasts are banned.

2017 Sony shoots two versions of *Wedding Crashers;* sells copies as censored or uncensored.

2019 Instagram shuts down my account for a photo of tattooed mastectomy patients, including a woman's reconstructed breasts with nipples.

Twelve

DRESSING FOR SEX
2008

Do you want to watch the Victoria's Secret Fashion Show?"
I looked up from the December issue of *Vogue*, hoping I'd
heard wrong. My boyfriend was pointing at the list of shows
on the DVR menu screen of his TV. Sure enough, there it was, between
Breaking Bad and *The Wire*. John and I now saw each other twice a
week when his travel and my daughters' schedules allowed. Tonight
was my turn to cruise the ten-mile canyon between the ranch house
where the girls and I lived in the Valley and his rustic home in Santa
Monica. Since he had to keep current with TV for work, he collected
shows for us to watch together. This would not be one of them.

"No, thanks."

"Are you sure?" he asked. "Adriana is wearing the fantasy bra with
five million dollars' worth of diamonds. And Allesandra is back from
having her baby."

I stared at this man I loved. After two years of dating, this was
the first I'd heard that he considered this annual underwear ad to be

must-see TV. I'd seen some of the hype before the big event the first week of December. It was impossible to miss.

"You know their names?" I asked.

"Of course. Heidi Klum is the host this year. You know Heidi. You love her. Everybody does."

We did both enjoy *Project Runway*, a competition that my first husband had made fun of me for watching. This man was more forgiving of my tastes, more appreciative of the creative arts. Or maybe he just liked seeing the models strip down for fittings. This underwear fashion show was far less subtle, a parade of women with figures most didn't possess. And they pranced across the stage, serenaded by rock stars. But John was at least half-kidding. Heidi Klum annoyed the hell out of him.

"Hon, don't get me wrong, you're the most beautiful woman in the world," he said. "You are, after all, Lady Beautiful. But these are Angels."

The flattering nickname did not help his case. "Sorry, I don't get pleasure watching women prance around half naked. Just proves that men run the TV networks."

He clicked the remote in search of a different show, so I decided to simply accept that he was a dude. We had recently been at a dinner party where the host claimed he divided everyone he met into two groups: "fight 'em or fuck 'em." He claimed the instinct was biological. Part of me was grateful that this man sitting beside me considered me beautiful despite his close knowledge of supermodels. The other part of me was jealous.

I tried to focus on my magazine. Unfortunately, now I was distracted by the way Jennifer Aniston leaned forward in her red dress to present her breasts on the cover. When I glanced back up at the TV, John was watching football highlights. I wondered if there would be a Victoria's Secret Super Bowl commercial this year. Would Janet Jackson's halftime nip slip have any lingering effect? The amount of breast to expose presented a fine line for network censors. Nipples, no; strutting sex objects, yes.

A few days later, it was John's turn to visit my side of town. After a casual dinner in Calabasas, we drove to my suburban neighborhood in Woodland Hills. We slowed to admire holiday lights wrapped around palm trees. There were just enough pine trees to make the chill in the air feel wintery. Chloe's scraped Nissan was blocking the driveway of our house, so we parked by the white picket fence, perfectly decorated with green garlands and big red bows. I climbed out of the car to adjust one, pleased that my daughter had plugged in the white lights along the roofline. We strolled hand in hand up the driveway and discussed whether I had enough logs left over from last week to light the fireplace. Then I recognized Eartha Kitt's voice crooning "Santa Baby" from inside the house. The wreath on the door window blocked the view, so we walked right in.

Across the foyer on the living room, Chloe and her friends were exchanging gifts by the Christmas tree. In their underwear. No, not underwear. Victoria's Secret lingerie. One girl, a tall brunette, wore a hot pink Santa hat with a matching bra, fur-trimmed skirt, and a sparkling belly button ring. Another wore candy-cane thigh-highs with a red bra and matching Santa skirt. Instead of a red hat, she wore a ribbon in her hair topped with a bow, like a gift. Still another wore white angel wings, and I wondered how she had paid for them, whether she had saved her allowance or her pay from Hollister or borrowed her parents' credit card—and did they know? Another friend wore a sequined burgundy bustier with her lowriders. Another made do with a push-up halter and Daisy Dukes. Chloe wore a leopard bra with a faux crystal appliqué where the cups joined, like the million-dollar bra in the runway show. When we stepped through the foyer, the only one dressed in a basic T-shirt and jeans sat back on an armchair and blushed. Perfectly groomed with long, silky hair, sparkling make-up, and shiny manicures, they were all slim, stunning, and scary. And they were all sixteen.

"Hi, Mother," Chloe said, acting normal so that I would. "Remember, we're having our Secret Santa party?"

I covered John's wide eyes, spun him toward the hallway and gave him a gentle shove toward my bedroom. Then I turned back to her and nodded. I never understood why she called me Mother and not Mom, but at the moment, that wasn't my greatest concern.

"I didn't know it was dress-up."

The girls giggled.

I stood there at a loss for words while they watched my face for a reaction. This was my own Victoria's Secret Fashion Show, Junior Edition. It felt horrible and shocking, and I wanted to scream. I was tempted to call their parents and kick them all out. But who was I to scold them when my very own boyfriend was one of the millions who watched the show that had inspired it?

I surveyed the lingerie peeking from gift bags and the ripped wrapping paper on the coffee table. Was our house chosen because I was divorced and therefore, by definition, easy on rules? Because there were no brothers or fathers around? Or was it simply our turn? For now, I just wanted them to cover up.

"Aren't you girls cold?"

They all shook their heads, so I hung my jacket in the closet and set my purse on the front table to buy time. The real fashion show was still on my boyfriend's DVR across town, and I hadn't made him erase it. Was that tacit approval? I looked past them at my bookshelf of parenting books, hoping for consolation. I spotted *The Female Brain*, which explained how hormones influence our lives. In it, Dr. Louann Brizendine claimed that communication between adolescent girls prompted such a strong hormonal rush that it was akin to orgasm. Had these girls dressed up and stared in their mirrors alone, they wouldn't get what they needed for self-assurance: peer approval. They were practicing being sexual, playacting what they thought was womanhood, and they could do it safely here. But it still made me uneasy.

ABOVE: Fashion Rule #1: Cover your nipples! Mom, my sister, and me, in Arizona, 1963. BELOW: Daddy's girl, 1964.

ABOVE: All American family in Ohio, 1965. Mom and Dad taught at OSU. CENTER: The orange bikini I didn't fill out, 1973. BELOW: Wedding diet disaster, 1986.

Nursing boobs! 1989.

ABOVE: Three generations under the Maypole, 1992. BELOW: The portrait of Grandma Bert, whose eyes followed me around the living room.

PRESIDENT
of the
★ UNITED STATES ★
Year 2030

ABOVE: With my sweet girls at home in Woodland Hills, 1995. LEFT: My daughter's campaign poster from later that same year. Fingers crossed!

ABOVE: Celebrating my 40th birthday with my sister, Tracy, in Ojai, 1999. LEFT: Author photo for my first novel (with padded bra), 2000. *Courtesy of Bruce Malone.*

ABOVE: In Santa Barbara, first romantic weekend with John (just before confessing that my boobs were fake), 2006. BELOW: On the beach in Cabo with the boobs I always wanted, 2008.

Practically bursting with joy at my wedding to John, 2010.
Courtesy of Megan Stark.

Our first dance, 2010. *Courtesy of Megan Stark.*

With my daughters at my wedding, 2010. *Courtesy of Megan Stark.*

With my daughters on Thanksgiving after chemo—with fake bangs, 2012.

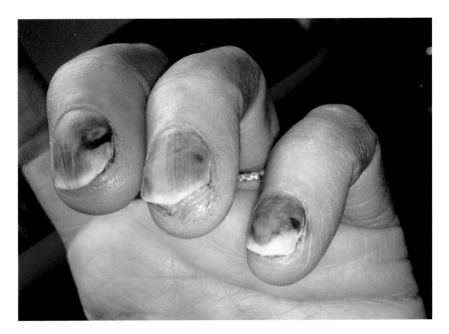

ABOVE: Chemo nails, 2013. CENTER: Impersonating myself in a wig and fake eyelashes for my book release at Barnes & Noble at the Grove in Los Angeles, 2013. BOTTOM RIGHT: Hair! 2013.

My first work trip in chemo curls. With my daughter at the Faulker Society's Words & Music Festival in New Orleans, 2013.

With John on his work trip for the Cinémathèque de Nice, France, 2014.

Celebrating the end of five years of breast cancer treatment in Paris, our first trip as a family, 2017.

With my daughter and niece at the Women's March in San Francisco, 2018.

When I got to my room, John was sitting on the pink velvet cover on my bed. The wall behind him was painted deep fuchsia. Juliette, now at college, had predicted that no man would ever go inside this room. She was wrong, but it wasn't until now that I realized why. My bedroom resembled a bordello, like the first Victoria's Secret stores.

"Don't you think that's a little strange?" he asked, pointing down the hall.

I shut the door. This man bought lingerie for me on work trips to Paris and Milan. He called me Lady Wonderbreast and had a nickname for each one. I thought he'd understand.

"They're just playing dress-up," I said, sitting on the bed beside him. "Like Halloween."

"Halloween for sex," he shot back.

Oh, please, I thought. Halloween was already for sex. Party stores sold leotard cat costumes for preteens. But I needed to stay on point.

"Don't be a hypocrite," I said. "They feel pressure because of men like you. You idealize the Victoria's Secret models—excuse me, *Angels*— who are so innocent in their fuck-me shoes and fantasy bras strutting around half naked on a public stage. First they starve themselves and get waxed and spray-tanned and—"

"But these are just girls," he interrupted.

"They didn't make these outfits on their own."

"The store makes them for women of all sizes."

"I doubt it," I said. "The average adult woman weighs 159 pounds."

He winced at that image, and I wanted to slap him, but first I needed to convince him this party wasn't weird. I needed to convince myself, too. I went to check on my garter belt in the dresser behind him. The first garter belt I bought, back in the eighties, was from the bridal section of a department store. Outside of sex shops, that had been the only place to buy lingerie. This contrast pointed directly at the transition from girl to woman, the official start of sexuality: the virgin sanctioned as sex object. Victoria's Secret made it fashionable to, I don't know, practice?

"Maybe I should hide my lingerie better." I said.

"Why? You're a grown woman. These girls aren't even eighteen."

"So what? Victoria's Secret sells a line called Pink specifically for teens and college students, but they don't ask for ID. It's practically a rite of passage for moms to take thirteen-year-olds there for candy-colored panties."

"Just admit it—this is weird."

"No," I said, pushing my garter belt to the back of the drawer. My stomach felt queasy, but I didn't want to shame these girls for being exactly what girls raised in America are pressured to be. I shut the drawer and looked at John.

"This is your fault for perpetuating that stupid fashion show."

"More women than men watch that show," he said.

"Sure, to see what they have to compete with. Aspire to."

"Are you mad at me?"

I shook my head. Mostly I was afraid for my daughter. But no way was this man getting laid tonight. We heard giggling and muffled voices as the girls went into Chloe's room and shut the door. I took off my high heels.

"You should go."

I locked the front door behind him and surveyed the remains in the living room. They'd done a good job cleaning up. I pulled a worn paperback from the bookshelf: *Reviving Ophelia* by Mary Pipher. The book reminded me that it wasn't just the fashion industry or the media that pushed a certain look or narrative on young women. These teen girls were judged every single day, by themselves and each other. Chloe's school outlawed narrow shoulder straps, but permitted short shorts and low-cut skinny jeans. After school, tube tops were all the rage. At parties, all bets were off. Only recently had I found my missing top, a sexy halter I'd splurged on for a summer event, scrunched under the girls' bathroom sink. And last spring, Juliette had remarked on how many of her high school classmates wore cute outfits in the morning but, when caught, were forced to change into their baggy PE uniforms for the rest of the day. Of course these girls wanted to wear what they wanted to wear. How could it be a surprise, when sexual attractiveness was the most obvious, often the only, form of power available to young women?

Above the fireplace hung a formal portrait of my late grandmother in a large gilded frame. I looked up and caught her green eyes watching in amusement. A vivacious redhead, my Grandma Bert's beauty was captured in the oil painting in 1957, when she was forty-two. She stood in three-quarter profile wearing an elegant strapless gown and posed against an emerald background. With her prominent cleavage in front and the large bow on her backside, the costume was reminiscent of a bunny. My male cousins called her "Tits" Turner, using the surname from her third husband, and they'd stored the portrait in a basement back east until I claimed it. Now she hung in my living room, a prime example of womanhood whose eyes followed me across the room like a modern Mona Lisa.

Was it ironic that her great-granddaughter aspired to the same kind of sexual beauty fifty years later? From a strapless evening gown to sexy underwear—same woman, different clothes.

Within a year of the party, Allen Edwards, the man responsible for Farrah Fawcett's do, saw Chloe at his hair salon and suggested she take up modeling. When Chloe said she was too shy, I was surprised, even a little disappointed. An all-star athlete whose injuries had ended her sports career, she had yet to find a new activity to help her build confidence. Did she recognize the emotional cost of beauty? Did she have a healthy fear of failure? Or was she simply a "nice" girl, caught between middle-class mores and a world that rewarded exhibitionism?

As we left the salon that day, I put my arm around her shoulder for a comforting squeeze. Her thin skin was dotted with surgery scars. My stomach seized at how deeply she felt them. I wanted her to experience the positive physical side of being a woman. If only I knew how to help.

Five years after the Santa party, my daughter's friends were finishing college and struggling to establish careers. Chloe was just as excited to share news of a friend with a scholarship for graduate school as she was the financial independence of a swimsuit model, or the fame of one who bared her breasts on *The Bachelor*.

Today, when high schools call girls "women," the demarcation between childhood and adulthood is blurry. The HBO show *Girls* was groundbreaking because it depicted the immaturity of a group of young white women with unblinking realism. Breasts were the most obvious fact of physical maturity, underscored repeatedly by Lena Dunham's nudity. Girls become women on a continuum, a sliding scale of emotional and physical development.

Living in Los Angeles, the entertainment capital of the world, makes it hard to ignore the images in movies and television. For me, it was a goal to get here. I never considered the impact it might have on my girls growing up. I'd like to think it's helpful to see how the sausage gets made, but maybe that makes it more depressing. The Geena Davis Institute on Gender in Media reports the obvious: women have far less screen time, fewer speaking parts, and are vastly underrepresented, even in crowd scenes. And we are six times more likely to be shown in revealing clothing.[1] Gratuitous boob shots are so common they were used like wallpaper in the first few seasons of *Game of Thrones*. I imagined if my daughters were those actresses calling home to say, "Look, Mom, I'm on TV!" A brand-new word was coined in 2011 to describe the technique of exchanging crucial dialogue during sex scenes: sexposition. How far are we from the seventies heyday of "jiggle TV" like *Charlie's Angels*, when so many female cops are not only model-pretty, but go undercover as strippers?

Even action stars are not immune. In 2017, when Gal Gadot, former Miss Israel, played Wonder Woman in the first major motion picture featuring a female superhero, she was slammed about her breast size from fans of the DC comic book character.[2] Lara Croft, the Tomb Raider cyberbabe introduced in a 1997 video game with a 36DD bust and the tagline "sometimes a killer body isn't enough," paid off with seventeen video games and three films. Shapely Angelina Jolie took the franchise success to the big screen in 2001, but when Alicia Vikander took over in 2018, the trolls came out to criticize her breast size.[3] It seems clear that fans missed the "eye candy," but did they equate breasts with strength? Maybe there is some truth to the idea that breasts are a kind of superpower.

From the moment my daughters started to develop, I felt anxious. How much influence did I really have over their sexuality, identity, and self-worth as women? Since parents are also shaped by our culture, we perpetuate a dangerous double bind. I wanted my daughters to be attractive in the very ways that could reduce them to the value of their attractiveness.

In 2016, approximately 800 million people watched the Victoria's Secret Fashion Show broadcast from Paris. Heidi Klum, who parlayed thirteen years of Angel wings into $90,000,000[4]—often estimated at $120 million today—went on to build Heidi Klum Intimates with the motto, "more boobs, less bra."[5] When Victoria's Secret—with over $6 billion in sales—talks about Girl Power, they aren't kidding. But there is no doubt in my mind which "girls" they mean. When I leaned into John's home office to ask if he'd be watching the Fashion Show, he paused ESPN and smiled. "Beautiful women walking around in their underwear? What could be better than that?"

I had no answer, so I turned to leave. Then I overheard him say, "I can't believe we get away with this."

But men do get away with it. How did John? Like Beyonce suggested, he put a ring on it.

• • •

After four years of dating, my kids were out of the house, I was ready to move back to the beach, and my boyfriend was still really cute. I took a deep breath and told him I'd changed my mind about marriage. A wedding band wouldn't feel like a handcuff if we kept the focus on fun.

To my surprise, fun for John meant a formal wedding. I was up for eloping, but he wanted his parents to witness the blessed event. And he wanted to prove to his college friends that Buddy Love, a nickname taken from *The Nutty Professor*, was finally taking the leap. There was no way around it. I needed a dress.

This made the situation more serious. Bridal gowns have been designed to display a woman's worth ever since special clothing was created to commemorate the event. Contrary to popular belief, neither the color nor the neckline of the white wedding dress originally symbolized purity. Since marriage was an exchange of wealth, everything was about status. When Queen Victoria married in 1840, she was already a monarch. Before bleach was developed, silver and loose jewels[6] were woven as "dowry" into white fabric "because it was so difficult to stay clean."[7] To stand out, Queen Victoria wore a pure white dress with a neckline cut low enough to frame the royal diamond necklace.

After World War II, when Americans were back in the business of having babies, weddings grew to be a social event. Just as buxom pinup girls became the ideal shape of the modern housewife, couture houses started closing their fashion shows with a bridal gown. This elevated the dress of every girl's dreams to the level of art. A new kind of "dowry" was displayed: the fleshy promise of fertility and motherhood.

In 1957, my twenty-two-year-old mother was escorted under an arch of swords held by naval groomsmen on the St. Regis Hotel roof. Her white satin dress with a sweetheart neckline was chosen by her father, perhaps to celebrate his immigrant rise to success. The look copied the new American royalty, Jacqueline Bouvier Kennedy, in her 1953 wedding to the future president.

During the swinging sixties, my sister and I spread flower petals in my aunt's path in the St. Regis ballroom. Her full lace skirt opened to reveal sexy hot pants, but the top was a turtleneck. Even the celebrities who wore miniskirts, from Yoko Ono to Raquel Welch, wore high necklines. Isn't it ironic that freedom was symbolized by the part of the body open for business on the wedding night, while the breasts remained hidden?

When I was engaged in 1986, there were few bridal magazines and no internet. During college, I was one of the 750 million who awoke before dawn to see Princess Diana's dress for her 1981 marriage to Prince Charles. Once revealed, the contradiction between her sexy date-night dresses versus this princess gown with childlike ruffles camouflaging her bust was right out of Roman mythology. Diana, goddess of the hunt, is not only a virgin praised for her purity, but also the goddess of fertility. The bridal industry exploded. To dress casually for a wedding now mocked the very institution of marriage. Eighties wedding gowns covered most of the body, so every inch of exposed skin alluded to what was hidden as both an object of desire and a vessel for future generations. I found a watered-down version of Princess Di's dress with an off-the-shoulder bodice and lace sleeves. The white corset with silky cups that I wore underneath completed the contradiction of "lady in the parlor, whore in the bedroom."

For my first marriage, like most brides, I wanted to look perfect. That meant I had to be as thin as humanly possible. Jane Fonda's workout video made the solution simple. "Feel the burn," she said, and we did, with aerobics and eating disorders. Anorexia became the "disorder of the eighties."[8] Fonda used diet pills for years and was also bulimic, but not one of us hungry girls knew that. We also didn't know she had breast implants. Thanks to the Zone diet and daily aerobics, whatever boobs I had when I bought the gown were long gone by our wedding day. The silky bra cups hung limp.

As the sun began to set that evening, 120 guests were seated on the waterfront patio of the Marina del Rey Hotel. The hotel staff stalled by serving champagne while my groom tracked down the missing DJ, then took his place at the gazebo. I tore my dad away from the hockey game on TV. With one hand on my bouquet and the other on his arm, we hurried down the Astroturf aisle. On the first step, I felt the lace front of my dress slip. With each subsequent step, it slipped a little more. I looked down to see the growing gap between the bodice and the bra cups, but all I could do was press my bouquet against my ribs to hold it up. When we reached the gazebo facing the waterway, I handed the flowers off to my sister. The dress sank. Fortunately, the lace caught on the top of the corset and stayed there.

Soon, styles rebounded with more streamlined, body-conscious silhouettes led by America's royalty: celebrities. In 1996, Carolyn Bessette, an executive at Calvin Klein, married John F. Kennedy Jr. in a clinging satin slip dress that set a trend. By 2001, Pamela Anderson, the buxom *Baywatch* actress, married Kid Rock in a white bikini.

By the time I got engaged to John in 2010, the wedding industry had waxed, waned, and was bouncing back from the recession. There were bridal magazines as heavy as doorstops, wedding guides at grocery stores, and bridal blogs on the internet. *Say Yes to the Dress* was in its third year on TLC. Even feminist Naomi Wolf, who wrote *The Beauty Myth*, was not immune. She justified her traditional dress as a costume that defined a woman as "sexually priceless."[9]

I wanted a simple, elegant dress. Been there, done the other. We found a small clubhouse in northern Malibu with easy access for my fiancé's parents and a beach for his East Coast friends. He invited thirty people; I invited ten. My father was not one of them. My mother protested his presence so loudly that by the time she relented a week before the event, it was too late to invite him. That was fine with me. Last thing I wanted was a repeat of the scene at my first wedding when Dad showed up with his second wife. He hadn't invited me to his third wedding, held in a park in Ohio, so I didn't think he'd mind. This wedding was for John.

After scouring clearance racks at bridal boutiques all over the San Fernando Valley, I found a simple goddess dress at Nordstrom. Excited about my bargain buy, I modeled it for my family. Big mistake. Juliette looked at me and shrugged. Chloe shook her head. My mother spoke up.

"John's family is not flying in to see him marry a woman in a nightgown."

"It's not a nightgown," I said. My twenty-one-year-old, who had already talked me into spending far more on a lacey chemise for the honeymoon (which was as awkward as it sounds) started laughing. I thought about John's elderly parents, married over sixty years. His father was a retired colonel and professor of military strategy who had taught at the Pentagon, and his mother, one of the first in the League of Women Voters, was still teaching current events at a college in Denver. They'd seen their son struggle and build a successful business, but they had never seen him married with a family of his own. Surely, they would be comforted to see how much I loved him. Did a dress really matter?

Apparently so.

A week later, we visited David's Bridal, the largest American bridal store chain. The rows resembled banks of puffy clouds with full skirts, beaded skirts, even feathered and frothy skirts. The gowns all had one thing in common: no straps.

I was no stranger to strapless. After wearing my mother's 1960s vintage cocktail dress on vacation in Mexico, I used the photo on our engagement announcement. The top defied gravity with internal boning, like the black satin gown Rita Hayworth shocked the censors with in the 1946 film *Gilda*. Back then, dresses that appeared to stay up from divine intervention were called the "naked look." They were banned by religious groups and outlawed on army bases. It wasn't until Christian Dior featured a flower-printed number with a full skirt in 1955 that the fashion trickled down to the masses. In the 1980s, my sister and I wore strapless sundresses as bridesmaids for my mother's second wedding. She had panicked and married an engineer who lived on a boat. After he moved into the condo she'd worked to buy for herself and had her doing his laundry, he insisted his name be added to the deed. She called her lawyer, but not for that.

At the bridal store, I asked the sales manager why strapless dresses were still so popular. She claimed everyone looked good in them. Judging from the wails emanating from the dressing room, I doubted that. Far more likely they were easy to alter and accessorize, particularly with the padded bras and plastic inserts on the nearby display table.

A few weeks after our shopping trip, *Bridalplasty* premiered on E!. Executive producer Giuliana Rancic invited brides to compete "for plastic surgery procedures that included breast implants."[10] Boobs, the ultimate bridal accessory.

Frustrated, I invited John to help. He wasn't a big shopper, but he was so enthusiastic about this experience that we planned our dates around it. He wanted to show me off. While flattering, I couldn't help feeling objectified. I knew he loved me, but he also wanted me to look beautiful for his friends. I wanted him to look handsome, too, but he didn't have to show skin to do it. I had to find a balance between elegant and tacky, sacred and profane, virgin and whore—when everyone knew what we'd be doing when the gown came off that night. To avoid feeling ridiculous, I pretended to be a model. Models monetized their physical appearance. That made them smart businesswomen, right? At least, no matter what gown we agreed on, it would not fall down in the front.

At a trunk show of clearance styles in Beverly Hills, we settled on a tulle-covered A-line skirt with a crystal bodice. I immediately visited the dermatologist to give my décolletage a youthful glow. When I returned for the fitting, it was perfect. All that was left to do was fix some beading and add bra cups. My car broke down the day before the wedding, so I got a rental, picked up the dress, and drove up the coast.

On my wedding day, Juliette and I spread the ivory dress on the empty seats of a limo and enjoyed a peaceful cruise along the ocean. The sun hit the crystals and sent sparkles all around, as if my fairy godmother had waved her magic wand. Once in the prep room, we could hear the guests arriving. My groom hummed as he strolled in and out.

Then it was all about breasts. My sister, Tracy, stopped in, wearing a purple V-neck dress. She tugged the fabric up to cover her bra then wished me good luck. My mother, stunning in violet silk, pushed her bra straps out of view, then changed her mind and switched to the strapless spare in her purse. Juliette's gold bridesmaid dress fit her so well, she flung her new bra back into her overnight bag. Her sister, always original, showed up in a tiny halter dress, like Tinkerbell.

When it was time to step into my gown, Juliette shrieked and pointed toward the mirror. My bridal shower thong, with the words "I Do" printed on the hip, showed through the skirt. I'd worn beige-colored panties for every fitting; how could I forget today? All that practice wearing lingerie, and I blew it. The only option was to go commando. Fortunately, there were eight layers of ivory tulle. No one would know. I took a deep breath and vowed to not let it bother me. Somebody helped hook the hidden belt and zipped me up. The dress fit perfectly. I felt fabulous.

Then I hugged Juliette and my boobs burst out. Not all the way to the nipple, but enough to look like they could. As long as my arms were down, all was well. When I lifted them up, the neckline cut into the swell of my breasts. Fuck. We unzipped the dress to take a closer look. The bottom of each sewn-in cup was a rubber bumper. The seamstress had sewn in the requisite push-up pads for brides, maybe younger brides. On me, it looked Victorian, like a presentation of breasts for m'lord.

The wedding coordinator who came with the party house peeked in to give us the "go" sign. It was too late to rip the rubber cups from my dress. On the bright side, I no longer cared about my panty problem. Now I was concerned about the impression I would make to the groom's proud parents. "What if John's folks think I'm a floozy?"

Juliette laughed at the old-fashioned word, but I was serious. My soon-to-be father-in-law had a doctorate in international relations. I had met my serious, soon-to-be mother-in-law on a book tour in Denver after reading the opening sex scene of my new novel when John and I were just starting to date. I hadn't known she was in the crowd with my eventual sister-in-law, niece, and twelve-year-old nephew. Now they might see me as a woman trying to deny her age and biology by flaunting her sexuality. Just when I was feeling safe, secure, and ready to be loved forever, I feared disaster. My groom loved my breasts, but he didn't want everyone to see them. Nor did I.

Juliette zipped me up. "His parents are probably just happy he's getting married."

"What about his best friends from back East?" Maybe they figured John was just tired of dating. Not only did he have sophisticated ex-girlfriends, but his female fans in Europe kept scrapbooks of his lectures like he was a rock star. He could have his pick. I wasn't naturally pretty, but I could pull myself together when I needed to, and I needed to *now*. At this moment, with hair and makeup, facials and fittings, I looked as good as I ever would again. I was fifty. Here was the downside of vanity: being judged by it. Oh, the double-edged sword of beauty.

I tugged up my top.

"They won't notice," Juliette lied.

Michelle, my hairstylist, repinned my veil so that it draped farther in front of my shoulders. "If they do, they won't say anything."

We could hear the music now, Rufus Wainwright's cover of "Hallelujah." The girls picked up their bouquets of white roses and daisies.

"Just think of *Legally Blonde*," one of them said.

We recited our favorite line in unison, "What, my boobs are too big?" and laughed.

"Thank you," I said. I grabbed my bouquet and followed the girls out.

During the ceremony, John and I paid tribute to our mothers by giving them each a rose. My mother was so ecstatic about the wedding that she spent much of the reception rejoicing at how I had beat the odds. She marveled that, at fifty, I had a better chance of being hit by a bus than getting married. She was misquoting the 1986 *Newsweek* cover story about single women over forty being more likely to be the victim of a terrorist attack than get married.[11] Even Meg Ryan's character in the nineties rom-com *Sleepless in Seattle* knew that wasn't true. But to many women, it still felt true. For me, getting married wasn't a fairy-tale ending—I knew too much for that. It was a new beginning.

For years, when I looked at our wedding pictures, cleavage was the first thing I noticed. As I walked down the aisle, my dress covered my cleavage perfectly. During the reception, when I raised my arms to dance or clapped at a toast, the view was R-rated. But no one said a word.

By 2016, bridal-wear accounted for 20 percent of the average American wedding budget. Strapless dresses soon shared the racks with off-the-shoulder, daredevil necklines, and sheer bodices. Yet even in 2017, former Victoria's Secret Angel Miranda Kerr covered up with a long-sleeved, high-necked gown to marry Snapchat founder Evan Spiegel for a "sense of purity and mystery." It struck me that my daughter and her friends had that lingerie party to look and feel like sexual women, while a woman who made her living being a sexy Angel wanted to prove she could be modest. Fashion highlights the evolution of our sexuality, as well as the contradictions. Brides today have unlimited options, but a wedding can require a tricky balance of showing respect for commitment, as well as the visual desirability that makes us "worthy" of it. In early 2020, the bridal wear industry was predicted to be a $74.9 billion business by 2025.[12] Surely, the global pandemic will damper sales indefinitely, but when it's over, what better reason to celebrate love with wedding traditions?

Later, when I asked John if he noticed my cleavage that day, he didn't need to look at our wedding album. He clearly recalled that my breasts had been more prominent than usual. Yet, the cut of my gown was so tight around the waist before flaring to the floor that the hourglass shape was balanced. Perhaps unconsciously, he saw the Victorian symbolism: the breasts as an anatomical dowry, a match to the long skirt that hid my most prized female parts. He says his main reaction was, "That is one gorgeous woman and I'm getting married to her right now." Of course, it's to his benefit to say something so ridiculously sweet, but this was years after the fact. His enthusiasm highlights the profound, truly transcendent experience of a wedding.

Everything I both loved and feared about being a woman was captured in those uneasy moments before I walked down the aisle. After that, we had a fabulous time, and I barely thought about my boobs.

Then they tried to kill me.

Secrets of Victoria's Secret

A Peek under the Fantasy Bra

History

1977   Founded by Roy Raymond for $80,000 to make buying lingerie comfortable for men.

1982   Sells for $1 million to Leslie Wexner of The Limited (L Brands, Inc).

1993   Sales top $1 billion; Raymond leaps to his death from the Golden Gate Bridge.

1995   Makes Fortune 500 list.

1997   Catalog distribution hits 450 million copies.

2000   CEO Sharen Jester Turney pushes the look from *Playboy* sex object for men to *Vogue* sex symbol for women.

2017   Comprises 61% of US lingerie market; earns $7.38 billion in US sales and $12.6 billion in annual international revenue.

2019   Comprises 24% of US market share; earns $6.8 billion in US sales.

   One hundred models of Model Alliance send open letter to address sexual misconduct.

   Women are added to the board of directors, shifting the board from 15% to 40% female.

2020   Owner Les Wexner retires at eighty-two amid complaints of misogyny and connections to the late sex offender Jeffrey Epstein.

2020 Social Media Popularity
   Instagram: 68.8 million followers
   Facebook: 29 million followers
   Twitter: 10.8 million followers

Angels' Spillover Success
   Highest net worth: Gisele Bündchen, $400 million
   Related business success: Heidi Klum, $130 million;
   Tyra Banks, $90 million; Adriana Lima, $85 million
   Average height: 5 feet,10 inches
   Average weight: 120 pounds

Fashion Show History

1996 $1,000,000 Fantasy Bra is worn by Claudia Schiffer on the
        runway.

1999   The first year online, 1.5 million users visit and crash the site.

2000 $15,000,000 Fantasy Bra is worn by Gisele Bündchen on
        the runway.

2001   2.3 million TV viewers; first show is held in New York City.

2003   Twelve-foot Angel wings are worn by Heidi Klum.

2011   Forty-pound Angel wings are worn by Alessandra Ambrosio.

2019   Canceled for lost viewership and "branding issues" after
        longtime chief marketing exec Ed Razek's comments on
        transgender and plus-sized models; he resigns.[1]

2019   One plus-sized model and one transgender model are
        added to Angel roster.

All estimates based on 2020 report.[2]

PART THREE

THE BREAST OF EVERYTHING:

Womanhood

Thirteen

KILLER BOOBS
2012

You have cancer."

I couldn't help but glance behind me. *You talkin' to me?* I wanted to ask, like Robert De Niro in *Taxi Driver*. But from the expression on Dr. Spinner's face, I doubted she'd have laughed.

"Are you sure you have the right chart?"

My doctor nodded and proceeded to go into all the gory details. I didn't hear any of them. That's why I had brought my friend Janet. She was the one I had been meeting to hike with—that's how stinking healthy I felt—when Dr. Spinner called. She refused to give me the biopsy results over the phone, and it was the Friday before Labor Day weekend, far too late to fight the traffic from Santa Monica to her office in the Valley. The fact that she had insisted on meeting on Labor Day, when most people were at a barbecue, made it clear that the news was bad. I immediately called my plastic surgeon, whose kind words helped me get through the weekend.

The room felt hot, so I gathered my hair up to air the back of my neck. When I came back to the conversation, Janet was asking detailed questions. I preferred working on a need-to-know basis. And there was only one thing I needed to know.

"Did my implants cause it?"

"No."

Dr. Calvert had said the same thing, but as the engineer of my curves, he had a conflict of interest.

Mammograms had been painful enough when I was flat. For the past few years, when the technician pulled flesh away from each silicone balloon and clamped it between cold plates, I was afraid it would burst. The tests were always hard to read, so when my recent results came back with a small dot in my right breast, I didn't worry. Plus, I was a glass-half-full kind of gal, content to follow the protocol and wait six months to check again. On a whim, Dr. Spinner had asked the radiologist for a second opinion. He agreed it could wait, but if I were his wife, he'd schedule a biopsy. And voilà.

The doctor stood and handed me a printed list of oncological surgeons (the first of many new terms for me) in Los Angeles. I was lucky to be in a city with so many good ones, she said. Then she pointed at her first choice and suggested I call immediately. Not when I got home, not first thing in the morning. *Now.*

OK, I thought. *Good to have a plan.*

Here's the thing about the "C" word: people pay attention. It was like having big boobs compared to little ones. Turns out, everybody knows someone who has had breast cancer. One out of eight American women are jinxed. Maybe that's why it sounded so cliché. Since over 3.8 million women in the U.S. have already had it,[1] this was less than original. Boring, even.

After a few rings, an efficient female voice came on the line. I recognized the brisk tone of an answering service, so I asked to leave a message. The next woman's voice was so gentle I wondered if she knew someone who was sick. Or, even though I sounded completely healthy, if she knew that it was me.

When I got home, I told my husband matter-of-factly. My sentence started with, "So." By the time I got to the end of it, I remembered that John's college girlfriend had died of breast cancer. He had every reason to fear I could be next.

As the sun filtered through the trees outside the window of the living room where we sat, I felt worse for him than for me. This was an analytical guy who'd majored in philosophy. Yet there was no logic here. We were pinned to the present, to this prickly moment on a new Crate and Barrel couch. We had bought it in beige, an easy color to fit into the first home we planned to buy together. Now, house hunting would have to wait.

He rubbed his palm against the nap of fabric in quiet protest. He didn't understand how it could happen to me. I had followed all the "rules" to be healthy. I ate more vegetables than anyone he knew. Plus, I hiked, practiced yoga, and went to the gym. This was random, beyond my control.

"Do you know what kind your girlfriend had?" I asked.

"No. I only know she went all natural, the holistic route." He turned to look at me.

"Don't worry," I said. "I have an appointment with an award-winning board-certified surgeon who invented some modern technique. I'll do whatever he says." We sealed my promise with a kiss.

This would be like learning the high dive when I was six, I decided. No matter how scared I was, I would follow directions. I would put my fingertips first, dive in, and earn the damn points. First, I had two weeks packed with medical tests to complete.

I called my mother and sister next. Now that I had a doctor's name, they could look him up and feel comforted by his credentials. I made them promise not to tell my girls. My role was to take care of my children, not the other way around. Besides, if the girls got worried, I would worry about them more. I couldn't manage their fear when the facts were still a mystery. I would tell them as soon as surgery was scheduled, the solution at hand.

When Chloe called about shopping a few days later, I didn't mention I was on my way to be felt up by a team of strangers. While I was in the waiting room, Juliette called to say the old couch I had shipped up didn't fit through the door of her San Francisco apartment. She heard the nurse call me in for an MRI and asked what was up. I mentioned routine tests. As far as I knew, the closest my daughters had ever been to breast cancer was when a friend's mom participated in the charity walk from Santa Barbara to Los Angeles. Personally, I hadn't heard about the disease until junior high, when it was considered an embarrassing female problem, like menstruation.

In order to answer questions without sounding like an idiot, I read up. While the history of breast cancer has been traced back to Ancient Egypt, there was little credible research. Most people died young and undiagnosed. By the eighteenth century, as women lived past the age of sixty, tumors had time to develop. Since there was no cure for cancer, there was great secrecy about this women's disease. By 1900, breast cancer was the biggest killer of women, and would remain so until 2004.

The women's rights movement of the sixties helped to open doors at medical schools in the seventies. As female doctors began to graduate, they expanded awareness of women's health. In the cancer field, however, breasts were the Rodney Dangerfield of specialties: they got no respect. Fortunately, Shirley Temple, the curly-topped child actress that my sister and I had adored as little girls, loved her breasts. Back then, doctors didn't bother with a biopsy. They hacked the whole thing off: the breast, the muscle tissue, and the surrounding lymph nodes. In 1972, after being diagnosed with breast cancer, Temple refused. Instead of a radical mastectomy, she insisted on a "simple" one to remove only the breast tissue. She dared to call her illness what it was—breast cancer—in *McCall's*, which was likely more controversial than her government appointments. Two years after that, First Lady Betty Ford announced on national television that she had breast cancer. Three weeks later, Happy Rockefeller, the popular wife of

Vice President Nelson Rockefeller, was diagnosed. The epidemic was out of the closet.[2]

Kinda. The lack of research in women's health created a gap in knowledge that affected both treatment and insurance coverage. It wasn't until 1998, four years after President Bill Clinton's mother died of the disease, that he signed the first Women's Health and Cancer Rights Act into law so insurance would cover breast reconstruction.

Here's my favorite statistic: between 1985 and 2004, more American women died of breast cancer than the number of Americans who died in World War I, World War II, Korea, and Vietnam *combined*.[3] It's true—I checked the math.

Soon after my diagnosis in September of 2012 , I had coffee with my friend Hope Edelman. I had picked up my biopsy slides in the Valley and was passing through Topanga Canyon, where she lived. Hope was famous for writing *Motherless Daughters,* a best seller that sprouted a national organization. It wasn't until I mentioned my errand that I remembered she had lost her mother to breast cancer. I wanted to crawl under the floorboards of the organic coffeehouse. She reminisced about buying her daughters coats in multiple sizes in case she got sick, too. Since I also had two girls, this was easy to imagine. We changed the subject to work, but later, as I pulled out of the gravel lot, there was a shift in my awareness. My breasts were part of a much bigger picture.

Driving slowly down the twisting canyon, I passed the stretch of road where I'd set the fatal car accident in my new novel, the spot where I—I mean, the mother character—drove off a cliff and barely survived. My own mother was alive, thank God, partly because it was my job to make sure of it. It was my job to care for many people. In my teens, I had picked the lock and counted her pills during her depression. In my thirties, I had pried the antique rifle from my husband's fingers during his depression, and in my forties, I had obsessed over my children's inclinations to follow suit. In every scenario, I was the mother. Invincible. This sickness was ironically specific. My breast, the very symbol of my mortal purpose, my human destiny to nurture, was now threatened by a disease that could keep me from fulfilling it.

By the time I reached the coast highway, my breast felt like a ticking bomb. There had been no cell signal in the canyon, so I pulled over to the gravel berm where a surfboard-laden van had just vacated a spot. I parked, put on my reading glasses, and checked the email on my phone.

My stomach cramped at the thought of my publisher finding out I was sick. The editor had bought my manuscript four months earlier, then asked me to cut a hundred pages. This was a tightly woven thriller. I couldn't just chop off ten chapters. I had canceled all my plans, including my annual mammogram, and had slaved over it all summer. If my editor thought I was too frail to polish and promote the book, she could shut down publication.

But I didn't want to lie to anyone. I just wanted to pretend this wasn't happening. There was so much I couldn't control. But I needed this novel. Due to my divorce, my children's health issues, and working to pay for it all, it had been four long years since my last book. And this was the big one I'd started years earlier, as a literary work in grad school. The structure had changed, but it was still about a mother who would do anything to protect her child. It was a culmination of everything I'd ever written, everything I knew about the desperate maternal love that still kept me on 24/7 emergency alert. I took my reading glasses off, put the phone back in my purse, and drove across town to drop off my slides at Cedars-Sinai Hospital.

A week later, the waiting was over. My draft was approved, the release date locked for spring, and Target was featuring it as a Recommended Read. I hit the highway to meet my surgeon. I circled the Beverly Center in West Hollywood, where a date had once abandoned me to drool over Angelyne. Then I found the Cedars-Sinai Saul and Joyce Brandman Breast Cancer Center, an entire four-story building for breasts, run by Dr. Armando Giuliano.

I pulled up under the archway in my old sedan. A valet opened my car door and escorted me out as if I were a VIP. Inside the waiting room, sunlight shone through the windows on quiet couples and families watching a game show on TV. I went to the desk and signed my life away, then took the elevator upstairs to another lounge, where a sign forbade the use of cell phones. Here, women with designer purses fidgeted across from women with plastic totes. Some pretended to browse health brochures.

I sat down in a corner chair, pulled a work file from my briefcase, and then skimmed through manuscript notes my editor had sent with the signed contract. One item she wanted clarified was about a minor character who had breast cancer. Startled, I closed the folder. I'd written that as a random affliction, like filling in the blank in a Mad Libs game. Just a coincidence, I told myself.

Soon I was ushered into an exam room, where I put on a cotton robe that opened in the front. Assorted men in white lab coats came in and felt me up far more thoroughly than any date ever had. After growing up in a natatorium locker room, I didn't mind being topless, but I felt sorry for some of the older women in the waiting room. We were all lab rats in a science experiment.

When the doctors left, I tied the cloth belt in a bow and finger-combed my hair just to feel human. A nurse in pink scrubs slipped inside and logged onto my computer records. Then a striking man with a wreath of silver hair and a tie peeking out from his white lab coat strode in with an air of brilliance. He'd recently won the Brinker Award for Scientific Distinction, the highest award given by the world's leading breast cancer foundation, Susan G. Komen.[4] Yet, when he took my hand and smiled warmly, he was a friend.

Tests showed that my tumor had more than tripled in size in less than a month. It needed to be removed right away. I regretted delaying my mammogram, so I explained why I did. The doctor's wife had just retired from the UCLA English department, so he understood about writers. And since I was headed to campus in a few hours to teach a novel class, we had a connection. Now the appointment felt more personal. He assured me that the delay did no harm. In fact, had I done my annual mammogram on schedule in May, the tumor might not have shown up at all. At this growth rate, by next May when I had another. . . . He shrugged.

Goose bumps prickled on my arms. He was quiet, watching me. I had never considered my own death before. I was invincible, or so I thought. This was humbling.

"Can you operate tomorrow?" I asked.

He chuckled and explained that he needed another biopsy, blood work, blah, blah, blah. He suggested we wait a few weeks. That sounded like forever. What if it tripled again and killed me? The image of a tombstone flashed to mind, but what would it say? My family knew I loved them; there was no unfinished business there. But would my life have meaning beyond the date I died?

I wanted to make some sort of difference. That's what I'd taught my children: that we should contribute, leave the world a better place. At least I hoped I'd taught them that. But had I made a difference to anyone? I thought of letters I kept, emails and cards from readers. In some way, to some women, I had.

I exhaled, realizing I'd been holding my breath. How strange to think that this novel, *What a Mother Knows*, had saved my life. When my editor had broached the new title, I'd laughed, thinking a mother knows *nothing*. Now I appreciated it, with a different interpretation. A mother knew she would do anything for love. If this were to be my last word, would it be enough? Yes.

You know how they say your life flashes before you when you face death? That didn't happen to me. When I felt the pressure lift, my next thought was about the future. Of course, I needed to get this book out. But there was more. I wanted to see both of my children happy. I wanted to enjoy being married to my husband. I wanted to live by the ocean.

We continued our conversation while he examined me, but I was nervous about my implants. Then again, we were in West Hollywood, so he must have plenty of patients who had them.

"Is it possible to leave my implant?" I asked.

"I'm the man," Dr. Giuliano said, grinning. He didn't mention his accolades or that he was the pioneering doctor who proved that lumpectomies were often as effective as mastectomies, but I knew what he meant. He was *The Man*. The previous year, he'd made news limiting the removal of lymph nodes in the arm. He was a preservationist, for sure. I felt incredibly lucky.

Then he asked if I was Jewish. I'd been raised Unitarian in Ohio, so I didn't feel Jewish. But my grandmother, an Irish Catholic, converted when she eloped with my Jewish grandfather, whose family escaped from Russia during the Bolshevik revolution. My dad's parents were German and Polish Jews. And I'd been to my cousins' bar mitzvahs.

I nodded, feeling more connected to my Jewish heritage than ever before. Dr. G asked if anyone in my family had had breast cancer. I shrugged. He insisted I take the BRCA test for the breast cancer gene, which is more common in Ashkenazi Jews like me, in case I needed to consider a mastectomy.

That evening, my husband was packing for Colorado to visit his dying mother. He hadn't told her I was sick, and I hoped she wouldn't be hurt by my absence. She was kind and accomplished and I liked her a lot. I also liked how patient my husband was while she told me stories during her visits that he'd heard many times before. She hadn't breastfed her children, but she had made them feel safe during countless international moves in the military. I couldn't say the same. I had breastfed, compromised my career, and tried my hardest to be a good mom, but my children's home hadn't always felt safe. And now it never would.

I needed my go-to comfort food—frozen yogurt with sprinkles—and fast. Everything felt better when I got back in the car across from the yogurt store. Then I pulled away from the curb in a U-turn and crashed into a van. A handicapped van. Driven by a disabled teenager. My bumper broke his axle, so he couldn't even get out of the car while we waited for the tow truck. I waited by his open window and could not stop apologizing. His father showed up with a fancy long-lens camera hanging from a strap around his neck.

"I might have to get my breasts cut off," I told the dad, but he hardly said a word.

The police arrived, and everyone took pictures. Then I went to say goodnight to the boy. He was writing a blog about the football injury that had put him in a wheelchair, and I was grateful to be able to offer writing help if he needed it. He was fine. I was fine. Neither of us was really fine, but the accident was just another bump in the road.

• • •

When I went to see the stern woman in charge of genetic testing, I had no idea about my family history. People were private in my family, and now it was going to cost me. I couldn't prove a need to get insurance coverage beyond the basic level of testing for gene mutations. The more in-depth test was $2,500. A new law would expand to cover more BRCA testing in January, but it was only September. Then the geneticist opened a small cardboard box pre-labeled with my name and pulled out the plastic tube inside. She suggested I call Myriad, the screening company in Utah, to rush the results. The nurse said they would save the sample in case I decided to test for the third level. That one cost $7,000. I started laughing. She warned that it would be helpful to know whether I could pass this down to my daughters. I stopped laughing, and spit in the tube.

Juliette took the news well when she called me back from San Francisco on her way home from class. I couldn't tell what she was really thinking, but by the end of the call, she was describing her new couch. I gave Chloe a rehearsed speech in the car after I picked her up at the mall in Century City. She immediately called her boyfriend to pick her up at the corner gas station. She didn't want to talk about it. Apparently, she talked about it with her sister, because a few hours later, both girls called me at home on a conference line. They insisted that I turn on the TV. The NFL players were wearing pink for breast cancer awareness.

As if I wasn't aware.

Since my diagnosis, the world had turned pink. From nail polish to tractors, there was no escaping it. The third time a store clerk asked for a donation, I pulled a doctor's bill from my purse and asked if she'd like to donate directly. How could pink socks on a bunch of overgrown millionaires throwing balls around help? Why not donate half their salaries? I used to love the color, from my favorite hot pink dress in high school, to the pastel OshKosh B'gosh outfits my girls wore as toddlers, to the fuchsia paint on my bedroom wall. Now I was sick of pink. Breast cancer ruined an entire color for me.

A few days later, I waited for surgery in my curtained-off pre-op room with tubes of warm air pumped through a plastic suit. I looked like the Michelin man, but boy, it felt good. I'd endured so many exams that even my husband no longer flinched when a stranger palmed me in front of him. Earlier that morning, a wire had been surgically implanted in my breast to stick out like a signpost for the surgeon. Now, finally, I could relax. This would all be over soon.

A nurse came in to check on me and I was tempted to kiss her in gratitude. I had never felt so cared for. All the nurses were incredible; surely, they took courses in "nice." She adjusted my IV and dimmed the light. Soon, Dr. Giuliano came in with his surgical team to say hello. He looked different in green scrubs and a surgery cap printed with hot-air balloons. The whimsical touch gave me full confidence I would wake up. Just in case, I told the anesthesiologist, a young woman, to be sure I did. As I went under, the team talked about vacationing in Greece.

On the following Wednesday, I brought my new book cover to the post-op appointment. Dr. G seemed genuinely happy as he removed the stitches from my puckered breast. He assured me the wound was healing well, but I needed one more surgery to clear the margins. He would go right back in the same incision, to be sure he got everything. I would be fine.

Whatever. What was another few weeks? I couldn't get back to yoga, but I could get back to work. "When should I schedule it for?" I asked.

"Friday," he said.

"The day after tomorrow?"

He nodded. He wasn't going to wait for the genetic panel. He was gambling that I wouldn't need a mastectomy, but he wasn't gambling on my life. Whatever was left inside me was as stable as a Molotov cocktail. Now I was both scared and relieved he was on top of things. I scheduled surgery and rescheduled everything else. I also added his name to the acknowledgments page of my book.

Forty hours later, Dr. G greeted me in his air-balloon surgery cap and the nurse rolled me back into surgery. My husband was still out of town, so my mother had slept over to drive me at dawn. This would be the last time; I'd make sure of it. She was so nervous I made her pull over so I could take the wheel. I hated having her worry in the waiting room. I begged her to go across the street to the Beverly Center when the shops opened at ten. I was going to be fine. Dr. G said so. But I was ready for Pinktober to end.

After another week spent prostrate from pain pills, I recovered and went back to work. I had classes to teach, blogs to write, and a new website to plan. I'd finally bought a new car. Life was good. The first review copies arrived just before my post-op appointment, so the following week, I brought a copy as a parting gift.

As always, Dr. Giuliano was happy to see me. Today he was dressed in a crisp white button-down and dress pants, probably on his way to give a talk somewhere. He examined my breast and declared me cancer-free. The nurse made notes on the computer screen as I covered up. Since it was my last time seeing him, I asked him what stage I had. I knew it was HER+, hormone positive and something negative spelled "Neu," but friends kept asking me the number.

"It doesn't matter," he said. "It's gone."

"Wonderful, thank you!" I hopped off the table to leave. He stopped smiling and blocked the door. Even though I was cancer-free, I needed more treatment. Preventative treatment. "What do you mean?"

"You're going to lose your beautiful hair."

I burst into tears and stood there, helpless. My hair? After a moment, he opened his arms and I stepped into them, sobbing against his crisp white collar. When my tears subsided, he reached into his pocket and pulled out his cell phone. He dialed a number and handed me the phone.

"Ask for Daniel Leiber and schedule an appointment to see him right away."

The nurse stepped behind me to get the room ready for the next patient. We stepped into the hall, where Dr. G waited with me for someone to answer on the other end. I didn't understand why I needed a different doctor. He explained that the lab tests showed a chemical makeup conducive to sprouting up somewhere else. This other doctor would be in charge of chemotherapy, radiation, and hormone therapy. I nodded but felt numb. I wanted Dr. G to be in charge. He told me I would be fine, and I believed him. I needed to believe him.

"I messed up your shirt," I said, pointing at the wet spot smudged with mascara on his shoulder. He shrugged, and then a man's voice came on the phone line.

I don't remember leaving or waiting for my car or driving away. A block from the hospital, a thought struck me. Years earlier, another writer had confided that she'd had a preventative double mastectomy. Maybe Dr. G hadn't suggested prophylactic surgery simply to spare me. My hair was different. It was long and thick and, except for a businessy bob in the eighties, had always been like that. I took it for granted. Not like my boobs. They'd been trouble from the start. When it came to life and death, I realized, they didn't matter. *I hated them.*

I pulled over to the curb on a residential street in West Hollywood and called the office I'd just left. It was urgent, I told the nurse. The wait was so long I started biting my nails, a habit I'd kicked years earlier. Why didn't I think of this while I was there? What if he was gone? I was about to give up when I heard his voice on the phone.

"Can you just cut them off, instead?" I asked.

"No." Dr. G explained that the cells could be left in the scar tissue on my chest wall. They could spread anywhere, anytime. Boobs or no, it wouldn't make a difference.

"I don't want to do chemo."

"I'm sorry, Leslie."

I hated hearing my name.

US Breast Cancer Statistics*

- 276,480 new cases of invasive breast cancer in women and 2,620 new cases in men are predicted this year.[1]

- 42,170 women and 520 men are expected to die from breast cancer in 2020.

- Breast cancer has caused over 2 million deaths since 1975.

- Over 3.8 million women in the US have a history of breast cancer.

- US women have a one in eight chance of getting breast cancer; the risk rises with age.

- US women have a one in thirty-seven chance of dying from it.

- Death rate is higher for black women than white women, other ethnicities vary.

- 5–10% of patients have the BRCA gene mutation.

- 85% of patients have no family link.

- Treatments: chemotherapy (100+ kinds), surgery, radiation, immunotherapy, targeted therapy, hormone therapy, stem cell transplants, precision medicine, holistic medicine.

Ways to Reduce Vulnerability to Breast Cancer
- Limit alcohol consumption to two drinks per week

- Adopt a plant-based diet

- Exercise

- Reduce stress and the burden of caregiving

- Meditate and practice mindfulness

- Breastfeed

- Get 7-8 hours of sleep per night

Sick of Pink?

Lest we forget we have breasts, there are plenty of pink products to remind us. For example . . .

Aerie T-shirts, Apollo Tools kit, Avon candles, Beistle paper plates and napkins, Bialetti fry pan, BIC pens, California license plates, Caterpillar tractors, Charter Club terry robes, Coach watches, Comfort Revolution memory foam pillow, Cuisinart coffee maker, Dooney & Bourke umbrellas, Duck duct tape, Eggland's Best Eggs, Eos lip balm, Estée Lauder night serum, Everlast boxing gloves, Evian water, Fabletics leggings, Felix the Cat animated wall clock, Flambeau Outdoors tackle box, Ford Escape, Gap lingerie, Geo Crafts doormats, GUESS watches, Loft necklaces, Master Lock combination padlocks, Morton salt, North Face rain jackets, OPI nail polish, Playtex gloves, Ralph Lauren fragrance, SABRE pepper spray key ring, Skil power drill, South Bay Seafood's Pink Ribbon Oysters, Sterling Forever rose gold ring, Sutter Home wine, S'well reusable water bottles, Swiffer mops, Thermos bottle, Timberland boots, Tory Burch fragrance, Wilson golf balls, tennis balls, and tennis rackets, and Woodchuck Hard Cider.

*Estimates as of 2020, breastcancer.org

Fourteen

CHEMO CHICK
2013

With a carry-on full of hairbrushes and curling irons I wouldn't need anymore, I boarded a plane to San Francisco. I wanted to physically touch my firstborn and let her see with her own eyes—big brown ones like mine—that I was fine. The medical appointments crowding the next twelve months would not change anything. This was the baby who had redefined my life, the shy little artist who drew animals, the sensitive violinist who played *The Phantom of the Opera*, the poet who dyed her hair blond in an ill-fated attempt at sorority life. Now she had found her place at a prestigious art school with a 94 percent graduate employment rate. I didn't want her to worry.

First, I told her the good news. The second panel of genetic testing had come back negative. There was 90 percent chance I was not a carrier of the BRCA mutation that could pass to her.

"Ninety percent is an A," Juliette said.

It was a B+ when I was in school, but close enough. I nodded. Did I want to break the bank to raise my grade with the third level of testing? My oncologist agreed it was a long shot, so I decided against spending thousands more. I was already draining my savings for hospital bills. I gave Juliette my hair appliances and shut up.

We spent the weekend sharing our favorite mother-daughter activities, like shopping at Target. Together, we chuckled over the pink ribbon nail polish on clearance. Soon, my nails would blacken and bleed, and a few would fall off. For now, the sale marking the end of Pinktober was simply a relief. Sick. Of. Pink.

Back in Los Angeles, I had surgery to implant a portocath just under my collarbone. The plastic pincushion sat just below the skin, connected to a catheter tube that snaked inside my neck before connecting to the vein that would disburse meds throughout my body. The tube was uncomfortable and made it tricky to turn my head or sleep on that side for months. But it would save my arm from being jabbed every time they pulled blood out or pushed chemicals in. Which was often.

Now I had scars on both sides of my chest. I needed shirts to hide them. I needed nontoxic toiletries, organic makeup, a soft cap for sleeping, and bigger scarves. I needed a skullcap to keep scarves from slipping off my head and a headband of bangs to make hats look normal. I had yet to brave a wig store. Soon I would avoid germ-infested crowds and wear gloves to the grocery store, so I had limited time to shop. And those were just a few of the things on the three-page list a friend named Cissa was kind enough to give me. She spent hours going over the ins and outs of treatment, all the things doctors don't know or are too busy to tell you. This was an act of sisterhood I promised to pass on.

Cissa's husband shared his experience with my husband. He said relationships change and often break under the pressure. He warned John of the dangers ahead as patient and nurse. That, I vowed, was not going to happen. First of all, John, the former bachelor, was a lousy nurse. Not only did he lack the caregiving gene, he'd never had children, or even a pet. He was happy to honor any post-op request, but when I resorted to calling his cell phone to request a drink of water, it was clear he didn't think ahead.

Next, I consulted a custom wigmaker. I had no idea Steven Tyler had extensions until I saw his picture in the lobby. The wigmaker created real hair wigs for orthodox Jewish women as well as news anchors. Who knew? However, one wig cost thousands of dollars and required a great deal of care. Instead, I collected a variety of wigs with nylon hair. My husband named them: "short and sassy," "lady beautiful," and "blond bombshell." The last was barely blond, but it was John's favorite, which kind of pissed me off.

When I couldn't sleep after my surgeries, I hung out in the cyber chat rooms of breastcancer.org. It was horrible to hear that some women's partners left during treatment. Who knew what my husband's reaction would be when I lost my hair and lay scarred, skeletal, and sick beside him in bed? Plus, his mother had just died. He deserved to get away and give seminars where hundreds of men praised his brilliance and women threw their panties. (OK, I never saw the panties, but I heard plenty of flirting.) So, two days before my first chemo, I dropped him off at the international terminal and picked up a friend at the baggage claim next door.

To be honest, I hardly knew this friend. Karen had graduated from my enormous high school in Ohio after me, but we'd met on the alumni website. She was also a writer, with a syndicated newspaper column called "BusStop Moms." She occasionally had business or sorority events in LA, so we bartered the use of my house and car in the Valley in exchange for housesitting. The mother of two herself, she knew what to do when Chloe totaled her car as I flew to Italy for my honeymoon. She also knew how to calm my worried mother over the phone. Best of all, she was an expert caretaker. She had just published *Knitting with Hospital Gloves*, a book about being a patient advocate, and wanted to start a blog. I had zero intention of writing about this. Living it was bad enough. So I gave Karen carte blanche on the condition that she kept me incognito. I didn't want to be defined by disease. She named the blog "Sick of Pink," after my alias on breastcancer.org. I was dubbed Chemo Chick.

The night before chemo #1, eight different pill bottles lined my bedside table, all with different directions. While Karen scoured the house with vinegar, her solution for everything, I made a schedule of when to take which pill and for how many days, with spaces to record the times actually taken. My chemo cocktail was scheduled for every third Thursday, so I'd be recovered in time to teach Wednesday night classes until Christmas. We decided to work the chemo lounge like an airplane ride, buckled in for the flight with a bag of amusements.

The steroids kept me up all night, so I was ready when the alarm rang. I pulled on a clean pajama top and leggings. Then we headed to St. John's Hospital. First, we stopped for an apple fritter. Because, why not?

After winding our way past exam rooms to the chemo lounge, we Goldilocks'd around the room to find the perfect Barcalounger by a window. I weighed in while Karen set up. The sky was gray. As soon as I sat down and spread a leopard print blanket over my lap, it started raining. Karen said the angels were crying for me. Talk about morbid. I opened a gossip magazine and said, no, the rain was just washing away all the bad for a fresh, clean beginning. I planned to make this a positive experience if it killed me. I refused to believe it might.

A nurse with a grim expression came over, pushed my pajama top aside and cleaned my port with alcohol. Her nametag read Maggie, but I immediately thought of Nurse Ratchet from *One Flew Over the Cuckoo's Nest*. The actress who played her was in a film I wrote, so the comparison was irresistible. But we had the wrong film. When the nurse raised her hand, clutching the dagger-like port attachment, and came at my chest, she was more like Norman Bates in *Psycho*. I leaned away in fear, so she missed. The bent needle had to pierce my skin to lodge in the plastic disc. She tried again. I closed my eyes. Score! Once attached, I felt like a marionette. I covered my bulging port with my polka dotted pajama top while she flushed saline through a tube. Then she took blood samples.

Karen and I tried to get back to which celebrity was cheating on which other celebrity while we waited for the lab down the hall to test my blood. I needed to be healthy enough for my chemo cocktail. The three components of mine were Herceptin, a new targeted therapy for my kind of tumor, plus Taxol and Carboplatin, essentially poisons I'd get six times over a period of five months. Together, they had the initials THC, like the component in marijuana. Nothing was as strong as the chemo cocktail. Patients are duly warned about side effects, but they stream out of doctors' mouths like the end crawl of pharmaceutical commercials. If you listen too closely, you'll be afraid of the cure.

As we waited for the lab results, a wigged woman in a chair across the room blessed her first bag of chemicals as if it were a magic potion. Another, in a headscarf and beaded earrings, swore this was her last dose and declared she would not continue on to radiation. The woman next to me insisted I go outside, smell the flowers, and lay down on the grass in a state of grace. This pissed me off; I was already a smeller of roses. I was already happy to be alive. I just wanted to be happy *today*. If not for the tube stretching from my chest up to the metal pole by my side, I wouldn't believe this was happening. I pulled up my fuzzy blanket and smiled when my doctor came to check on me.

If you looked up "mensch" in the dictionary, a picture of Daniel Leiber would be there. Where Dr. G was a benevolent emperor, Dr. Leiber was the favorite uncle. He answered every question and when he didn't know the answer, he immediately called a specialist in New York or Canada to find out. One of his clients, a writer on the TV series *Parenthood*, modeled the oncologist on the show after him. He showed me the blood work, as if I could decipher the numbers, and said we were good to go.

When he left, Karen and I were laughing. Nurse Ratchet returned with the first two pouches of chemicals, hung them up, and shut us down. She sat on the wheeled stool in front of me without a word. She made me nervous. I closed the magazine and looked around at the scarecrows in the room.

"I'm too healthy to be here," I explained. "I feel like I should cry, but I don't want to."

The nurse leaned close to me until her forehead was touching mine. "I want you to cry," she said. "This is real. It's going to be hard."

I cried.

Like the mean teacher on the first day of school, Maggie became my favorite chemo nurse. The various bags of medicine and antibiotics took six hours to surge into my system. By the time we walked out, I was cold and jittery, from the inside out. And I understood what she meant.

My breasts had warned me of every pregnancy. Now there was a different awareness, a waiting. I slipped into bed and logged on to the chat rooms of Breastcancer.org. On the website, there were groups of women trading notes. I found a group starting chemo the same week and joined. Some drove hours to get treatment, while others were unsure about the drugs they had chosen, as if they had picked a door on *Let's Make a Deal*. Some complained about doctors as glorified mechanics. I knew doctors were only human, but I trusted them. I had to. At the very least, they had gone to medical school, and I had not. My lifelong method of working hard to get results wouldn't help this time. I could put my fingertips first and aim down from the high dive, but there was no telling what lurked in the water below. My boobs were a wake-up call. It was time to "let go and let God." I was going to find out what that meant.

The first twenty-four hours felt easy. The next afternoon, Karen drove me back to the hospital for Neulasta, an expensive shot for white blood cells. I felt OK, so I was excited to splurge on a late lunch from a trendy new café on the way home. But by the time we pulled into the parking lot, a burning pain rose up my legs inch by inch. I couldn't move them. What a strange sensation to have your bones hurt. When we got home, Karen helped me into the house and down the few steps to the living room, because the hallway to the bedroom felt too far. She made soup while I prayed for the pain to pass. I took a few bites, then lay down on the wooden floor. Big mistake. My insides flamed and my back was on fire. I got to the steps and sat up, but had to lean forward to breathe, cradling the weight of my skull in my hands. I had never felt this kind of pain, not during the heartburn of pregnancy or the torn flesh of childbirth. For the first time, I felt surrender. My body put words in my mouth and pushed them out in a whisper.

"I don't think I can do this," I said. I was ready to die.

Karen looked up from the old club chair across the room, where she was on the phone confirming her flight home. She hung up.

"I'm staying," she said. And called the doctor's cell phone.

By morning, I had two more pill bottles and a jug of vile anti-ulcer liquid to drink thirty minutes before each meal. As if I could eat. Here was the first unexpected side effect that wasn't on any list. At three in the morning, a woman on Breastcancer.org mentioned taking Claritin before the shot to lessen the bone pain. My doctor had no idea why it might work, but it couldn't hurt, so we put it on the shopping list. Getting chemotherapy had sounded like the worst part, but it wasn't. The worst was what came after, when it started working.

Soon I could no longer keep track of the times between meds. I couldn't read the books I'd gathered in anticipation of down time, or finish an article in a magazine. I even gave up on fashion magazines. The Guess models had such fluffy breasts, not to mention a Lolita vibe, that I just couldn't deal with it. I'd stockpiled chick flicks on the DVR, but one was *Sleepless in Seattle*, written by Nora Ephron. She had just died from a blood disease related to her breast cancer chemo. Instead, we turned to the Hallmark Channel for "Countdown to Christmas."

The simple plots and happy endings were perfect. Plus, they never showed breasts. Most of the lead actresses had long hair and dead mothers, like in Disney movies, so that was familiar, too. I could doze off and wake up without any confusion as to what was happening. Real life was not the same.

On day three, the power went out. John and I lived in an older house in a gorgeous neighborhood, but now it was dark and cold. The house was surely toxic with mold and ancient plumbing, but this was no time to move out. Electricians hooked up a generator for the weekend, then I crawled into bed and stayed there. I could feel the curtain fall. I couldn't read or write and my words were mixed up. The next days were a blur. We got power back on just in time to watch my favorite show, *The Good Wife*. Alicia was defending Christina Ricci's character for baring her breasts on a late-night TV show for a mock breast cancer PSA. A horn honked to mask the word "tits."

I slipped back under.

By the end of a week, the sun came up and I started to feel like myself—if I were a hundred years old. I bundled up as if for a moonwalk, then shuffled around the tree in the backyard. That's all I could manage. A few days later, we took a walk on the beach and it felt glorious. I ran my fingers through my hair . . . and a handful came out. I pulled more out in clumps, like a party trick. It didn't hurt. I let a few strands go, and the breeze took them. Maybe a bird would use them to build a nest.

I couldn't bear the sight of waking up to hair on my pillow. Nor could I tolerate an ice cap on my head, an imperfect method to keep it. I called a few friends to have a head-shaving party at the wig store in the Valley. After dropping Karen off at the airport, I found she'd left a bottle of my favorite wine in the car. My mouth was full of sores by now, but as I sat in that chair while a woman buzzed my head, I sipped the wine anyway. This was a celebration, dammit. Of life.

Being bald was strange, but mostly it was cold. Wigs felt weird, itchy. A writer I barely knew, Bernadette Murphy, knit me the softest cap I had ever felt. When my bald brother-in-law stopped by, I pulled it off to show him we were twins.

"Bold move!" he said.

I loved that. That was how I wanted to be: bold. But it wasn't easy. My sister visited with her family, including her husband, who was still weak from lung cancer. Her preteen daughters played dress-up with my hats. I was reluctant to share my wigs, but not out of selfishness. When the nine-year-old tried "blond bombshell" and turned to show me, I thought, *You, too, can get breast cancer.*

Juliette flew down for Thanksgiving, and for the first time, I ordered a turkey precooked from a store. It was our second Thanksgiving with John as an official part of the family. I wore a headband of plastic bangs beneath a felt hat that swam on my scalp. Chloe piled her plate high with mashed potatoes and her favorite green bean casserole. But when I handed her a fork, she pulled away. She didn't want to touch it. She was afraid I was contagious. My husband stood over the table with the butcher knife in his hand and raised his voice for the first time since we'd met. Juliette sobbed. Slowly, John carved the turkey and passed me a plate. After dinner, the girls cleaned up until the kitchen sparkled.

There were some good days, and I had work to do before the next round. I wrote as fast as I could, blogs and promotion and polishes on the book. My husband flew out again and Karen came back. She had now driven my new car more than I had. I taught the next class on a rainy Wednesday night while on pretreatment meds. Some of the students, lawyers and computer experts writing their first novels, had no idea I was sick. Others watched me with suspicion and eyed Karen, standing guard as my "guest." I felt like one of those animatronic characters at Chuck E. Cheese who came to life for the show, then drooped as the lights dimmed. After walking slowly back through the puddles to the parking lot, I called another instructor to take over.

By round two, I thought I understood the drill. I swallowed dozens of pills, for bone pain and infection and nausea and sleep and this and that, every few hours. A few fidgety days later, the curtain came crashing down right on schedule, but this time it was different. I would come to understand that every time would be different. As the chemo took hold, my body shut down more and fought back less. The schedule was planned so the worst chemical doses ended in March. Then I would start radiation, which would end just in time for my book release. After that, I'd start years of hormone blocking pills, each with its own side effects.

My fingernails turned black and curled like claws, leaving blood on the keyboard as I typed. And I typed a lot, as many hours as I could sit upright, on the days before the curtain came down. My big toenails fell off. The same drug made my nose bleed, and when it wasn't bleeding, it was a leaky faucet. I stuffed Kleenex in every sleeve and kept packets in every drawer. Soon, scar tissue grew over my tear ducts so I couldn't see past my watering eyes. Every few weeks, an eye doctor probed my tear ducts with inch-long needles to keep them from closing. Each time, I thought of Jack Nicholson in *Terms of Endearment* when he said he'd "rather poke needles in his eyes" than fall in love with Shirley MacLaine, whose daughter was dying of breast cancer.

I don't remember Christmas.

Sometime around New Year's, my father and his wife flew in from Ohio. For the first time, I made him change his entire travel plan. He delayed their trip for a week so I'd gain more resistance to germs and enough focus to drive a car. Now, white bumps covered my tongue, so I sucked on lozenges to swallow. Worse, I had lost my sense of taste.

The morning of my father and his wife's arrival, I painted my face to hide my pallor and brushed my best wig. Tracy and her family drove ninety miles to meet us for brunch at The Huntley, a rooftop restaurant with an ocean view. She had just been nominated for an Emmy for covering a big fire in Santa Barbara, and was describing how her shoes melted. When it was my turn, I answered questions about work and pretended the $15 oatmeal didn't taste like sawdust. My father had told me I could do anything I set my mind to. I set my mind to being strong.

No matter how frail I felt, I couldn't bear to blame my breasts. I didn't want to play like a girl, or to be evidence of a weaker sex. As soon as we said our goodbyes and they headed to the airport, I gave the car keys to my husband to drive. When we got home, I pulled off my wig, washed off my mask of makeup, and climbed back into bed.

• • •

Some women on breastcancer.org were taking antidepressants; a few were still cooking for their families; others were slowly dying. When the internet crashed during one of my short windows of clarity, I panicked. I had crafted deadlines with a careful eye on the calendar. There was nothing brave about having breast cancer. All that warrior talk was bullshit. You do what you need to do, or you don't. You can only do so much.

I counted down the chemo sessions, at least the toxic ones. The infusions of Herceptin would continue being injected into my porto-cath every three weeks for a year. At chemo, I recognized a mom from the Valley who had been diagnosed with the exact same thing before Herceptin was available. She would die before my treatment was finished. When it became clear that some of my side effects would be permanent, it didn't matter. I would be alive to feel them.

Sometimes I shuffled around the block by myself and met up with an old man moving at the same turtle pace. He was between chemo treatments for something else. This was a secret society of walking skeletons. When I ventured to the grocery store in my headscarf, I wondered where the others hid.

Another time, when I was shuffling around the neighborhood in a felt hat and a faux fur vest over my pajamas, Bradley Cooper came out of a modern mansion and climbed on a motorcycle. He said hello, and I nodded like a little old lady. I had seen him before, back when I was healthy, but hadn't recognized him until after he waved and passed by. Now, it was my turn, so bony and slow that he didn't recognize me.

Like Dracula, I avoided bright sun and human contact. Women online were getting pneumonia and worse. I didn't want to delay treatment. My fingers and feet swelled and went numb, my weight dropped, and bruises bloomed out of nowhere. My skin thinned so much that when my shin grazed the bed, it bled for days. Anyone who dared enter the front door had to use the giant bottle of hand sanitizer before stepping beyond the foyer. My husband showered after traveling before hugging me.

Soon, I lost track of things and paid $2,000 to the wrong doctor. I missed other payments altogether. When I called Nordstrom customer service to explain, they sent flowers. It was strange how even during the darkest time, my faith in humanity grew. And then someone would email me an article suggesting that the myth of a thing called "chemo brain" might actually be true. Sigh.

I made a list of people I wanted to see and those I didn't. I needed mothers, women who were nurturing and patient, whom I could call on to bring me a California roll, since soy sauce was the only thing I could taste. My friend, Cathy, the one whose triplets had gone to preschool with Chloe, climbed into bed with me. We spent hours online shopping for tiny earrings to go with my headscarves. I never bought any.

When I finally confessed that I had cancer on Facebook, old classmates messaged from across the country to wish me well. I was grateful. Other friends either disappeared or called too much. I shortened my list to those I wouldn't need to entertain, people who would just walk me around the block and go home. My mother was angry that I didn't want my sister to come help; she thought it would hurt her feelings. But Tracy was already working full time, helping a sick friend, and had been through hell with her husband's illness. I didn't want Chloe to hang around, either, so I just smiled when she dropped smoothies off at my bedside. I couldn't bear the weight of their heavy hearts.

For my third round, Karen came back to what she now called Chemo Canyon. We hung out in bed with her wine and my pills and enough magazines to make it a slumber party. We also fast-forwarded through *The Bachelor*, an exercise in public humiliation with the voyeuristic thrill of a train wreck. I enjoyed the faux romance, but the tears after their meta-dates were a horrible advertisement for women. The previous season opened with the usual presentation of breasts as assets in evening gowns. It was like Miss America, complete with swimsuit competition. Then bachelorette Courtney Robertson took off her bikini top too soon and became the villain. Apparently, the others forgot they were competing to fuck the bachelor in the Fantasy Suite and snag a diamond ring.

The new season starred a straight arrow named Sean. During Karen's visit, she went to a sorority event at UCLA and found a live celebration of "Bachelor Nation." Karen crashed the party and shoved a camera in front of Bachelor Sean. He recorded a personal get-well wish.[1] It doesn't matter whether I'd like him in person. He will always have a place in my heart. As will she.

Who else but Karen would alert me by email when actress Charlize Theron shaved her head for *Mad Max*? Theron told a reporter that "being bald is so liberating, every woman should do it."[2] Who else but Karen would call laughing months later when Theron "fumed" at doing it again?[3]

My husband was back in town for the last three sessions. On Valentine's Day, I got dressed up for a romantic date by the fireplace. I couldn't feel my numb fingers enough to latch stockings to a garter belt, so I substituted thigh highs that barely clung. My bridal negligee hid all my scars except for the bulging port. I wore the blond wig, glued on false eyelashes, and pulled on a pair of opera gloves to cover what was left of my bloody fingernails. I buckled high-heeled sandals on the loosest hole to squeeze over my swollen feet. Then we put on soft music and sat by the fire. I couldn't taste the champagne or the chocolate, but for a few golden moments, we could pretend. Then, smoke began to rise and the scent of burnt plastic overwhelmed my Opium perfume. The back of my wig had melted. We laughed, moved away from the fire, and carried on.

By the next round, there was no carrying on. My husband and I watched *Project Runway* while he rubbed my swollen legs in bed. I felt the heat rise until my skin was slick with perspiration. I was hoping he wouldn't notice, but he lifted his hands as the heat rose up to my head. I took off my knit hat. Now I was as hairless as a Chihuahua. I fanned my face with my left hand and tried to ignore the sight of my nails. Thick and blackened, they no longer bled, but now my fingers were numb. The Roto-Rooter eye appointments were slowing my faucet of tears, but I kept Kleenex in my right hand for my runny nose. My body was bloated, my weight had gone up, and my doctor had no idea when or if I would have feeling back in my feet. As we watched Heidi Klum prance in her stilettos, I couldn't help but glance in the mirror. Never had I felt so ugly.

My skin chilled, and my husband put his hands back on my leg.

"This is the perfect date," he said, and looked back at the screen.

Haha, I thought. He was teasing. I was overcome with guilt at getting him into this. I swallowed the last of the lozenge soothing my dry mouth and forced out an apology.

"I'm sorry," I said. "You didn't sign up for this."

He turned to face me. "Neither did you." He turned to the TV screen.

That was it? It felt too easy. He had been flattering me with compliments ever since we started dating, but I always assumed he was being playful, feeding me lines. He still called me Lady Beautiful. What more proof was there? Past experience proved that I had only myself to rely on, so I took pride in being independent, in control. Now I was neither of those things. And yet he was still watching TV happily, as if this truly was the perfect date. My breasts, now pitted and scarred, had held me back when I saw them only as sacred maternal organs. For the past five years, when they made me feel sexy, I had known it was another limited version of myself. Here was a partner who saw me beyond the boobs, beyond either of these roles. I had underestimated him. Our relationship was more than I imagined. I didn't have to be pretty, I didn't have to make dinner, and I didn't have to prove myself. All I had to do was breathe.

After the sixth and final round of chemo, I looked forward to the Academy Awards as a celebratory event. Since both John and I were movie lovers and had written a few of our own, this was an annual ritual. I still dreamed of walking down the red carpet in a sparkly gown. I was blurry from the meds as I sat in bed, marking my newspaper ballot. I had a tendency to vote for my favorites, so I usually lost to my husband. This year I felt confident about everything: I was alive, and I was going to win. My mother and I had already exchanged long-distance phone calls during the red-carpet show, when we rated the gorgeous gowns. I was primed for the opening performance with antinausea pills and a bowl of popcorn.

Then Seth MacFarlane opened with the song, "We Saw Your Boobs." I laughed. Then I thought better of it and blamed the meds. He wasn't joking about those trashy websites that collect X-rated clips. He was referring to Oscar-winning films in which women used their bodies as instruments for their performance. Or was that just what they were supposed to think? It was hard to believe that the Academy had approved these lyrics, let alone that the director and orchestra and cameramen had all practiced this ahead of time. How many millions of people around the world were laughing along with this song? I looked down at my boobs and wondered if they, too, could be movie stars. Or if they would always be fodder for jokes. Even those who protested afterwards couldn't erase the memory of it. I looked forward to photos of actresses at the famous after-parties, but it was hard to appreciate their beauty without thinking about their boobs.

A week later, I met my radiologist. He was so cute and charming that when he listed the possible side effects that could linger for years, I brushed them off. Surely he was just being polite, required to read me the fine print. Six weeks of radiation sounded easy compared to eighteen weeks of chemo. It even had a fun nickname: "rads."

The myriad appointments necessary to get set up before radiation were far more mysterious. Every time a new medical technician led me from the dressing room into a chilly room with a machine, I marveled at the number of occupations in the medical field. I didn't ask a lot of questions because I figured they were tired of explaining. I didn't want to be a pain in the ass. I didn't need to know why the white slush didn't taste anything like the pineapple flavor they promised. The truth was, I didn't want to know. I was afraid.

It was easier to smile, shut the fuck up, and get handed off to the next person for X-rays. It reminded me of square dancing in fourth-grade gym class—you just go with it. Besides, had I known what the contrast MRI entailed—an IV of blue dye taped to my arm while laying on my belly with my breasts hanging through holes on a plat-form that moved back and forth into the clanging machine—I might have run. When I learned I'd play flying Superwoman twice a year, maybe forever, it was TMI.

One afternoon, I found myself in a white cube of a room on my back with my arms up over my head. I was strapped in to stay still. The weight of my arms would shape the soft plaster cradle that would keep them out of the way every day during radiation. There I was, laying on my back wearing another pale green smock that opened in front, trying not to scratch my itchy nose. Just as I wondered if I would have to carry this cradle to radiation every day myself, a man came at me with a long needle and a dish of black liquid. This time I asked, "What the fuck?" Only more politely. I hated needles, partly because nurses had a hard time jabbing my veins. That's why a portocath still bulged from the skin below my left collarbone. I had finally learned when to apply numbing cream before Nurse Ratchet hammered the attachment to my chest for the drug infusions I needed every three weeks for a year. Where was my numbing cream now? What kind of needle was this?

The nurse opened my robe and jabbed a series of dots in a horizontal line below my breasts. He explained—a little late, I thought—that these were tattoos. The dots would pinpoint the exact latitude and longitude for the radiation beam. I was torn between laughter and tears. Juliette had a mustache tattooed between her fingers. She did it so she could hold it up to her mouth and make people laugh. I was not a fan, but at least it was clever. Had I known I was getting inked, I would have asked for a mermaid.

The actual radiation sessions were in a different medical center with four floors. My job was to change into yet another front-opening smock, then wait my turn in the hallway to enter a cavernous radiation room. An older man and a young nurse helped me up onto the table. One opened my robe and lay my arms in my cradle. The other pulled the heavy radiation beam close and locked it overhead until it cast a network of red lines across my chest. A woman's disembodied voice from a booth behind me guided their efforts.

Then everyone cleared the room.

This was the scary part. I could hear them in the booth, settling in for the scan. I didn't like being strapped in like that. Not the naked part, but being alone. What if there was an earthquake? I made nervous conversation until they told me to be quiet. If I breathed too much, my chest would expand, and they would have to start over. As a last-ditch effort to delay, I asked about the large wall that curved around the bed. A technician spoke up. That wall, and the thick ceiling, protected the people in the rest of the building from this radiation beam. This beam, aimed at my bare chest.

"Ready?" the voice asked. "Don't breathe too much."

Normally, I am not prone to panic attacks. But now I was trapped in a concrete bunker. I imagined hearing the theme song from *The Twilight Zone*. The machine hummed and cooked like a giant microwave. I closed my eyes and prayed. She hadn't said not to breathe at all, just not enough to expand my chest in a way that would misdirect the aim of the radiation beam. How much was too much, I wondered, needing a deep breath badly to stay calm. I tried to envision walking on a beach, but mostly I lay there and waited.

"OK, breathe," she said.

There was a series of clicks as the beam moved a few millimeters for the next scan. I felt like my brain was disconnected from my body, a flesh and blood form clamped like a slide beneath a microscope, all for these stupid breasts that had betrayed me. My life was on hold as the world spun beyond the white walls without me. I felt lonely.

The sessions were every weekday at the same time. The people there became family, chatting about weekend picnics and crafting projects as they strapped me in for target practice. I shared concerns about my daughters and filled up with their friendliness. Too soon, it was time to shrink back into a mere organism. The flesh on my breast reddened, burned, and bubbled. I rubbed aloe on it twice a day and bought a loose cotton bra to protect my tops from staining.

At the end of the first week, I waited in the exam room for the cute radiologist. He examined my breast, then made conversation. He told me about his toddler's ballet class and a new vegan restaurant in Venice. I still couldn't taste anything, but I played along. He was helping me feel like a person, not just a patient. Yet, as we chatted, I despaired over whether to my close my robe, how to do it without being obvious. He'd already seen me topless. This was just my doctor and me. Nothing sexy about it. But still.

All the doctors warned that the effects were cumulative, both in effectiveness and fatigue. I didn't realize what that meant until I tried to live normally and do three errands in one day. The next day, my limbs felt too heavy to move. I couldn't get out of bed for the rest of the week, except to go to radiation. One day, there was an annoying twenty-something in the waiting room who was training for a 5K and invited me to meet at happy hour. Or maybe I just saw her on a good day. I smiled and said no, thanks. One of the big benefits of being sick is that it gets easier to say no. As friendly as I was on the way in, I was just checking this errand off my list. On the way out, I kept to myself.

During the second week, I felt a shift. I was used to waiting for appointments, for my turn, for the doctor, for the all-clear to leave. Yet it didn't feel like waiting anymore. Once preparations were made, and I lay on the table with my arms over my head and red lines bisecting my breast as the machine hummed over me, I was resting. Instead of feeling alone, I started to feel more connected. To all these people and this equipment, to everyone who had invented and installed each piece, all there to keep me alive. Thanks to their effort, I could just lay there and be. This process would either stop the cancer from returning or it wouldn't. Letting go of control offered a sense of calm. A state of grace. I was no longer afraid of dying.

Thanks to my breasts, the world was expanding. As I lay there, I sensed the people buzzing around me in that room and the clinic and the neighborhood and the city and in ever-widening circles, to where strangers were going about their days. I wanted them to feel my gratitude, to spread this love for humanity in its wake. Now, instead of quietly returning to the dressing room, I thanked everyone in my path. I chatted with people in the waiting room, joked with the parking attendant, complimented the grocery bagger, and called my daughters from the car. I'd always been friendly. My shy husband appreciated my presence at parties because I actually enjoyed making conversation. Juliette and I enjoyed a made-up game where we had to offer compliments to three strangers a day. During chemo, I'd forgotten. Now, my breasts had given me the gift of community. And every moment mattered.

On Sundays, I went to a healing yoga class wearing a nylon cap over my hairless head. When I had energy, I swam a few laps at the local high school pool without any cap at all. It was a goof to smile up at the lifeguard as I adjusted the goggle straps over my bald head. The water felt soft and cool. I threw my life savings at holistic massage and tried acupuncture to soothe my aching joints. I was starting to feel more alive.

The clouds were clearing, but one problem remained. The fountain of inspiration I had counted on for as long as I could remember was dry. I could respond to and analyze existing ideas, but was at a loss to think of anything original. After an agonizing day trying to write an essay but stumbling over typos and twisting my words, I joked about it on Facebook. The next thing I knew, a dozen Sprinkles cupcakes were delivered to my door. Susan, the wife of the film school friend who'd immortalized my breasts in our student film, read the post and sent them. Never had I appreciated social media so much. Each pair of cupcakes had a colored button to display the flavor; they looked like six sets of nippled breasts. I stood in the kitchen in my bathrobe and laughed, then ate two straight from the box. Finally, I could taste chocolate again. Call it a Happy Meal.

On the last day of radiation, the technicians awarded me a certificate of graduation, which seemed silly. They also gave me a congratulations card that everyone had signed. I gave them a thank-you basket of flowers in return. For six intense weeks, they'd been my family. For months, my car would steer there automatically.

The last day of radiation was publication day for the novel that may have saved my life. This X on the calendar was the best reward, the goal that had kept me going during the long days of darkness. Two days later, we celebrated with a book release party at the Grove, a fancy shopping center in Los Angeles. I pulled on a wig, false eyelashes, and a new dress that covered my port. My husband took a photograph of me under my book picture in the window of Barnes and Noble. I looked almost like me.

Feeling a bit shaky, I wandered back inside to greet my friends and do my reading. The host, Lita Weissman, had presented one of my first book parties two decades earlier at a long-closed bookstore in the Valley. My husband was doing the Q and A with me, focusing on the writing process. Chloe arrived with a friend, as usual, still dressed in her chef's uniform from class at Le Cordon Bleu. She sat smiling with her friend and a few others she knew in the front row. The other half of the audience had no idea I was sick. For a few precious minutes, I almost forgot, too.

When the wine and cheese were gone and the chairs were folded, I went downstairs to sign the extra books. On the shelf behind the register was another new release, Florence Williams's *Breasts: A Natural and Unnatural History*, destined to win the *LA Times* Book Prize for Science. This manifesto about toxic breast milk was being compared to *Silent Spring*, the groundbreaking 1962 environmental classic by Rachel Carson . . . who died of breast cancer. Why did breasts get more respect when they were toxic? I stood at the counter and leafed through it for a few minutes. I knew I should buy it, but not yet. I wanted to extend this happy evening. I needed more time to forget.

A few weeks later, I began immunotherapy, a fancy name for pills that block the hormones related to my cancer. Women in treatment take various pills depending on whether they are pre- or post-menopausal. I wasn't sure where I fit in, since there wasn't enough time to take blood tests between stopping birth control and starting chemo. The hot flashes started immediately, drenching my sheets. I put plastic beneath them like a bedwetter. After holding hands between the pillows for a few minutes each night, my husband surreptitiously slipped away. I was still getting infusions every third Thursday, but a drippy nose seemed like the worst of it. What could go wrong with a pill?

A few days in, I woke up with my hands like claws. My feet were so curled I couldn't walk. I took deep breaths and pressed my palms against the side of the bed, then stepped gingerly on the floor to stretch out my toes. I felt like a witch. Was this what arthritis felt like? These meds were known to make bones brittle, so after a few more tests at various doctors' offices, I added a bone strengthener to the regime. This made my joints ache, and my shoulders curl forward, especially on the side of my surgery. At my biweekly blood tests, my oncologist prescribed physical therapy, but that wasn't going to fix it. As long as I spent half an hour each day doing exercises, my shoulders would stretch out. When I stopped, so did my shoulders.

Soon I was taking one pill to counteract another, plus vitamins and whatever side effect–battling supplements that my doctor would allow. I used to pride myself on not having any medicine in my bathroom cabinet, as if being healthy was something I had control over. Now, every Sunday, I jammed seven pills into each compartment of a long purple pill box. When Jimmy Fallon made a joke on *The Tonight Show* about old people's days-of-the-week pill cases, I was too tired to be angry.

In the chat rooms, women were giving up. One wrote that the quality of life was too compromised to continue. She didn't want to live longer if the living was like this. All this effort was a gamble anyway, to raise our odds of survival. We were no longer sick; we were trying to avoid getting sick again. I understood, but I was still so surprised about getting sick in the first place that I wasn't about to quit early. I begged my insurance company to approve the brand-name pill, which had a more consistent delivery method and known fillers. Even then, it cost hundreds of dollars a month. I spent the summer and fall trying new pills to find one I could live with. Or perhaps I grew used to the stiff joints, hot flashes, and dry everything.

I was still desperate for one more pill, something to cure chemo brain. My left brain seemed sharper than ever, but my imagination was gone. I wrote blogs, spoke at conferences, and returned to consulting. Yet the last story I had started just lay there. My pages were still blank.

My oncologist sent me to an expert at UCLA doing a study on post-chemotherapy cognitive thinking. She said my changes were too subtle to be measured and compared it to an athlete complaining about a particular muscle. She suggested this was either a result of the toxic chemicals that still lingered in my body, or a result of the hormone blockers halting the lubrication between the two halves of my brain. The only way to know for sure was to stop treatment. I didn't care *why* the right side of my brain was slow, I just wanted it back to speed. Still, it wasn't worth risking my life to find out. This was collateral damage. I had to live with it.

By summer, Angelina Jolie had announced her preventative double mastectomy in the *New York Times*. Magazines reported so many women following suit that it sounded like a trendy new excuse for breast implants. When people learned I'd had treatment, they looked at my boobs as a bonus. Yet only 35 of every 100,000 breast cancer patients who had mastectomies opted for reconstruction.[4] Part of this was due to the lack of information provided by their oncological surgeons. But women with the BRCA gene mutation had been undergoing this procedure for some time—now they are called "previvors." And most did have reconstruction. The rate of procedures didn't rise, but testing sure did, at least for those who could afford it.[5] Jolie's glamorous after photos were everywhere while I was still bald and bloated. It was hard not to be jealous. Petty, I know.

Now I was back to real life between infusions. Chloe broke her arm on the same side where hooks had been implanted to keep her shoulder together after a sports injury years earlier. She needed two titanium rods and twelve screws implanted that would require several surgical adjustments. I pinned sparkly broaches on my stretchy hats and ferried us between her medical appointments and mine. The cycle of caregiving continued.

I counted the days until my hair came in. When it appeared as salt-and-pepper stubble, my first venture out was to Juice Crafters. Jamie Lee Curtis was there waiting for a smoothie. We'd never met, but I thanked her for wearing her short hair with such style. Gracious, she said I looked great. That made me feel better for a day or two. Then I tied my scarves back on. I added Bioten, a hair-growing supplement, to my multitude of meds. A few years later, an oncologist said in *Elle* that when a woman "wants to restore her looks to her pre-cancer state,"[6] it bodes well for treatment. Whatever it takes, I guess.

On the bright side, every three weeks, when I returned to the chemo lounge for my infusion, it felt like home, a place where everyone understood what you were going through. And now I could teach the newbies how to tie a scarf in a pretty bow. My hair grew back in curls. After a year of avoiding germs, I was excited to fly cross-country to a conference. The airport security officer scanned the image on my driver's license then squinted at me. "That you?" his eyebrows asked. "Used to be," I nodded. He shrugged and let me pass.

A year after my first chemo session, I had surgery to remove my port. Some women keep it longer in case they need it again, but why tempt fate? I wanted it out. I was ready to make up for lost time, to go places where no one knew me as Chemo Chick. When the bandages came off, there was a rude scar on my chest. The clumsy surgeon assigned by the hospital turned out not to be in my insurance network. That year, when I didn't dare change doctors, also happened to be the year Anthem Blue Cross stopped covering out-of-network providers. Cancer is expensive, and I still had years of meds and testing ahead of me. Meanwhile, Chloe was diagnosed with complex regional pain syndrome (CRPS), a chronic pain disease requiring intensive treatment. The hits just kept coming.

Yet, there was pride in picking up the reins where I had dropped them. It was easy to slip right back into my old routine of driving and shopping and cooking and cleaning and loving and worrying and saying yes. Of all the women I knew, me and my bosom buddies in the Breastcancer.org chat rooms seemed to be most overwhelmed by the lives of those around us. We were in this together. We were also back to work.

At a literary conference a few months later, my copanelist cancelled, so Mary Menzel, director of the California Center for the Book, affiliated with the Library of Congress, interviewed me for ninety minutes. We sat at a table stacked with my entire oeuvre: nonfiction books, novels, a coffee table book, and essays. She was the only person I'd ever met who'd actually read them all. She saw the pattern: new mom, working mom, divorced mom, paranoid mom. As I watched the women in the audience listen and nod, it was clear that they could relate. I was nobody special or famous, so I was honored to be sitting in the chair. I was Everywoman. Yet, when my host stopped exploring my work and started summarizing my life, it sounded like a retrospective. I tugged at the tangle of chemo curls at my temple and realized they all thought I would die.

After two more surgeries and five more years of hormone therapy, my oncologist said I had completed treatment. I was cancer-free—and the odds against reoccurrence were high.

At first, I was thrilled, eager to embrace a new normal. I gave up on my eyebrows growing back and had them tattooed. I accepted that my eyes would stay dry, my sinuses wet, and my nails ugly. But my hair was growing, my shoes fit, and I could almost raise my arms up over my head. A jubilant week passed. Then I woke up with a new feeling: fear.

When I was first diagnosed, it felt random. The news hit like the Northridge earthquake: unexpected. For five years, I did everything humanly possible to prevent aftershocks. Now I had no protection. No poison, radiation, or pills. As I lay awake at night, I had a sense that this wasn't so random at all. My San Andreas Fault lay deep inside.

Stress can be described as the body's reaction to an event, challenge, or demand. When it prompts negative psychological emotions, such as worry, anxiety, depression, anger, fear, frustration, grief, or helplessness, our bodies have a physiological response. That response raises the level of cortisol, often called the "stress hormone."[7] Chronic stress lowers our immune system response and creates inflammation. These mind-body connections vary from person to person, but when we experience negative emotions repeatedly, over a long period of time, they can burn holes in our natural defenses. A science report in the *Journal of Clinical Investigation* connected the dots to breast cancer. Just as we are at our most vulnerable, stress triggers a gene called the ATF3, which acts as a "master switch" to cancer cells.[8]

My first reaction was to blame every tornado, earthquake, and person who'd ever caused me distress. While I'd taken my mother's suicide attempts and my ex-husband's anger in stride, perhaps I was in denial about their lingering effects. My attempts to control situations led to anxiety and my constant state of preparedness led to exhaustion. Then I realized I had chosen to get involved in my loved ones' lives, to sacrifice whatever it took to help. This prompted a new wave of guilt and regret. I needed to step back to take better care of myself. If I didn't, how could I care for others, even when they asked?

We know that stress causes us to lose sleep and skip exercise. It also increases our tendency to self-medicate with unhealthy eating, smoking, and drinking. My doctor warned that the latest statistics showed that more than two drinks per week, for any woman, raises the risk of breast cancer the way cigarettes raise our risk for lung cancer. So much for that glass of wine in the bathtub. Stress also causes us to isolate ourselves from friends and family who could provide emotional support. As Dr. Kristi Funk puts it, "the stress is killing you."[9]

The challenge of self-care is counterintuitive to the lifestyle of most women. Everyone has breasts, but women are 100 times more likely than men to get breast cancer.[10] Since the number one determinant of breast cancer is being a woman and the risk rises with age, one might assume the disease is nature's signal that we have outlived our biological purpose. Yet, it strikes younger women more and more. Could the very capability of reproducing be a factor? Surely our biological role of caregiving is embodied by our mammary glands. Nurture is our nature. When the American Academy of Family

Physicians warns about caregiver stress, the photographs accompanying the articles all depict women.[11]

As we "lean in" to the workforce, we still carry the burden at home. When the women in Silicon Valley invent a hands-free nursing machine to pump milk during meetings,[12] they aren't "having it all," they are *doing* it all. I used to think it was odd that aristocratic women employed wet nurses even after bottles were available, but now I understand the nutritional benefits. It's also clear that turning blood into milk burns an enormous number of calories, a valuable form of energy. We underestimate the way women deplete biological resources as if strip mining, to get the most from every pound of flesh.

Beyond the physical drain, there is an emotional and physiological strain from nurturing other human beings. With or without children, women bear pressure from society to take care of mates, businesses, and often the greater good. Certainly, there are hormonal and genetic links for breast cancer. But for most cases, like mine, there is no one scientific source. It takes many years for cells to mutate and grow unchecked, escaping the immune system until they develop into tumors.[13] And the immune system is compromised by many activities common to women.

Before a recent birthday party for my yoga instructor, I learned that he also taught spin classes. I expected two opposite groups of women: mellow and aggressive. After the initial small talk, it became clear that every single woman I met had something else going on, some exhausting duty. Exercise was a mutual escape from the emotional burden of loved ones with challenges, from infancy to addiction to Alzheimer's. At first, this depth of responsibility struck me as a coincidence in a small sample of women. Then, a few weeks into the fall of 2017, I was in an email loop with a group of authors across the country who took turns blogging on the Girlfriends Book Club website. We were considering shutting it down due to a lack of time. These women had chosen careers in which they could work at home, partly to create a better work-life balance. But one author broke the unspoken rule to limit our emails to business by apologizing for her delayed response. She blamed family issues. All business conversation ceased. Within hours, over a dozen other authors emailed back to confess their summer vacations had consisted of caring for loved ones. Even for women in control of their careers, stress is the norm.

Three years later, the COVID-19 pandemic put this in stark relief. When both partners were working from home, it seemed logical that caregiving responsibilities would be split evenly. But that was not the case.[14] Working mothers, already pulling a double shift between their day jobs and caregiving responsibilities at home, were now burned out from doing what Sheryl Sandberg called a "double double shift."[15] One might argue that women bowed to the fact that they earned the lower income, or had the kinds of jobs that were more flexible so they could spend more time parenting on top of their jobs outside the home. But this only circles back to the initial challenges faced by women who want to both work and have children. Now, these very women were left without vital outside help, which mostly came from other women. Many would consider one of the effects of this global tragedy to be a setback for feminism. I suspect the pandemic will also mark setbacks for women's health.

Flight attendants have always advised adult passengers to put the oxygen mask on first to better help those around them. Women need to stay healthy to care for our families. Emotional support is part of the cure. Mutual intimacy and caring strengthens our immune systems. Just as lifestyle changes can modify disease at the cellular level, self-care that builds resiliency can stave off stress. While we can't control the weather, or "people, places, and things," as the recovery movements say, we *can* control our reactions. We can try to avoid conflict, be mindful, and seek serenity. Arianna Huffington suggests we learn to "thrive."

But we must also tend the community gardens. It does take a village. In addition to improving treatment for women of every race and budget, and searching for a cure, we must work to prevent cancer on a universal scale. As other countries catch up to us in modernization, their breast cancer rates have risen, too. The United States is last in every aspect of government support for families, from nursing to parental leave. We must fight for affordable childcare and healthcare to share the weight of what is clearly a deadly burden. When the medical community expects hundreds of thousands to be diagnosed each year, the burden is on us all.

We have lost invaluable assets to this disease. In May 2017, Maryam Mirzakhani, the only woman to win the Fields Medal, considered the Nobel Prize for mathematics, was cited as a prime example of scientific potential in an award-winning journalist's book *Inferior: How Science Got Women Wrong*.[16] This forty-year-old mother of a little girl discovered the physics of "how the universe came to exist."[17] Science doesn't get any bigger than that. What else could Mirzakhani have discovered had she not died two months later of breast cancer?

I broke down and bought a pink Bic fireplace lighter. There is no ribbon logo, no promise of a donation, and the color is so stereotypical that it's now discontinued. But I needed it. My boobs will affect my life forever. No one ever calls it boob cancer, yet these are the same body parts we refer to in fun. And every time I light a candle with my pink lighter, I am reminded to eat clean foods, to exercise, to limit alcohol, and to avoid toxins. I remember to slow down, spend time with friends, and to rest. I am no longer sick of pink. I am grateful. If you know someone with breast cancer, you understand. If you don't, God bless you—you will.

Over forty-two thousand American women will die of breast cancer *this year*.[18]

A Few Americans Diagnosed
with Breast Cancer

epidemic *noun* ep•i•dem•ic e-pə-ˈde-mik
1. an outbreak of disease that spreads quickly and affects many individuals

—*Meriam-Webster Dictionary*

Bella Abzug	Vanessa B. Calloway	Edie Falco
Kathy Acker †	Edna Campbell	Caitlin Flanagan
Claudia Alexander †	Diahann Carroll †	Drew Gilpin Faust
Barbara Allen†	Rachel Carson †	Deanna Favre
Anastacia	Julia Child	Carly Fiorina
Elda E. Anderson †	Lois Chiles	Peggy Fleming
V. C. Andrews †	Jackie Collins †	Jane Fonda
Christina Applegate	Mindy Cohn	Betty Ford
Fay Baker †	Sheryl Crow	Kay Francis †
Brigitte Bardot	Yvonne Craig †	Georgia Frontiere †
Jillian Barberie	Bette Davis †	Helen Gahagan †
Judi Bari †	Ruby Dee	Greta Garbo
Kathy Bates	Sandra Dee	Barbara Gittings †
Frances Bavier	Janice Dickinson	Kim Gordon
Meredith Baxter	Shannen Doherty	Paulette Goddard
Ingrid Bergman †	Elizabeth Edwards †	Nanci Griffith
Rose Bird †	Shirley G. Du Bois †	Alaina Reed Hall †
Judy Blume	Barbara Ehrenreich	Fannie Lou Hamer †
Erma Bombeck	Jill Eikenberry	Dorothy Hamill
Eileen Brennan	Linda Ellerbee	Virginia Hamilton †
Nancy Brinker	Melissa Etheridge	Ruth Handler
Blanche Calloway †	Judith Exner †	Julie Harris

Samantha Harris
Teresa Heinz Kerry
Heidi Heitkamp
A. "Lady" Hitchcock
Judy Holliday †
Shirley Horn †
Mary Hubbard
Laura Ingraham
Molly Ivins †
Kate Jackson
Ann Jillian
Betsey Johnson
Jennifer Jones
June Jordan †
Helen Kane †
Joan Kennedy
Margaret Kilgallen †
Hoda Kotb
Evelyn Lauder
Sandra Lee
Shari Lewis
Audre Lorde
Julia Louis-Dreyfus
Juliette Gordon Low †
Myrna Loy
Marilyn Lloyd
Geralyn Lucas
Lorna Luft
Joan Lunden
Linda McCartney †
Claire McCaskill

Rue McClanahan
Hattie McDaniel †
Kylie Minogue
Andrea Mitchell
Janet Napolitano
Olivia Newton-John
Cynthia Nixon
Tig Notaro
Kim Novak
Sandra Day O'Connor
Grace Paley †
Minnie Pearl
Kelly Preston †
Giuliana Rancic
Judy Rankin
Betsy Rawls
Nancy Reagan
Lynn Redgrave †
Minnie Riperton †
Amy Robach
Cokie Roberts †
Robin Roberts
Happy Rockefeller
Ann Romney
Calypso Rose
Rosalind Russell
Debbie Wasserman
  Schultz
Eve Sedgwick †
Bershan Shaw
Jean Simmons

Carly Simon
Nina Simone †
Naomi Sims †
Jaclyn Smith
Dame Maggie Smith
Suzanne Somers
Susan Sontag
Wendie Jo Sperber †
Dusty Springfield †
Gloria Steinem
Susan Strasberg †
Marcia Strassman †
Gloria Stuart
Jacqueline Susann †
Deborah Sussman †
Wanda Sykes
Shirley Temple Black
Maura Tierney
Marietta Tree †
Linda Tripp
Danitra Vance †
Vivian Vance †
Janice E. Voss †
Margaret Walker †
Marcia Wallace
Pat Ward†
Anne Wexler
Rita Wilson
Elizabeth Wurtzel †
Laura Ziskin †

† Died from breast cancer

Fifteen

HOW *NOT* TO BE
A ROLE MODEL
2013

Mom, can I get breast implants?"

The words made me freeze in my desk chair. I struggled to compose my face into a benign expression before swiveling to greet Chloe in the doorway of my home office.

"Hi, hon," I said, pausing so she could see me clearly. Not just me as her mom, but as a breast cancer patient wearing a cotton cap covering her head, still bald from chemo. Was this ironic? Was she that insensitive? Or had I done such a good job acting perfectly fine so my daughter wouldn't worry that she had taken my recovery for granted? I unstuck my T-shirt from the salve on my radiated breast and chose Door Number Three.

The last time we had been in the car together, and I mourned my reflection in the rearview mirror, she shut me down by saying something nice. Apparently, it was right for me to look ugly now. Survival preempted vanity. And maybe she was right. When she complained about her smudged mascara, I kept quiet about my total lack of eyelashes. All her life I had tried to be a good role model, with everything from a strong work ethic to good grooming. That day, when she came in and saw me working, was a prime example. She had followed my lead directly into the double bind of boobs.

"Hon, you already have a beautiful figure." I gestured at her skinny jeans and the sweater that scooped to expose a lace bandeau. This was a sophisticated look, consistent with the rest of her wardrobe. High fashion favored the flat-chested. She was model thin—maybe too thin. If she gained some weight, I thought, she would gain up there, too. She had barely shaken a virus that had lingered long past the holidays, so it could be she just needed time. I sure did. But I didn't dare say that. "Can we talk about this later?"

She eyed the stack of work on the desk behind me and nodded before lifting her gaze to the window. "Thanks for watching my baby."

When I turned around, I could see her beloved pit bull chewing on a stuffed mallard in the backyard. At least it wasn't a real baby. Then her breasts would be a different concern. Clearly, I needed a twelve-step meeting: *Hi, my name is Mom and I am a hypocrite.* Or were implants a common parental problem now, something to discuss at Mommy & Me? I'd read about teenagers in Newport Beach getting breast implants for high school graduation. Some of those girls also got a Mercedes when they turned sixteen, but that didn't mean Chloe expected one. If she were under eighteen, I would forbid augmentation. Now she was nearly twenty-one, and I feared it.

With one sniff of the air, the dog abandoned his toy and bounded across the overgrown lawn. As Chloe strolled into view, he nearly knocked her over in his attempt to nuzzle her. The only reason I babysat today was so that she could drive across town to Pasadena and take care of some business at Le Cordon Bleu. Now the beast was licking her face, and she was hugging him in a love fest so touching it looked like they had been apart for days. This was clearly unconditional love. She was getting him licensed as a service animal and dreaming of the day when a pit bull would be welcome in restaurants. *Dream on,* I thought. The dog was truly a sweetheart, but I still wished it were some fluffy little mutt with a better reputation.

That was how I felt about breasts, too, I realized. My prejudice against them was more about their bad reputation than the reality. Soon, my daughter would be so busy with culinary school that she would forget about breast implants. At least I hoped so.

While Chloe wrestled a leash on her lovestruck pup, I googled "young women" and "breast augmentation." No specific studies came up. Several articles on plastic surgery claimed that teens were the most likely "to be dissatisfied by their appearance," but most grew out of it. When I heard her bring the dog through the house to say goodbye, I clicked to a different screen and spun my chair around.

"I'll talk to Nana," she said.

Oh, crap, I thought, smiling. As the family matriarch, my mother wielded great influence. She would empathize with Chloe, who had been through some rough years. Between the rocky divorce, her sister leaving for college, and the water polo injuries that turned an all-star athlete into just another babe in La La Land, I'd dragged her to half a dozen therapists. Then I remembered that my mother was a therapist, as well, only recently retired. She had once trained other therapists. Surely, she would help her granddaughter explore the reasons she felt surgery would make her happy and find a better solution.

We hugged goodbye as if nothing had happened, but I couldn't get her request out of my mind. The problem was, I didn't know any other mothers who had dealt with this, and I felt embarrassed to ask around, especially in my condition. It made me feel as if I'd not only been a bad influence but had taught the wrong values. Worse, the only boob job I'd truly noticed on someone her age was during my divorce ten years earlier. I was buying a slipcovered couch to fill up our empty living room. The salesgirl looked like she stuffed baseballs in her tube top. A delivery guy entered the open doorway with a vase of long-stemmed red roses and set it beside an identical flower arrangement on her desk. When I asked if it was her birthday, she said no, they were from her boyfriend. I pictured a middle-aged man in a sports car.

Too distracted to return to writing book club questions, I researched breast augmentation again. There was nothing about age groups beyond the numbers. Surgery was on the rise for teenagers, but reductions were reported most often because of the struggle to get insurance coverage for them. Even though the FDA declared that augmentation was beneficial to a woman's quality of life, reductions were elective. Saline was approved for women over eighteen and silicone for women at twenty-two. Board-certified surgeons wouldn't go against FDA guidelines, but plenty of other surgeons would. Hell, my dentist's new partner offered Botox. There was no law against it.

By the time Chloe was six years old, forty of the fifty-two state winners in Miss USA had implants.[1] In 2009, the Miss California Pageant admitted to buying implants for Carrie Prejean. She may have won Miss USA had she not spoken out against gay marriage. Pageant officials immediately revealed an old sex tape to discredit her. They demanded she resign—and reimburse them for the implants. Donald Trump, who owned the pageant, let her slide. When questioned about the implants by a Christian newspaper, she said, "I don't see anywhere in the Bible where it says you shouldn't get breast implants."[2]

In late May, several months after Chloe's request, I flew to her sister's graduation from the Academy of Art University in San Francisco. Juliette sent me two of her four tickets, so my husband would meet her dad for the first time. I'd only seen Drew twice since our divorce, but I still got nasty emails. Fortunately, my mother was there to see her eldest granddaughter graduate from college, so she sat with my ex in the enormous auditorium. After the ceremony, we met outside the crowded entrance surrounded by a rainbow of helium balloons.

This was two weeks after I completed radiation treatments, but I had six more months of infusions. The bump of my port was concealed by a thick sweater. Perhaps the obvious wig above my gaunt cheeks and drawn-on eyebrows contributed to our calm meeting. We took an awkward picture with the graduate, then split up for the day.

On Sunday, Juliette was all mine. While my husband read in our hotel room overlooking Union Square, I spent an hour online looking up local bookstores. Since I didn't have the energy for a proper tour, Juliette and I planned to spend the day handing out bookmarks and book club guides from Oakland to Pacifica. I dressed to impersonate myself again, but with thick eyeliner instead of fake lashes. If they didn't believe I was the person the back of the book, the grad could vouch for me.

Juliette picked me up in front of the hotel in my hand-me-down Acura. She wore a sundress. I understood she was used to the cool weather, but I couldn't help notice the low neckline cutting across her cleavage.

"Do you need camisoles?" I asked, mindful of her student budget.

She laughed and pulled up the front of her dress. "I have some. I just didn't have time to do laundry." She wasn't trying to be sexy; she was oblivious. But I didn't want anyone ogling her boobs. I wasn't using sex to sell books.

"You could always join #FreetheNipple," I teased, as she drove over the bridge. I'd just read about it online while waiting for her. It had started as a documentary by Lina Esco, an outspoken feminist,[3] in support of a woman arrested for being "topless" on a beach. Being "shirtless" is legal for both sexes, so perhaps the police simply needed a dictionary. The woman sued and eventually won. The protesters supporting her paraded bare-chested in an effort to desexualize their body parts. Twitter banned their boobs, so celebrities stepped in and posted their own topless photos. I wasn't sure how much was for the cause and how much was for publicity, but it didn't matter. I'd rather have my daughter strip for a cause than for *Girls Gone Wild*.

"No way," Juliette laughed. "I'm not a feminist."

What the fuck? My breath caught in my chest. I tried to control my rage at this denial of everything I believed in, every effort to raise her as a respectable human being from the first moment she suckled at my breast. Clearly, I had not done my job as a mother of girls. I counted to ten slowly until I could speak in a calm voice.

"Hon, you are a female. By definition you are femin-ine, femin-ist. Don't you want to get the same paycheck as the guy who sat next to you at graduation yesterday?"

She took her gaze off the traffic to give me the side-eye, as if I was the crazy one.

I pushed on. "You're OK making seventy-six cents to his dollar? Lucky you're not black or it drops to sixty-three cents. If you were Hispanic—"

"Mom!"

"Sorry, I looked it up when I compared your tuition to average salaries for copywriters. I love that this school has a 94 percent employment rate, but there's no law saying you'll make the same as your classmates."

She shot me a look. Then she explained that the F-word made it sound like women were superior. She was referring to the "man-hating women's libbers" from her nana's day. She thought their bad reputation made them fail.

This was a classic "straw man" argument. Since those who opposed feminism couldn't argue against equal pay, they claimed these women hated men. It was completely unrelated but repeated so often that any woman talking about equal pay got a bad rap. The failure of that first wave was just as my mother had predicted: a lack of focus on child-care. Twenty years later, the same roadblocks led to my own career change, and the compromise I made to care for this entitled brat sitting beside me.

I rolled down the window to get some air. I didn't want to make Juliette feel guilty about the choices I made; I just needed her to understand. Feminism is about equality, not superiority. When I started working at home, her father took pride in paying the mortgage. But didn't she hear how he mocked my income? Did I have to remind her of the time he hit me when dinner was late? She saw me on the floor, my bruised lip, my utter failure. Money is where the power lies. She was lucky she hadn't faced the hypocrisy yet, at least not enough to notice. Oh, how naïve.

"What if you get pregnant?" I said. "Do you have any idea how much that would slow you down compared to the baby daddy?"

She was quiet, probably thinking of famous female business leaders. But they were exceptions, not the rule. As long as women had babies and breasts to feed them, we would be dismissed. Or was the word "oppressed"?

Maybe the word "feminism" did sound superior, but that was merely semantics. In any negotiation, don't you fight to compromise for what's fair? Even Harvard graduates hadn't solved the motherhood challenge. The majority of them stayed home. The only playing field I'd seen leveled was the divorce court. Several of my hardworking girlfriends paid alimony to deadbeat, cheating ex-husbands. But that wasn't the point.

We drove past an adult video store displaying a poster of a half-naked woman wearing star-shaped nipple pasties. I looked over at my beautiful daughter behind the wheel while she steered us through the city with ease. Her dress had slipped down again. My pride was mixed with concern about her false confidence. Juliette trusted that she would be treated fairly, not exploited for her body, and that was my fault. Instead of raising her to expect equal rights, I should have taught her how to fight for them. But how?

At City Lights Books, the bearded manager was polite. I autographed the books in stock as he looked at the cover depicting a little girl running into the woods. I felt compelled to explain that the girl in the story was actually a teenager involved with sex, drugs, and a murder trial. Then he opened the book club guide, a stapled collection of discussion questions and ideas. He saw recipes for Hawaiian dishes, since an important chapter takes place there, and I felt feminine in the weakest sense. I turned to the page with a Spotify playlist of Doors music, since rock lyrics are clues in the book. Then I waved Juliette back from the rack of Neil Gaiman books to raise my hip quotient.

As I signed books from one end of the city to the other, I wished I'd used unisex initials instead of my feminine name. When men wrote about families, it was considered "real" literary fiction. Men got automatic respect, like when dads "babysit" their own kids. I kept finding my novel shelved in rows labeled "women's fiction." Eighty percent of book buyers are women, but this was not the high-status shelf. I did find a bestseller by Nicole Krauss with the mainstream fiction, but she usually wrote from a man's perspective. And she was on record saying she'd been pressured to wear low-cut dresses for publicity pictures.[4] Thanks partly to the rants of best-selling author Jennifer Weiner, a female reviewer had finally been hired at the *New York Times Book Review*. But I didn't expect much change. The problem was similar with popular fiction. Look at any best-seller list. Mostly male authors ruled especially when writing detective and crime. These were popular genres, so they earned big advances, lots of promotion, and sold a lot of books. It was a self-confirming cycle.

I had another idea. Instead of using initials to pretend I'm a man, why not give men what they really want? I vowed to put boobs on my next cover. I chuckled to myself. Juliette looked over, but I didn't explain. This would sound like sour grapes, and I wanted to have a nice day.

As we headed over the Bay Bridge to Oakland, Juliette's phone buzzed. Her boyfriend had already checked in, so she expected it to be her dad calling en route to the airport. I shrugged to let her know I didn't mind her answering. Happily, it was her sister, so she clicked the speakerphone button, and we both shouted hello. While the girls planned a private call for later, I took out my own phone to email some graduation pictures.

The image prior to the first balloon-filled shot was a photo of Chloe in her chef outfit. She looked so cute, completely hidden in white, with her name embroidered over her chest. If not for her smiling face, it could have been someone of either sex.

"Did you see her uniform?" I waited until we were stopped at the next light to tilt the screen toward her. She nodded. I didn't know how often they talked, but surely there were no secrets. I couldn't resist. "Has she mentioned wanting a breast augmentation?" I was too embarrassed to say boob job.

"Mother," she said, "Who cares?"

"Apparently, your sister cares," I said, wishing she would just call me Mom. "And she's not alone. I read that over three hundred thousand American women will get implants this year. But you already have curves."

"Just lucky, I guess." She laughed and pushed her thick hair behind her ear before continuing. "My only concern is, what if she changes her mind? She's pretty indecisive these days. Like about quitting culinary school."

Oh, crap. My silence prompted a furtive glance from Juliette, so I pretended to already know this. "Those pots are heavy."

"Especially with those hooks in her shoulder," she agreed.

"And the ex-gang member who's always texting her," I said. Chloe couldn't block the man's number when he was in every class. She had complained to the instructor, but all he could do was warn the man, which made it awkward. The class was small and she was one of the few females. That archaic belief that women belong in the kitchen referred only to the ones at home.

"Maybe it's just not as fun for her to cook anymore," Juliette suggested.

"Could be. It's just as important to find out what you don't want to do as what you do." I checked the map and pointed to a shady cul-de-sac of shops. "I'm more worried about the boob job idea."

"I don't think she'll try out for *Playboy*, if that's your concern."

"It wasn't until now, thanks."

She wasn't referring to a potential mother-daughter legacy. She had no idea what I'd done. This was the upside of the narcissism of youth—they didn't want to hear their parents' stories. By now, *The Girls Next Door* had run its course, but *Keeping Up With the Kardashians* was another freight train to hell. Without *Playboy*, could the Kardashians have launched a financial empire from a sex tape? Chloe claimed to watch because she missed our old house, and their store was so close that our former mailcarrier could be spotted on their show. I just hoped she wasn't one of the millions who broke Twitter after Kim posted another "liberating" boob shot. Some said she was the most influential person on social media. And I was just as guilty of reality-show rubbernecking.

"What about *The Bachelor?*" I asked. "You guys are both the right age." I heard myself say guys instead of girls, but I didn't know why. Did the male word sound more powerful, even to me? Then I realized that show had a similar allure as the one I felt answering the ad for *Playboy* back in the day. I wanted public approval that my daughters were pretty enough to be picked. They'd look gorgeous in evening gowns. But the thought of seeing them fall for the fantasy made me shiver.

"That show is so stupid," Juliette said. "All those people competing to get married."

"See, you are a feminist!"

After we parked in front of A Great Good Place for Books, an independent bookstore that lived up to its name, I reached over the car console to give her a hug. In real life, of course, I wanted her to be happily married someday. I hoped she and her sister would find partners who loved and respected them as equals. That was my fantasy. I picked up my last box of book club guides and climbed out of the car.

On the way back to the hotel late that afternoon, the tented booths of a street fair blocked our route. Juliette pulled to the curb beyond the clanging cable cars at Union Square a few blocks from my hotel. I gave her a long, hard hug. I was flying home in the morning, so it was impossible not to cry. Now she would be looking for a job and starting her grown-up life. We released our embrace, and I saw her blue bra strap slip down her shoulder, a sign of poor fit. The towering glass entrance of Victoria's Secret was visible, so I pointed in that direction. It was a plea for more time.

"Hey, want to shop, then watch *Mad Men* with us at the hotel? With your degree in advertising, it's practically research."

"Thanks, but I just want to go home and watch *Game of Thrones*."

I nodded, and climbed out of the car. She didn't care about history; she was all about the dream.

"Any last thoughts about your sister?" I asked. Stalling, but serious.

"It's her body."

Smarty-pants. I thanked her for the day, climbed out to the curb, and shoved the door shut. "I love you!"

She blew me a kiss and drove off. I waved goodbye, picturing her with pizza and beer and her boyfriend, watching the flat-screen TV I'd sent last Christmas. Did she notice the bare breasts more in high definition or did they look like wallpaper in the background? She rooted for the Mother of Dragons, but for every queen, there were dozens of exploited slave girls. Did she take the female nudity for granted, see it as something that just happened on TV? Did she equate it with the kind of sacrifice she might have to make to launch her own career? Or did she simply watch it the way it was written and directed, from a male point of view?

After I lost view of Juliette's taillights in the stream of Sunday night traffic, it hit me that she said she was going *home*. My baby was never coming back. Home was here in San Francisco, far away from me. I missed her already.

Sobbing, I turned toward the hotel. Thank goodness it was Sunday night. Then I panicked that the hotel might not have AMC. Without the distraction of *Mad Men*, I would be sad all night. Juliette surely had it, since her other favorite was *The Walking Dead*. The zombie apocalypse series featured death and dismemberment every week, but I'd read that when a machete sliced off a woman's bloody breast, the censors made them blur the nipple. Had she noticed that? I wiped my eyes with my sleeve and took a deep breath.

She was gone now, from my sight and my influence, and I feared for her worldview. Exhausted from the long weekend, I trod down the sidewalk and narrowly dodged a group of girls. They were giddy with triumph, pink bags in hand, outside the gilded doors of Victoria's Secret.

Back in Los Angeles the next afternoon, I stopped by Chloe's studio apartment to drop off a bag of Ghirardelli peppermint bark, her favorite. When I knocked, she shouted from the couch to come in. She was lounging in sweatpants while she looked at her computer screen. She pushed a few bottles of nail polish aside, so I could see the face of a high school girlfriend, a familiar brunette with a trembling smile who was overseas in the Israeli army. Oh, the miracle of technology. I made small talk, brushing off a compliment about the bandanna tied around my bald head, then excused myself to go to the bathroom and give them privacy.

There was only one square of toilet paper clinging to the cardboard roll, so I opened the cabinet under the sink. No Charmin, but I did spy a familiar striped pink shopping bag in the back. It was filled with a jumble of rubber blobs that lived up to their nickname, chicken cutlets. There were also foam bra inserts, some covered with so much lint that I suspected they'd been fished from my own trash can years earlier.

Until recently, I had put Chloe's figure in the category of the high fashion models a few inches taller. Maybe she wanted to be closer to the Victoria's Secret Angels. Many were rumored to have small implants, called the "Brazilian B."[5] Apparently plastic surgery is no big deal in Brazil, where many of the current models were from. Women boasted about it. In America, we pretend not to paint our faces or dye our hair. We want to be as naturally beautiful as the Victoria's Secret Angels. OK, maybe not everyone. But here was the ubiquitous pink bag right under the sink. Since it wasn't within easy access to her underwear drawer, she probably wasn't using them. She wanted real ones. I pushed the bag back where I found it and grabbed a box of Kleenex.

The following Saturday, my mother sat in my living room, resplendent in navy blue slacks, a matching top, and simple gold jewelry. Chloe sat across from her with shining hair and manicured nails. She wore a white T-shirt and jeans in a way that looked equally elegant. My mother's poodle, Pierre, a cliché that made me bite my lip, yapped at my heels as I served them sparkling water.

After retreating to my office, I hovered in the doorway to eavesdrop. I failed to hear a word, so I tiptoed back to my desktop and typed "boob jobs," the only phrase I hadn't googled yet. Wow, lots of links for this. I clicked on celebrity quotes and learned that actress Kaley Cuoco got one at eighteen and said it was the best decision she ever made.[6] Naya Rivera, who also got one at eighteen, was so excited she told all her teachers at high school.[7] Denise Richards regretted hers at nineteen, but mostly she blamed herself for not checking out the doctor. Same with Tara Reid, famous for her botched boob job. Oh crap. Kate Upton, that year's *Sports Illustrated* swimsuit edition cover girl, was Chloe's age. Wait, Upton's boobs were real. How was that fair?

I was still reading about celebrities when I heard the click-click-click of Pierre's nails on the hardwood floor. My mother's footsteps followed, then she leaned her blond bob into my office. I stood to face her. The slam of the front door echoed from the hall behind her. It sounded angry, so I tried not to smile.

My mother announced that her granddaughter understood that surgery wasn't the answer to angst over life in general. However, she did believe that it could make Chloe feel more confident. She said it couldn't hurt to look into it, but only with a board-certified surgeon. I was disappointed, both at her response and the idea I'd let any doctor who wasn't board-certified lay a hand on a child of mine.

Eureka! That was the solution: take her to *my* doctor. Dr. Calvert was her doctor, too. Years of softball had periodically dislocated her shoulder, but an aggressive water polo game caused the most damage. An orthopedic surgeon installed hooks in her shoulder and neurologists shrugged at her concussion results. Dr. C had grafted skin from her scalp for her sinus repair, so he was the perfect person to consult. We both trusted him, and now he had four children of his own. Surely, he would talk her out of it. I'd get all the credit and none of the blame.

A few weeks later, we sat at the end of a leather couch on the tenth floor waiting room of the Beverly Hills surgical office. Several doctors held office hours that day, so the chairs were full of men and women—but mostly women—in pursuit of perfection. Chloe texted someone while I retied my headscarf and read about our doctor's Patients' Choice Award. The twenty-something woman in the velvet chair beside us kept glancing at me as if we'd met. She flipped through a scrapbook of photographs, then she moved to squeeze in beside me on the couch. Chloe moved over to give us room.

At first, I feared she recognized me from the before and after boob book. I sipped my complementary bottle of water and hoped the photo showing my collarbone hadn't given me away. Then I realized there was a big lump from my port there now, and no hair grazing my shoulders. She pointed at the article I was reading and bragged that she was seeing the same doctor. She said he was such an expert that he'd just returned from a European lecture tour. She had exactly enough time between graduate school semesters to get her nose done. Her nose looked fine to me. When I smiled, she mistook it for interest and showed me the photographs of her favorites. I was about to say I wasn't sure it worked that way, but she was already describing her ears and her chin and the parts she would fix next.

Chloe and I exchanged eye rolls in a sweet moment of bonding.

"What are you studying?" I asked, to be polite.

"I'm going to be a psychologist," she said.

I stifled a laugh. Chloe's eyes widened in horror before she turned away. When a nurse called the woman in, I felt guilt by association. She was an example of my greatest fear, being here, as they would say on *The Bachelor*, "for the wrong reasons."

Chloe's name was called. I held back. This was her deal and I wanted no part of it. But she waved me in, so I grabbed my purse and followed. If she thought this was a show of support, she was mistaken.

In the examination room, Dr. Calvert asked how I was doing. He had been my first call when I was sick, so I appreciated his friendly concern. I also appreciated he didn't mention how different I looked from when I saw him last. Then I went to look out the window at the Hollywood Hills to stay out of the way. Also, to signal him to dissuade my daughter.

First, he checked the swathe of bare scalp hidden beneath her hair. He said he could fix that whenever she was ready.

"We met a woman in the waiting room who was having a bunch of stuff done," I said. "She mentioned being here because you are famous for noses. Is that all you're doing now?" I smiled, hoping he would get the hint.

He chuckled and sat down on the rolling stool.

"I don't limit my practice. I do limit my patients, though." He shook his head. "That woman had issues that surgery would not fix. I turned her away."

Chloe and I exchanged grins, then I sat down on the stool in the corner. This was the equivalent of a salesperson telling me the dress I was trying wasn't right. I trusted him even more now. Chloe worked in a clothing boutique, so we'd discussed this as a sales strategy. But she told me she did it honestly. It led to repeat customers. And voilà, here we were.

"So, what's up?" Dr. C asked. "What brings you here?"

Chloe explained that she had been waiting all her life to have breasts. She always wanted them, but they never came. She saw me shake my head before I knew I was doing it. She turned on me. "How could you not know that?"

I shrugged. She had never mentioned it that I recalled, but it had been a busy bunch of years since she hit puberty. The divorce, her sports injuries, her sister going to college, working my ass off to pay the bills, my cancer . . . She never wore baggy clothes to hide her figure. She spent money on lip gloss and nail polish. She was aware that people considered her pretty, even if she didn't think so. She had so many other challenges smack in the middle of adolescence that her looks seemed fail-safe. To me, anyway.

After Chloe put on a paper gown, the doctor returned with his assistant, Orla. I was tempted to ask Orla about her new baby. This, however, was not the time. When the doctor opened Chloe's robe, I kept my eyes averted. I hadn't seen her naked since the days when she changed in the back seat of the car on the way to softball games. No reason to invade her privacy now. I was no expert. I just wanted him to tell her what not to do.

He closed her robe and nodded to her.

She smiled.

I panicked. "Maybe if she gains weight, she'll gain all over."

She shot me a look so hot, I felt sunburnt. I gave Dr. C a pleading look.

He wrapped his fingers around her thin wrist. "She's small-boned. Her body structure won't support enough weight to make a difference."

Strike one. I tried again. "Maybe she's still growing."

He looked up at Chloe, who had at least three inches on me. "How old are you?"

"Twenty-one."

He looked at me and shook his head.

Strike two. Why had I not emailed him in advance? Did he think my presence condoned this? He took the measuring tape from Orla and started measuring my daughter's ribs.

"Shouldn't she wait?" I asked, flailing now. "Even car rental companies have an age requirement of twenty-five. That's when the brain is mature."

"Why not enjoy them when you're young?"

Or when it's fun, he might have said. I wasn't sure. He wasn't talking to me. But I refused to strike out on this one. The twenties is a dangerous decade of life, when everyone is young and foolish. Didn't I flaunt my body then? I was angry now, frustrated at the fashion magazines that showed us the importance of looking sexy. Teen magazines and twenty-something websites were just as bad. Hell, I could barely read the cover of *Cosmo* at the grocery store without blushing. Sure, it was our biological imperative, our hormones, that drove us to compete for the most capable father to our offspring, to promote the very survival of our species, but geez. The whole thing had gotten out of hand.

Now Dr. C was telling Chloe how one client nearly caused a car accident just by walking down the street.

"She already does that," I said. He was no help.

"I don't doubt it." He looked up at her face. "Plenty of women would like your lips."

She had my mother's full lips, damn it. She turned to me.

"Don't worry, Mother, I don't care about that. Boys are stupid." We exchanged chuckles, both thinking of a ditty that a friend of hers sang on her voice mail. *I like boys, boys like me. . . .*

Dr. Calvert returned to the purpose of her consultation. Her purpose, not mine. "How big are you thinking?" Small, I wanted to say, in proportion. In my anxiety, I missed her answer.

"What are you, five-seven? Five-eight?" He studied her with his chin in his hand like Sherlock Fucking Holmes. He called numbers out to Watson over there with the clipboard.

"Why not the smallest you have?" I asked, a scientific query, as if I had no agenda at all.

"Since she's tall, her ribs are wider apart," he said. "One size does not fit all." He glanced at me as if protecting my privacy, as if she didn't know what filled out my blouse.

Would she even be here if she didn't know I had them? Would she be comfortable to go under the knife if I hadn't? That was the real problem, I realized, leaning against the counter in the tiny exam room. I felt like a horrible role model. I had tried to teach her the value of hard work, a healthy lifestyle, and the golden rule. When she was young, I countered Disney princesses with Brio trucks and drove her all over the city to build character in sports. She knew real beauty comes from inside. Yet I'd also demonstrated that external beauty matters, at least to me. And it could be bought. This was not a family tradition I wanted to start. I was still judgmental about breast implants, even though I had them.

"Shouldn't she wait until after she has children?" I asked. "So she can nurse?"

"She can still nurse," Dr. Calvert said.

Strike three. I was out. As he went over the risks with her, I heard something about nipple sensitivity and had one last thought. Did she know this was about sex? About the irony of having breasts that lured men's mouths, but no longer felt so good? Probably not. But I didn't feel comfortable enough to explain.

"Let's take some pictures," the doctor said, and stood up.

I escaped to the waiting room to stew. After a few minutes of tapping my feet, I realized I could feel my toes again. The neuropathy had finally passed. I was smiling to myself when Cerissa, the finance person, led my daughter through the waiting room to her office. She waved. I waved back. A young professional, she wore a silk blouse with slacks. I couldn't tell if she had implants, which was comforting, since Chloe adored her. She was a good role model.

Chloe emerged a few minutes later, eyes cast toward the marble floor. A sheaf of papers protruded from her faux leather purse. She now knew that in addition to the doctor's fee, there is a high price for the supplies, the surgery room, the anesthesiologist, and a series of pre-op blood tests. The implant manufacturer also advised replacement after ten or so years. Twenty percent of patients have complications. This was a budget decision for life.

Now I had her. I reached up for her hand to help me off the deep sofa. Then I lowered my voice. "Look, hon, I will support you in whatever you decide to do. But I won't pay for it. You're an adult. This is your deal."

She nodded, quiet as I said goodbye to the receptionist and opened the door. In the hallway, she turned back and smiled. "I can't wait to fill out a bathing suit."

A few years later, I mentioned my obsession with breasts at the start of a luncheon at Spago's in Beverly Hills. I wore my best dress in a sea of suits, women at the top of male-dominated professions. Two hours later, I dug out my parking ticket and looked up to see a dozen women surrounding me. They all had daughters who wanted breast implants. These women danced on the double-edged sword of attractiveness in their careers. They did what they needed to compete. Yet, many were also mothers and, like millions of others, they were conflicted over the message of beauty. They looked to me for answers. I could only shrug.

As we headed outside, a bank director spoke up. "My grandmother celebrated her ninetieth birthday last week."

"That's wonderful," I said, relieved to change the subject.

A smile played around her lips as she handed the valet her ticket. "She only has one regret in life: not getting breast implants."

We laughed. No matter how young or old, the dream of perfect breasts can be alluring. It seems like the answer to everything. The reality is not always so sweet.

Breast Myths and Facts

Myths

1. Looking at naked breasts is good for men's health.

2. Sagging can be avoided by: wearing a bra while sleeping, avoiding exercise, avoiding nursing.

3. Small-breasted women are less likely to get breast cancer.

4. Breasts can grow with special cream, pills, massage, or exercise.

5. Breast cancer is caused by: antiperspirants, storing cell phones in bra, implants, caffeine, tight bras, abortion.

Facts

1. Breasts, also known as mammary glands, are the only human organs with no medical specialty.

2. Humans are the only primates with permanent breasts.

3. Women are less likely to get CPR due to rescuers' fear of touching breasts—and the lack of dummies with breasts for training.

4. Age of breast growth is usually eight to nineteen.

5. Drooping occurs when fat replaces connective tissue during aging.

6. The left breast is usually up to 20% larger.

7. There are different nipple shapes: protruding, flat, puffy, or inverted.

8. The average breast contains 4 to 5% of body's total fat and weighs 1–2 pounds.

9. Breasts can grow up to a full cup size during the menstrual cycle.

10. Pregnancy often causes nipples to temporarily darken.

11. 200,000 Americans are born with three (or more) nipples every year. Most of that number are men.[1]

Sixteen

PICASSO BOOBS
2014

I was upside down in yoga class when I noticed something was off. Seconds before, I'd been in a state of bliss, gazing up through the window at a palm tree rising into the blue sky. Our instructor, Jeff, was blasting music ranging from the Rolling Stones to Rihanna. My hands were clasped under my arched back as I pushed my knees up in bridge position. My flexibility was compromised by meds, so when Jeff said to push higher, I lowered my gaze from the window to try. That's when I saw it. The mound of my left breast obscured my view as it should, but on the right, I could see my ribs, my hip bone, and Jeff's bald head in the front of the room. Where the hell was my breast?

Oh, there it was, pointing at Debra. She was next to me in the back, where we'd met when I was a newlywed with a ponytail. Now my head was covered with chemo curls and I was whispering to her in desperation.

"Does my boob look funny to you?"

Debra shrugged the best she could with her shoulders pinned to the mat. "Nobody's looking at your boob."

I knew what she meant. We weren't in the back just for fresh air, but also to avoid comparison to the younger, hotter contortionists in the front. Debra and I, both over fifty, shared everything from fashion magazines to frisky ideas for date night. I rolled over and reached for the crumpled Kleenex on the floor behind us.

"Are you crying?" Debra sat up and drank from her water bottle. At least it wasn't pink plastic with a ribbon logo, like the one by the woman's mat in front of me.

I shook my head no and wiped my drippy eyes. The damn chemo had burned out my nasal passages. A new song filled the yoga studio with a woman's strong, clear voice. I raised my eyebrows, or at least my forehead where they used to be, and pointed to the stereo.

Debra mouthed, "Madonna," and got back into position.

Ugh, I should have known. Jeff and his husband loved Madonna. I refused to put her on my playlist. When my girls were little, it was a struggle to keep them from seeing her sexy music videos. When Madonna had kids, she banned them from watching TV. Hypocrite. Her breasts weren't as nice as Emily Ratajkowski's, bared beside two fully dressed men in last year's record-breaking video for Robin Thicke's "Blurred Lines." But Ratajkowski, called the "Mozart of breasts,"[1] defended Madonna's right to show them. Yet even Ratajkowski's perfect orbs had been airbrushed by a magazine to be perkier.[2] As someone who needed more than airbrushing, I hated them both.

At home, I stripped off my sports bra and stared in the mirror. The radiologist had warned about "capsular contraction," but that was in the fine print for any implants. This was not just hardening scar tissue. This boob had balled up and rolled clear to my clavicle. Happy Pinktober! Again.

It occurred to me that my breast had burned to the touch for a few weeks now. I had figured it was just a phase and stopped sleeping on that side. It *was* a phase, but one that was getting more painful. How had I thought I'd skate past thirty-six blasts of nuclear radiation?

The more I looked at the reflection of my chest, the more it reminded me of the Picasso painting on my late grandfather's wall. A Russian Jew whose family escaped the Bolshevik Revolution, he'd worked his way up to the American dream and celebrated his success with the purchase of *Standing Nude and Seated Musketeer*. As a little girl, I had stared up at the painting in his living room. The naked, pink woman stood behind and to the left of an enormous man dressed in a fancy blue suit. A black circle represented the woman's left breast. There was a tiny black circle higher up on the right, but I wasn't sure whether it was the other breast or a hole in her neck. The painting was donated to the Metropolitan Museum of Art before I had the courage to ask. Perhaps Señor Picasso was simply expressing his cubist view of boobs. I was not a fan.

Then again, most people loved Picasso. The Keep A Breast Foundation raised money by selling plaster casts of women's chests as sculpture.[3] Maybe I could donate a cast of my Picasso boobs—I mean, breasts. Boobs might sound derogative. Better than a hundred other nicknames, though. A couple of tweens in Pennsylvania had been suspended from school in 2010 for wearing "I Love Boobies" bracelets on Breast Cancer Awareness Day.[4] That seemed crazy, since "boobies" was already a cartoon word. These girls had the balls to fight the school district in court. "Balls?" Yikes, did I really use a male metaphor for strength? Everyone knows balls are more delicate than any pussy. "Balls" is just easier to say.

My schedule was checkered with doctors' appointments that week, so I could ask about my chest. Two years out from diagnosis, medical surveillance was still my lifestyle: MRIs with intravenous ink, PET scans, prescription adjustments, blood tests, and more breast exams. The only doctor out of the loop was my radiologist. When I called the clinic, I was told he'd moved. At least he couldn't say, "I told you so."

In the quiet waiting room at the Breast Center, I skimmed a pile of dog-eared celebrity magazines. On the bottom lay a subscription issue of *New York* with a winking yellow emoji on the cover. Up for some cheer, I opened it to learn I'd just missed "Pretty Hurts" week. That reminded me of Beyoncé's recent song of that name. The title video opened with her in a cone bra, then showed cleavage to compete with anorexic beauty queens in a pageant. She sang about the evils of perfection while wearing sparkly bunny ears for the talent portion. The video ended with her trashing a bunch of trophies. In reality, Beyoncé's postbaby bod looked so amazing that it undercut her message. I chuckled. A woman with her eyes closed in meditation looked up. Now I felt bad. It was hard to keep a sense of humor in cancer world.

Twenty minutes later, I was in the exam room, sitting on the end of the table and baring my lopsided breasts for Dr. Giuliano. A nurse in her sixties who was updating my file looked over. I joked that I was no longer a science experiment; now I was a work of art.

"You know, like Picasso?"

No one laughed. Dr. G shook his head at the clumsy stitch marks under my left collarbone where a random surgeon had cut out my portocath. I tried not to wince as he pressed the thin white seam above my right areola and nodded at his superior handiwork. He'd excavated tumor and tissue multiple times with nary a mark. The nurse smiled.

"Thank you," I said. "But see how this breast is so much higher than the other?"

"The good news is your scans are clear," he said. "The bad news is that this mutation could get worse."

The word "mutation" made me cringe. "Can you fix it?"

"Why risk another surgery?" he asked.

Humbled, I dropped my gaze to his lab coat, embroidered with his name and a trail of initials. This was the man in charge of the entire Breast Center, among the finest in the country. He practically invented Save the Tatas. He'd given me two lumpectomies instead of a mastectomy, all in the service of saving my life. I was alive and that's what mattered.

The nurse patted her own chest. "You get used to it."

My shoulders instantly relaxed. It helped to have another sister in pink present. Apparently, my Picasso was not a limited edition. But did she mean I would get used to the pain?

As Dr. G probed the divot in my otherwise rock-hard breast, I realized I'd gotten used to a lot of painful things. What was one more? I peered around him to peek at the nurse's chest. It was impossible to determine what lay beneath her scrubs. That was the point of clothes anyway, right? Maybe my fashion days were over. Some women lived with ugly boobs and, lo and behold, it didn't ruin their lives. The nurse caught my eye, so I smiled to be polite. How long had she lived like that? Did it still hurt? Then I noticed her plain gold wedding band and wondered about her sex life.

"I do appreciate your work to keep me alive," I told Dr. G. "But I'm kind of newly married." After eighteen months of treatment, date nights were finally manageable again, at least after a glass of wine. Now I would need two, and a turtleneck.

Dr. G's face crinkled with kindness. "Your husband loves you," he said. As if a good husband wouldn't care.

He was right. I was being shallow, vain, and ungrateful. I gave him a goodbye hug that had to feel lopsided, but, apparently, he was used to it. He said he'd see me again in a few months and strode out of the exam room. I wasn't going to argue, to demean my husband for being a regular guy. He wasn't a boob man, per se, but. . . . Honestly, I didn't know how my husband would feel, but I knew how I felt: frustrated.

After they left, I strapped on my brassiere. My left breast plopped firmly into the cup. The right one stayed where it was. I needed to stop seeing my chest as half empty and start seeing it as half full. As I buttoned my blouse, my wrist brushed against my boob. Ouch.

Wait! I forgot to tell him how much it hurt. This was the doctor who mourned my long hair, who held me as I cried over chemo. I opened the door and scanned the hospital hallway, but it was full of women, some tearful, some stoic, but all in white waffle-textured smocks being escorted to and from sterile rooms. Nurses in pastel scrubs were deep in conversation at the appointment desk. My doctor was off saving someone else's life. This was silly. I could handle this kind of pain. It wouldn't kill me.

For the next few weeks of yoga, I wore a baggy T-shirt. At home, I wore a bathrobe until the lights went out. On date nights, I wore lace lingerie and refused to take it off. When I got a postcard from Nordstrom to buy a breast cancer gift card, I threw it away without complaint. My implant grew harder and higher every day.

I dug out my medical records and saw there was nothing listed as a lumpectomy. Must be a nickname. My procedures were both labeled: Mastectomy, Segmental. In the notes, Dr. G reported discussing a mastectomy. I did not remember that discussion. Did any woman hear everything that was said in such moments? The medical record also noted that I understood there would be "deformity." But what could I do now? Since a mastectomy wouldn't raise my odds of survival, I'd never explored reconstruction.

Besides, I figured everyone would choose a lumpectomy if they could. According to statistics, I was wrong. A lot of women didn't want to risk a mutilated breast. They wanted a brand new one. More intriguing was that more and more women chose to cut off both breasts when only one was diseased.[5] Some didn't want to live with a ticking time bomb. Others wanted some semblance of control. The fear of being powerless was familiar. I had never imagined this would happen to me. Now, every morning as I gulped down half a dozen pills, I was humbled.

At my next oncology appointment in October, the lab technician drew enough blood to feed a vampire. The little stuffed Dracula that hung from the lab ceiling with a paper clip looked like he was laughing. In the exam room with Dr. Leiber, I reported all my current meds: hormone blockers, bone meds to counteract the blockers, seven daily supplements for other side effects, Latisse to grow eyelashes, preservative-free eye drops, dry mouth lozenges, and various ointments to urge my fingernails back to normal. I asked if I could take an herbal remedy for the hot flashes that had been hitting every few hours for two fucking years. My husband still kept to his side of the bed in fear of drowning. The doctor said no, there was no testing that proved it wouldn't hinder the hormone blockers. I had three years to go; better sweaty than dead.

He noticed my Picasso boobs as soon as he did the usual breast check. There was no way to palpitate the hard one. He offered to prescribe the third level of BRCA testing, which had come down in price, in case the cost had influenced my decision.

Since Angelina Jolie's recent *New York Times* editorial about her prophylactic mastectomy, there had been a noticeable uptick in genetic tests. I heard her doctor, Kristi Funk, speak at a luncheon where she mentioned writing a blog about Jolie's difficult reconstruction with implant expanders that were filled up over a period of months. It sounded like slow torture. I hadn't read it yet. Like most women, however, I saw the impressive results in her low-cut top.[6] They were known as "bomb boobs," a nickname that harkened back to those 1950s bombshells.

A friend of mine endured a more natural alternative, a DIEP flap surgery that used her own body fat, like liposuction. This kind of surgery had so many risks of infection, open wounds, and other problems that hospitals like Johns Hopkins no longer offered it. Other flap surgeries posed risks as well. Many factors were considered in these choices, generally made under duress. A more futuristic option was to grow breasts from regenerative stem cell properties. Cytori, the San Diego company developing the process, was still working toward FDA approval for clinical trials.[7] So far, it was the breast cells that worked best to repair damaged tissue of other organs, including hearts. Reports noted the difficulty of shaping a breast to look natural. And by "natural," they meant perfect.

Everywhere I looked, from *Woman's Day* magazine to BodyRock-Fitness.com, breast shape was touted as an indicator of personality. While that was absurd, how much of this seeps into our perception? Is this why we focus so much on the appearance part of cancer recovery? Reconstruction surgeries were up 7 percent.[8] The number was rising, but it was still low, due to lack of information offered by the cancer doctors and the low availability of plastic surgeons. Doctors who supported reconstruction took it as a sign the patient was committed to recovery. A female doctor suggested that those surgeons preferred reconstruction because they were proud of their ability to do it. I wondered if they also feared losing the hard-won insurance coverage. Then I read that the president of the American Society of Plastic Surgery (now head of plastic surgery at University of Chicago) emphasized the visual benefit of being "more youthful, with a better aesthetic" than before.

When my breast started throbbing, I considered whacking it off like an Amazon woman. According to myth, they sacrificed a breast to excel at archery. But there was no evidence to prove it.[9] Greek storytellers, all men, probably made that up. How else could they get men to believe that a real tribe of tall, strong women could be such successful warriors?

During another sleepless night, I found a TED Talk by Darryle Pollack, a former TV anchor. She went through every kind of treatment for breast cancer, as well as every kind of hell. She started out well-endowed, but her body rejected reconstruction. Her TED Talk warned against perfection. Boy, did she hit the bull's-eye. ("Boy?" Here I am using male words again.) At this point, Pollack was a ceramic artist who created collages called Boobalas to show that "women's breasts don't define who we are."[10] Breasts had become her business.

In an impulsive moment, I emailed Pollack. She emailed back. Ah, the sisterhood. She told me about a textile artist named Melanie Testa. When Testa rejected reconstruction of her DDs, her doctor suggested she see a psychiatrist.[11]

In honor of Pinktober in 2014, Today.com featured a story about Barbie Ritzco, a Marine gunnery sergeant who ignored the growing lump in her breast to lead her troops, then stayed flat to be "free of things most women worry about their whole life." What a relief to know that a war hero had these same issues. She helped start a Facebook group called Flat and Fabulous to help others in a "breast obsessed world."[12] More proof it wasn't just me. I scrolled down to see a closer shot of her tattoo, a heart of flowers.

I loved the idea of chest art. Every man I'd ever met said that women were the real works of art. They meant it as a compliment, but maybe that's why we accept the constant display of our bodies. We are flattered into being objectified, reduced to our female parts until it's normal to see breasts everywhere. Except for nipples, of course—that's pornographic. Fox News would soon blur the naughty bits of a real Picasso on the air. CNBC would blur the nipples of a Modigliano portrait that sold for $170 million.[13]

My breasts looked like a Picasso now, but without them I could be whatever I liked. The only tattoos I had so far were the dots around my rib cage to help technicians aim the laser beam of radiation. Why not grow them into a chest full of flowers? Better yet, a mermaid. If I needed more treatment, that's what I would do.

When I reached to turn off my computer, I noticed the dates under Ritzco's picture. Even the Marines can't beat cancer.

I was lucky. A few nights earlier, as I avoided the painful boob in bed, Chloe had called. The mother of an elementary school friend who had the same type of hormone positive cancer as I did, but was diagnosed before Herceptin was available, had died. That drug, injected through my port every three weeks for a year, saved my life.

A few weeks later, it was November, and 2014 was declared as the year women "reclaimed our breasts."[14] Jessica Valenti, one of my favorite writers, applauded Keira Knightley's topless shot in *Interview* and comic Tig Notaro's comedy set after a double mastectomy. Chelsea

Handler was angry that her breasts were blurred on Instagram, and Facebook was finally lifting the ban on breastfeeding shots. Yet Valenti also admitted that breast cancer supporters were shouting "Save the Tatas," instead of "Save the Woman." It sounded like breasts were our priority, the part worth saving. She had a point.

To think that women were in charge was wishful thinking. This "year of the breast" looked like every other year, with cleavage over-flowing in holiday ads and novelty gifts, even a shampoo dispenser called Jingle Jugs. I wondered whether Valenti would reconsider when she read about vacation breasts in HuffPost.[15] Women in New York were getting temporary saline injections for special occasions. By December, the Sony hack revealed that people with breasts, from Academy Award winner Jennifer Lawrence to people in the executive offices to the production staff, were paid less than people without.[16] Yet breast augmentation was the most popular elective plastic surgery in America, with close to 300,000 procedures.[17]

I could relate. I'd had my implants for nine years now. The recom-mended term was ten. I was relatively safe from the cancer while I was on the hormone blockers, and the odds favored another negative BRCA test. What was I waiting for?

A week later, I was in Dr. Calvert's office on the examination chair, clutching my complementary bottle of water. Orla stood with the clip-board ready. Dr. C studied my chest quietly, like a problem to be solved. After a moment, he closed the flaps of my paper gown and sat back. I'd already told him how my oncology surgeon said I should leave them as is. Because I was, you know, alive. "What do you think?"

"I think he should cut his balls off and see if he feels like a man."

Laughing, I dropped my water. "I'm going to tell him you said that."

He shrugged, unthreatened. Dr. C was an internationally renowned expert in his own right. He helped people with horrible injuries. He had a wife, four young children, and commuted a hundred miles between offices in an energy-saving car. I'd even bumped into him late at night at a local pharmacy buying generic ice cream sandwiches to help a child swallow medicine. He was a good guy. And he was still shaking his head in my defense. I picked up my water bottle. If he thought breasts were as important as balls, then bravo. Except for one thing.

"Will insurance cover it?" I asked.

He nodded so hard a lock of dark hair fell to his forehead. "This was caused by cancer treatment. You need reconstruction. But radiated skin doesn't react like regular skin. It's tricky."

I nodded. Whatever. I knew that just as cancer could sprout up somewhere else, radiation damage could be found in cells forty years later.[18] Feeling invincible at the prospect of putting this whole nightmare behind me, I brushed it off. If anyone could help, he could.

Dr. C devised a plan to use the same size implants since the "pocket" of flesh was already there. The gap from the tumor was a problem he'd solve by padding it with AlloDerm, a bioengineered tissue. I wasn't sure if it was made from pigs or cadavers—and I didn't want to know. He said after the normal swelling, the implant should fall into place over time. He would need to do a lift to even out my nipples. I could handle the surgery and icky drains hanging off me for a few days, but I dreaded the sight of more scars. They'll fade, Dr. C assured me. A year from now, I'd barely notice.

Orla shot some before pictures of my Picasso boobs. I was tempted to ask for a copy to hang on the wall. I could frame it next to a print of *Standing Nude and Seated Musketeer*.

Standing Nude, No Musketeer.

After scheduling all the pre-op tests, I settled on the week before the holidays, and canceled other plans. On Sunday, I went to my last yoga class. This would all be worth it, I told myself. I had every right to have nice breasts. Soon, they would be perfect.

Or so I thought. Breasts, the gifts that keep on giving.

A Few Nicknames for Breasts

The word "boob" does not mean stupid. Or at least, it didn't used to. While Henry Miller is often credited for using it first in his 1934 erotica *The Tropic of Cancer*, "bubbies" can be found in a 1686 poem by Thomas D'Urfey, possibly baby-talk for the Latin "puppa," for "little girl." The fact that sixteenth-century sailors called the blue-footed Sula bird "booby" is a coincidence.

Airbags
Assets
Babies
Babs
Babushkas
Babylons
Balcony
Balloons
Bajongas
Bazongas
Bazookas
Bazooms
Bean Bags
Bee Stings
Big Ones
Bitties
Blinkers
Bolt-Ons
Bongos
Boobage

Boobies
Boobs
Bosoms
Boulders
Breasticles
Bubbalas
Buoys
Bust
Cannons
Cans
Cantaloupes
Cha-Chas
Charleys
Chest
Chesticles
Chest Puppies
Chestnuts
Cleavage
Coconuts
Cream Pies

Cupcakes
Cups
Cushions
Dinner Plates
Dirty Pillows
Double Ds
Double Lattes
Dream Team
Dumplings
Elmer Fudds
Feeders
Flapjacks
Flotation Devices
Flying Saucers
Fog Lights
Fun Bags
Gams
Gazongas
The Girls
Golden Globes

Goodies

Goodyears

Grapefruits

Grenades

Guns

Hangers

Headlights

High Beams

Honey Hams

Honkers

Hooters

Jingle Bells

Jugs

Kahunas

Kettledrums

Knockers

Lady Lumps

Liberty Bells

Life Preservers

Lollipops

Lunchables

Lungs

Mammaries

Maracas

Marshmallows

Meatballs

Melons

Milk Jugs

Milkers

Missiles

Mounds

Mountains

Mosquito Bites

Muchachas

Mudflaps

Na-Nas

Nectarines

Nips

Nuggets

Orbs

Pair

Patticakes

Peaches

Peaks

Peepers

Pillows

Points

Puppies

Rack

Rattlers

Rocket Launchers

Set

Shelf

Shoulder Boulders

Snugglepups

Softballs

Speedbumps

Squeezebox

Sweater Meat

Sweater Puppies

Swingers

Tatas

Tater Tots

Tats

Teats

Tennis Balls

Tetons

Tits

Titties

Torpedoes

Tracts of Land

The Twins

Twin Peaks

Udders

Umlauts

Watermelons

Wawas

Whoopee Cushions

Whoppers

Winnebagos

Wonderpeaks

W.M.D.s

Yabbos

Yahoos

Yams

YumYums

Seventeen

THE DEATH OF DADDY'S GIRL
2016

A year after stepping out of the shower and noticing that my nipples were cross-eyed, I had learned enough to understand how I became obsessed with breasts. But I was still unhappy with them. Now they were a work of art more like a Monet, pretty if you squinted from a distance. The left one was *Playboy* perfect, but the right, the one that tried to kill me, was still a bit higher, fuller, and pointed politely away. It was tempting to blame my doctor, but he warned me about radiated skin. He had a new plan to make them match, to fix them for good, but I hadn't scheduled the surgery. It would validate the belief that I was broken. This pursuit of perfection was troubling. But one thing was clear: I wasn't crazy.

At the YMCA, I climbed on the stair climber below a row of televisions offering sports, news, or entertainment. E! was showing graphic images of a woman's breast implant surgery. I was horrified, but none of the men working out missed a step. My eyes met those of a woman on the rowing machine. Her shrug gave me the courage to stop my workout and ask the manager to change the channel. There was power in numbers.

Soon after, I caught a rerun of *The Tonight Show*, with Jimmy Fallon playing a word game with Miley Cyrus. She shut him down by shouting, "I have boobs. I win!" I laughed so hard, I spilled tea on the bedsheets. So what if she stuck out her tongue and dressed in balloons? Her entire life had been dictated by men. After being controlled by her father, music producers, and TV executives, she was up for a fight. Weeks later, she'd been on *Jimmy Kimmel Live!*, where she pointed out the irony of the network censors approving the nipple-pasties under her barely there cape. Why is underboob, which only women have, acceptable, while nipples, which everyone has, obscene? I found the clip online one night and called my husband in to watch.

He froze the video and pointed out the heart-shaped pasties on Cyrus's nipples. "Because that's where you suck."

By "you," he meant everyone who mattered. Not babies. Men. Nipples were the intersection of the sacred and the profane. They were available for sucking far beyond the childbearing years. Why else were we the only mammals who spent most of our lives with developed breasts? Our bodies evolved to attract and enhance intimacy. This was about sex and the art of sex, a human activity designed purely for pleasure. And breasts were right here on our chests like targets.

"Sure," I said, "but why do they have to be plump and pert as in that brief window between puberty and pregnancy?" Now I was talking in circles, so I got up to brush my teeth. With such a fuzzy line between empowerment and exploitation, I wasn't alone in my confusion.

America, a country in adolescence, was stunted at second base. We couldn't have these pleasure domes distracting us from our productivity, so we hid them with clothing. But we also displayed them to be in fashion, a business based on the striptease. We took titillation for granted so much that it seemed normal even to women. And that made me want to punch someone. But who?

When my husband settled in beside me, I resisted taking it out on him. Sure, he was another white man, a part of the patriarchy. But it wasn't his fault. Our culture beats women down so consistently that we barely noticed. Like any victim of Stockholm syndrome, we identified with our captors to be safe. We pretended we didn't care until we truly didn't. It was too much fuss. We smiled to get along and hang tough with the boys and used their words to feel equal. But we were the furthest thing from equal. Not just by law, but by definition. We could change how we react, but we couldn't change the fact: We. Have. Breasts.

Eyes wide open, I couldn't un-see the endless attack on our bodies. When *The Good Wife* focused on breast censorship in the episode guest-starring Christina Ricci, critics called it a ratings ploy and advertisers argued all the way to the bank. When Kim Kardashian's topless tweet got 38,000 hits in ten minutes, she was praised for her marketing savvy. Popularity equaled success, even at the lowest common denominator. Nobody cared when Facebook proclaimed National Cleavage Day, and nobody blinked when Jenna Marbles's 17 million YouTube followers made "How To Trick People Into Thinking Your Boobs are Bigger" a favorite. Brock Allen Turner, the Stanford rapist, texted his friends a topless shot of his unconscious rape victim, and got off with a slap on the wrist. Because he was a good swimmer, the judge said. Rachel Bloom's hilarious boob videos were a springboard to her network TV hit, *Crazy Ex-Girlfriend*, where she got away with singing about big boob problems because her character was "crazy."

Just as the NFL players started pulling on those Pepto-Bismol colored socks, I cleaned out my bookcase and came across last Pinktober's *New Yorker* magazine, with a poem entitled "Breasts" by Erica Jong, famous for the risqué novel *Fear of Flying*. Soon after, Carrie Fisher, most famous for playing Princess Leia, died. *Star Wars* fans paid homage with photos of her in that iconic gold bikini, largely ignoring Fisher's confession of how degrading it felt to wear it. Two months later, Oscar-nominated actresses were gifted breast lift coupons in their Academy Award swag bags. Headlines declared that men didn't care about breasts anymore, but the source was a porn site rationalizing a decrease in profits. Of course, men didn't pay to see boobs anymore—they were everywhere, for free. *Vogue* magazine claimed boobs were in fashion, then out, then in again. When I saw a skit on *Saturday Night Live* called "God Is a Boob Man," I kissed my husband and rested my case.

Yet, when I laughed about the skit during a walk with a writer friend, she claimed to not care. Some men don't care about breasts, either, or so I'd heard. But there is no denying that they mattered to the patriarchy. Even my friend was affected by it.

Within weeks, my personal angst was played out on the public stage. The first American with breasts to run for president in a major party, Hillary Clinton, battled the most chauvinistic, antiwomen candidate that had ever run for American office. Photos of young white women, their breasts bursting from star-spangled bikini tops, popped up on Twitter in support of Mr. Trump. In the beginning, I thought he was running as a joke—at least I hoped so. Within days, recorded interviews of Trump talking about boobs and judging women by their bra size turned the Republican Party into a frat house. In 2005, Trump declared that "a woman who is very flat-chested is very hard to be a ten." When this "Christian values" candidate was asked about his ex-wife Marla Maples, he said, "nice tits, no brains."[1] But he didn't respect women with brains, either. He called one of his own attorneys "disgusting" for requesting time to breastfeed her baby.[2] On the record, he told Howard Stern that if his third wife, Melania, was in a car accident, he'd worry about her boobs.

Souvenirs at the Republican National Convention included buttons describing Hillary Clinton as a Kentucky Fried Chicken meal featuring "two small breasts." Aside from the bad taste, it was slander. That inch of skin that got Senator Clinton in trouble on C-SPAN in 2007 seemed especially ridiculous in 2016. The naked breasts of Melania Trump could be seen by anyone with an internet connection.

The day Hillary Clinton won the Democratic nomination, I bought airline tickets to Washington, DC for the inauguration. I didn't have tickets to get in, but I was going. I invited my sister and found us a place to stay with an old swim team friend who worked for DC's mayor. I implored my daughters to vote. Juliette volunteered at election sites during high school, but Chloe had never voted before, and during my last visit I spied Fox News on her boyfriend's TV. I prayed she would vote with her head, not her heart. When men's opinions counted more, then identifying with our own sex was a dangerous act of rebellion.

The day I published a political essay, which had sounded shocking a few weeks earlier, it was swallowed up by a news cycle of sound bites about pussy grabbing. For the sake of entertainment, the media kept Trump in the headlines. There was no balanced news when a celebrity goosed the ratings. I prayed the rich white man who claimed to side with unemployed blue-collar workers was playing this as satire. Instead, he proved that all publicity was good publicity and winning was all that mattered.

After the high of seeing selfies of my daughters wearing "I Voted" stickers, my husband and I hunkered down to watch the election reports. A few hours later, I joined the majority of American voters who put the champagne back in the fridge and climbed into bed, too horrified to sleep. How could I explain this to my girls? Whether I blamed the electoral college or Russian interference, nothing could change the facts. I had birthed human beings into a world that refused to treat them with respect. Their breasts would deprive them of comparable pay, control of their bodies, and care for their children. This handicap garnered no government assistance, and now it would only get worse. I grieved for their loss. At dawn, I sat down at my desk and wrote them each a long letter of apology. Then I canceled my tickets to Washington.

In the dark days that followed, some friends took to their beds. Others took antidepressants. Republican women were photographed on the front lines giving victory speeches as if their breasts were powerful weapons in the battle against themselves. These women were so tough, or so brainwashed, that they took boob jokes and body slams in stride. They didn't need to be equal, because they were better. They had money and white men to make it so.

When the first daughter was sixteen, her father said she was so "hot" that if he wasn't her dad, he might be dating her. Now that she was primed for a power position, I gave my Ivanka Trump boots to Goodwill.[3] Yet, as the topic of climate change loomed, even the princess was held back. Her power lasted as long as she agreed with Daddy. Is it any coincidence that her husband, another white boy rich by inheritance, was proud that she could do "anything she set her mind to"?[4] Now that quote sounded condescending. Worse, it sounded familiar . . .

I learned my father voted for Trump on Facebook. A cousin on his side of the family, a large, tight-knit group on the East Coast, posted that my dad was the only winner. My father was a longtime Ohio Republican, but he was also an Ivy League intellectual, a scientist whom I hoped would see the big picture. I felt punched in the gut. He taught me I could do whatever I set my mind to, as long as I worked hard. He never saw me as a pinup with staples in my belly, but as his Mini-Me. Now I understood that when he hung me by the ankles and dropped me off the high dive all those years ago, it was a baptism into the deep pool of patriarchy.

A week after the election, my father emailed his flight confirmation for a Christmas visit. I ignored it. I was so heartbroken, so ashamed, so furious, I didn't want to see him at all. After several weeks of emails, I broke down and responded.

Dad, you have two daughters and four granddaughters. How can you betray us?

Give him a chance, he wrote back.

My chest constricted when I read those words. As abortion clinics closed, and the number of hate crimes rose, my father remained oblivious. He emailed about skydiving and triathlons until I surrendered, ready to relate on a personal level. Then he emailed what time to watch him on Fox.

My father was and still is a climate change denier. When his face appeared in the shadows of a newspaper ad for a documentary, I felt embarrassed to share his name. I don't believe his claims were due to ego or ignorance, but to perspective. My father is a statistics man with dozens of books to his name. When I suggested his statistics were skewed, he didn't bother to dispute it. There was no need.

Ever since Darwin, "survival of the fittest" has been the prism for all biological science. When social Darwinists speak about mankind, they mean *man*kind literally. Darwin did not believe that women were equal to men.[5] He felt that intellect required engagement with the world and women were limited by their need to be home to nurture the next generation. This conceit has colored much of science since. The belief that all *men*—meaning white men—are equal is a self-fulfilling prophecy.

I deleted the email of my father's itinerary and recited the Serenity Prayer. I could not change him. He voted as a Republican above everything. For me, everything was about my daughters, and theirs.

When my sister volunteered to pick him up from the airport, I decided to treat him like a guest I had just met. If he didn't talk politics, we could have fun. I plugged in the Christmas tree lights by the fireplace and opened the door to the deck for some ocean air. I stepped outside to see if the funicular was working, so he could take a ride up. After a cycling accident at an unmarked construction site, he had his hip fixed with a metal rod positioned so he could ride rather than walk. I planned a bike ride in Venice, a swim in the Pacific, and a screening of *La La Land*. He and his wife would be in town for twenty-four hours, short enough for me to love him without judgment and maintain emotional boundaries.

Tracy had no such boundaries. She arrived in full makeup and a red blouse, wired from a three-hour drive after covering a fatal fire in Santa

Barbara the night before and hosting a holiday parade that morning. Apparently, the half-hour ride from the airport with my father and his wife was limited to pleasant conversation. Once they brought their carry-ons inside and we hugged hello, she laid into him.

The quickened pangs of a panic attack closed like a cage around my lungs, so I excused myself to start dinner.

"How's your mother?" Dad called after me, to stall. Mom was not feeling well, so I glanced back at my sister in commiseration and kept walking.

In the kitchen, I took a deep breath, opened the fridge, and pulled out salad fixings from the farmers market. My dad's voice was already bouncing off the living room walls and invading the space where I sorted vegetables at the butcher block island. My husband was out of town, and I wished he were here to figure out the damn Sonos speakers and play some music. Instead, I heard my dad say he loves women so much that he provided employee flex time decades before anyone else. When my sister went off on his love of women outside our parents' marriage, his wife came into the kitchen to help me.

She was only a few years older than me and generally called him on his crap. As his third wife, she was also the charm, and had been around since my girls were toddlers. She gave them bubble baths. Not only did I like her, I was grateful for her existence. I suspect she voted along with the Ohio Republican party line, but I didn't ask. I didn't want to know whether she voted out of loyalty to my father, or to the egomaniac about to take office. I handed her a cucumber, mindful of the Freudian shape, then chatted over the argument in the living room.

"I'm jealous you'll be having dinner with Juliette tomorrow night," I said.

"It's an easy flight to San Francisco," she said. "Did she get her raise?"

"I wish," I said, finding the peeler for her. "She's been waiting for months. She was the thirteenth hire of two hundred. It's a typical start-up, but now her assistants make more money."

"Do you think she'll quit?"

"I don't know," I said. "She's worried that the Fair Pay Act will allow a potential employer to ask about her salary. This low pay could be used against her." I put a few ears of corn in the microwave and started it. "She thinks she needs a better title, too. I emailed her an article saying men go for jobs without meeting the requirements and get hired for potential, so she should just go for it, but . . . "

Tracy's voice raised over the hum of the microwave. We talked louder to ignore it.

"How about Chloe? Does she like Colorado any better now?"

"Hope so," I say. "She keeps moving for her boyfriend's job, so she can only do school online and work part-time. I worry that she plays housewife by default."

"Maybe they'll get married."

"Maybe," I said. "But if she gets pregnant before her career takes off, he'll always call the shots."

My dad's wife nodded. "And if they ever split up . . . "

I met her eyes over the chopping board. I was impressed by her ability to compartmentalize. She saw the injustice when it was applied to women in our family. And we both struggled to support our children single-handedly after sacrificing career time to raise them. But she probably voted for Trump.

She pointed at the bottle of cabernet already set out on the counter. I smiled.

When she reached for it, her ample chest was directly in my line of sight. I looked down at the tomato I was slicing, realizing that all three of the adult women here, the primary females in my father's life, had breast implants. Was it him or was it endemic, a symptom of American ideals?

Now my daughters, his granddaughters, faced the same challenge. This was his fault. Not him personally, but everything he stood for, everything that shaped him up to the moment he punched that misogynist's square on the presidential ballot. When the microwave dinged, I stabbed my knife into the cutting board.

I grabbed a bowl of grapes from the fridge and took it into the living room by the chair where he sat while my sister had her say. He smiled pleasantly, still Teflon, not only to the past, but to any opposing thought. He nodded as if I'd come to save him. That wasn't my intent. Tracy shot me a look as if passing a baton, then excused herself to go wash off her TV makeup.

"Dad, you know how you taught me that I could do anything I put my mind to?" I asked.

"I didn't tell you to work in Hollywood," he said, chuckling. He was an extra in every movie I worked on, and disappointed when I left production to write. He tore some grapes from the stem, then threw me a bone just as I turned back toward the kitchen. "Did I tell you I'm reading a novel?" he asked. "By a woman."

I hesitated, feeling hopeful. We had long debated the emotional truth of fiction over the science books he reviewed.

"*Atlas Shrugged*, by Ayn Rand," he continued. "Do you know it?"

"Yes," I said. "But that has no literary merit at all. It's propaganda. And if Rand were alive today, she'd identify with males, very young males." I felt a hot flash that I couldn't blame on my cancer meds. "Did you know when Rand died, one of her disciples put a dollar sign made of flowers on her grave?"

My dad was intrigued, an impartial pupil. That was his saving grace—always interested in debating on an intellectual level, safe from personal attack. I glanced back toward the kitchen, where his wife was filling wine glasses. I wanted to join her, but there was something frightening about Rand's "objectivism." No, not something: everything.

"You know how you used to pretend to be Superman?" I said. "You ripped open your shirt to show the big S? That was fun, because Superman fought to save the world. And he had a human side in Clark

Kent. John Galt, Rand's Superman, is different. He's the individual who triumphs over everyone else, no matter the cost. There's no freedom or justice. He's a millionaire who will stop at nothing to win." I'm tempted to mention that Trump loves this book, too, but I was wary of losing him. I tried another tack.

"*Atlas Shrugged* is a male myth, Dad. Like 'no man is an island.'"

"John Donne," he said, scoring points for sourcing the quote.

I smiled. "John and I were just talking about the fact that there's a female myth, too."

Dad pursed his lips in thought. As a fellow Princetonian, he respected my husband's philosophy background. Plus, Tracy was emerging from the bathroom, ready for round two. He avoided her glance.

"Like Katniss in *Hunger Games*," he offered. "Loved that movie, except for the violence."

"That's what makes her a warrior. Still a male myth, but she fights for the greater good. The female myth includes the nurturing of children. Even if the hero leaves, she circles back to rebuild the community, or she builds a new one."

My sister's phone rang. She took it outside on the deck to talk.

We both watched, anticipating the arrival of her daughters. The spell was broken now, so it was too awkward to tell him the female myth is a reality. My efforts to make a fancy dinner for him, a man whose views I despised, purely because he had spawned me, was proof. Which reminded me to take the salmon out of the fridge. I headed to the kitchen. Feeding the family was what mothers did.

I grabbed the full wineglass that awaited, thanked his wife, and took a grateful sip. Granted, my father didn't know much about what made a good mother. He grew up in boarding schools and summer camps and was abandoned to neighbors for months at a time. He was schooled by modern American culture. Did I ever tell him how I had been harassed, underpaid, and judged for my breasts my entire life? That was the real reason he lost movie roles, why I quit production to write.

No, I didn't. I never complained to him. I wanted him to be proud, so I acted like it didn't matter, like I could do anything I set my mind to, just as he promised. Anything less felt like failure. I stormed back out to the living room.

"It's not true, Dad," I said. "The whole self-determination thing. Hard work isn't enough for women to succeed. We need laws."

My sister came back inside. "They're here, climbing the stairs." She hurried past the bookshelf to go out the front door and meet her family.

My dad watched her, his eyes glancing across the row of books with my name on them. Then he turned to look out the window, where clouds blotted the blue sky. I waited for his answer.

"You girls turned out great," he said.

Ugh. "That is completely beside the point. I had every advantage as a white, middle-to-upper-middle-class American. But imagine how much more I could have accomplished if I were a man! You told me that I was invincible, and I believed you. I wanted to make movies to change the world, to feed the poor and cure cancer, all those cliché things to make the world a better place. I have this huge pit of regret, even though I tried to make the best decisions every step of the way. I do. It still drives me crazy. And what about my daughters, your granddaughters? Don't you want them to have the same opportunities you had?"

Tracy's voice mingled with the high pitch of her daughters' voices as they appeared at the door.

"Here they are," Dad said, pushing his battered body up from the armchair to greet them.

I nodded and shut up, fighting my impulse to help him stand. He was part of the culture against women, but he didn't see it, and he never would.

My brother-in-law appeared first, huffing from the stairs due to having only one lung after losing the other to cancer. He was carrying a crate of strawberries from the fields by their home in Oxnard.

I opened the door wider. Marie Claire, my seventeen-year-old niece, entered clutching a battered computer against her tie-dyed T-shirt. Next, her thirteen-year-old sister, Josilynn, dragged a trash bag full of Christmas gifts over the threshold. When she set it by the fireplace and turned back for a hug, I blinked at how much she'd blossomed since Thanksgiving.

These girls grew up watching modern cartoons like *Tangled* and *Frozen* between surfing and soccer. Yet even the latest Disney princesses were drawn with *The Animator's Survival Kit*, written by Richard Williams, the Oscar-winning creator of the incredibly sexual Jessica Rabbit in the Hollywood animation film, *Who Framed Rogert Rabbit.*[6] Since only 25 percent of working animators had breasts, most cartoons with cleavage were still "sexpots." The thought gave me pause as I hugged Joss, whose chest strained against a top she had clearly outgrown. She had more cleavage than me.

I pulled her aside. "Can I ask you a weird question?" My niece nodded, never one for talking to grown-ups. "What's it like to have boobs already?"

"I don't know," she said, pulling away. She spotted the cat and chased her out to the deck.

"Sorry," I called, then turned to my sister. "I didn't mean to embarrass her. She has no idea what she's in for with that body."

"Neither does she." My sister pointed across the room to Marie Claire, a high school senior, who was listening to Grandpa's enthusiastic pitch for Princeton. "I want her to take self-defense as an elective. One in four college coeds get raped or assaulted. My news team did a report on it during sweeps."

Her daughter accepted a hug from Grandpa, then bounded toward us and offered me the laptop. "Will you read my admissions essay for Berkeley?"

I accepted it like a gift. My girls never let me read their work, let alone asked for help. Maybe because I was a writer. Maybe because I was the only one at home, so any judgment would have felt harsh. Or maybe I *was* too harsh, too afraid of any failure. My nieces had a stay-at-home dad, a retired grandmother who lived with them half the year, and an aunt who was happy to help. Their mom was the worker bee. It occurred to me that when a dad worked, mom did everything. When a mom worked, it took a village to pick up the slack. Then again, I was jealous my girls didn't have a village.

"After dinner," I said. We could hear my father's cheerful voice and his wife's murmur in the kitchen. I wanted to hate him, but I loved him. I wanted to fight him, but how? My sister told her daughter to help set the table.

"I'm sorry I sold those plane tickets to Washington so fast," I said. "We could have gone to the Women's March. Do you want to go to the one in LA?"

"It's on a Saturday," Tracy said. "I have to work." We watched her daughter disappear into the kitchen. "You'll like her essay. It's about the childcare room in her public high school, for students who didn't have access to birth control."

My sister's eyes met mine, and I felt a new bond with her. We were on the same team now, and it wasn't the weaker one. We were fighting for our daughters. There was strength in our unity. I don't know who said it first, but we made a deal. My niece was coming with me to the Women's March. For the first time in a long time, I felt hope.

Women's Legal Rights

US Population: 51% women[1]
Representation: 24% in the Senate; 26.9% in House of Representatives; 33% of Supreme Court (as of 2021)[2]

1777 Women are prohibited from voting by law in the original thirteen states.

1920 Nineteenth Amendment gives women right to vote; this did not include women of color.

1921 American Birth Control League is founded by Margaret Sanger.

1941 3,000 federally funded child care centers are opened following the Lanham Act.

1946 All 3,000 childcare centers are closed.

1960 Birth control pill is legalized for married women. Twelve years later, the Pill is legalized for unmarried women

1963 Equal Pay Act passes, but is not enforced.

1964 Civil Rights Act prohibits discrimination due to race, creed, ethnicity, nationality, or sex.

1965 Black women get the vote thanks to the Voting Rights Act that prohibits discrimination.

1966 National Organization for Women (NOW) is founded.

1967 Affirmative action is expanded to apply to women.

1971 Discriminating against mothers of young children in the hiring pool is outlawed by *Phillips v. Martin Marietta Corp.*

1972 Equal Rights Amendment (ERA) is passed by Congress.

1972 Title IX of Education Amendments prohibit sex discrimination in education and athletics in federally funded schools.

1973 Abortion is legalized by *Roe v. Wade*.

1974 Housing discrimination against women is outlawed.

1974 Pregnant women gain the right to work, according to *Cleveland Board of Ed. v. LaFleur*.

1974 Single women can apply for credit without a man via Equal Credit Opportunity Act.

1975 State juries can no longer exclude women due to *Taylor v. Louisiana* ruling.

1978 Pregnancy Discrimination Act bans employers from discriminating against pregnant women.

1979 ERA misses ratification deadline with thirty-five of thirty-eight states needed.

1994 Gender Equity in Education Act, Title IX, is amended to require full disclosure of gender equity in federally funded schools.

1994 Violence Against Women Act supports victims of rape and domestic violence.

2003 The Chicks (then known as the Dixie Chicks) are blackballed for a casual anti-war comment against President Bush.

2006 Tarana Burke, a black woman, creates #MeToo.

2013 Ban against women in military combat positions is removed.

2013 Violence Against Women Act expands to Native Americans, queer women, and immigrants.

2017 *Time* cover shows white women as #MeToo "silence breakers."

2018 Supreme Court justice Brett Kavanaugh confirmed, despite allegations of sexual assault.

Number of women in Congress jumps from 16% to 24%.

2019 House of Representatives passes 2015 Equality Act for LGBTQA+ rights after singer Taylor Swift's petition.

2019 Title IX is expanded to include sexual harassment.

2020 25% of contenders for the Democratic presidential nomination are women.

2021 Women's rights are still not guaranteed by the Constitution.

Eighteen

BOOBS"R"US
2017

On January 20, Inauguration Day, Trump took the throne. By nightfall in Los Angeles, Mother Nature was freaking out. Heavy storms downed power lines all over the city. The highway patrol barricaded the roads around our neighborhood all along the Pacific Coast Highway. Between emergency sirens, I could hear the ocean's fury. When I peered down from the bedroom window, the water was alive with whitecaps, stripes of sputtering foam in the darkness. They reflected my feelings exactly. We could rage all we wanted, but what good would it do?

Close to midnight, when my phone could barely find a signal, my sister texted from her TV station in Santa Barbara. Landslides were blocking the mountain passes. Her daughter, Marie Claire, had her driver's permit, but the weather was dangerous. She could get to my place in a friend's truck if I could take them both. I'd love to, I told Tracy, but I was trapped, too. Nothing was certain, except that Obama was history, my husband was out of the country, and Mom's cancer was back.

The sirens wailed all night. I gave up on sleep and peered behind the blinds. Thunder crashed and lightning danced along the horizon. I feared the march would be canceled. How many car accidents would block the slick roads? How many people would walk in the rain? The thought of missing this chance to protest was physically painful. It felt like surrender.

The power blinked out. I grabbed a flashlight and laid in bed fully clothed for hours, as I had during the Northridge earthquake. This, too, was a shifting of the very soil beneath our feet. I had to do something. I found an old poster board and drew a simple sign. The heavens thundered in approval.

At dawn, the flashing lights faded and the skies began to clear. It felt like a miracle, just in time. I changed into fresh clothes, including my sturdiest bra. I was armored for action.

The power returned and the TV sputtered back to life, showing the Women's March starting in DC. An aerial shot revealed throngs of people, dotted with pink pussy hats named for a pun that, until now, implied weakness. I wondered if my mother would consider it vulgar. A close-up on the small screen showed placards reading, *My arms are tired of holding this sign since the 60s,* and *Do I have to burn my bra again?* Now I really wanted to call my mother, but it was too early to wake her. I would see her soon enough.

There was a knock on the door. Marie Claire had arrived with her friend, whose name was perfect: Harmony. We were doing this. I handed them plastic bags with protein bars, then we descended the stairs and loaded the car. The roads were eerily empty. We made it downtown in twenty minutes. Soon, people of all shapes and sizes flooded in from every direction by train and subway and bus and carpool. Families held hands and wove past in the crowd. Like many, this was our first true protest, and the adrenaline was contagious. We wove our way to the street with our handmade signs and squeezed through the masses for a glimpse of celebrities making speeches.

An hour after the march was supposed to begin, we stood shivering, trapped in the crowd between tall buildings. We waved at the news helicopters buzzing overhead and shouted to hear each other. We laughed with strangers, shared hugs and high fives. At long last, the mass of mostly women lurched forward. The narrow route was overwhelmed and we were forced to stop at every half block. We heard rumors of our numbers, each more fantastic than the next. So many were here, expressing our voices, peaceful and proud. We felt united in making history. Tears came unbidden.

At the end of the route, marchers pushed past us, flooding back between buildings. Clusters of balloons escaped to the sky. Women with megaphones were shouting. We tracked the voices to a stage and clung to a wire link fence to watch. Women of color dressed in army pants, not pussy hats, were railing about hunger, not hope. I looked at my niece and her friend, whose skin was different than ours. For the last six hours it hadn't mattered, but now I was reminded that it did. The opportunity and earnings that white women marched for were riches compared to the basic needs and safety that others lacked. We had to expand the scope of our fight to make all women equal. Only then could we truly work together to be equal to men. The mood shifted at the enormity of our task.

As we listened, the weather warmed up and we stripped down to our T-shirts. My niece, braless in her Planned Parenthood T-shirt, picked up an abandoned Nasty Woman sign.

A twenty-something man with a goatee approached and eyed the girls hungrily. I stepped closer to my nubile niece. He caught my glare, and moved on. The elephant in the room was still attached to our chests. Maternal instinct kicked in and I handed them each a box of raisins from my bag. It felt like the party was over.

"Ready to go?" I shouted over the noisy helicopter blades, whirring above us.

We left the shouting behind us and found our way back to the route. We pointed out protest signs discarded at the curb. A drawing of breasts reminded me of a *Saturday Night Live* skit that had aired the previous week, so I pulled out my phone and found the YouTube clip to cheer up the girls. It was an interview with the filmmakers of a fake movie called "Hot Robot 3: Journey to Boob Mountain," in which the hot robots returned to the factory to make their boobs larger. The director said, "If we could all harness our boob energy, who knows what we could accomplish?" [1] The girls looked at each other and laughed.

Word spread that 750,000 people were marching with us that morning. The staggering number reflected the largest public demonstration in history. Phones out, we compared pictures and posed for more. The sun was shining now. Around us, marchers bumped into friends and hugged hello. A rainbow-colored crew of millennials was picking up trash. Police were on every corner, helping orange-vested workers direct the flow. My niece and her friend were smiling again, with pleasure lit from within. This power in numbers gave our lives political significance. We were a link in a human chain, part of a greater good. A warm feeling spread though my chest. It was the feeling of my flesh and bones making a difference far greater than the weight of them.

Now my job was to set the girls free and send them home safely. We joined the crowds hiking back to the train station, where I gave the girls directions, hugs, and emergency cash. Then I hustled the mile back to my car. As part of the sandwich generation, today I was the bologna.

My car was the last one in the lot, so I checked that my suitcase with four days of hormone-blocking meds and side effect supplements was still in the trunk. Then I drove 130 miles to Palm Desert, where my mother lived with her poodle. My boobs practically throbbed with responsibility.

Three hours later, I drove past towering white windmills, and was tempted to wave hello. Palm Springs sprouted from the desert, and the aerial tram marked the last twenty miles. My bra straps dug onto my shoulders; I couldn't wait to take it off. After exiting on Washington, I nosed past Jefferson and Sinatra and Cook, newly aware that the streets were all named for men. At Trader Joe's—yet another dude—I bought soft foods and a spray of tulips, then loaded the bags on top of my battered pink protest sign in the trunk. The ERA logo looked like an ancient artifact.

As the sun drifted down behind the purple mountains, I parked in the driveway of Mom's golf course condo. I pulled down the rearview mirror and squinted in the last rays of light to apply the lipstick I had slipped into my purse at dawn.

My mother opened the door and I rolled my suitcase inside, past portraits of my daughters and my sister's family. I stopped short at the new picture in the number one spot: a framed pinup of Marilyn Monroe. She grinned.

"Do you recognize that?" Mom said.

"The famous calendar shot." I'd read that Hefner bought it from a photographer for $500, then used it as the cover of the first *Playboy*. Monroe was not consulted. "Where'd you get it?"

"I found it rolled up at an antique store. It's valuable," she said, turning to admire Marilyn's naked curves. "That's how we all looked, nice and round."

Beneath the girdles, I thought, *and the pointy bras*. Of course, now we had Spanx and silicone. My mother still had fine curves and, for another week or two, a full head of blonde hair. Back in the day she was a brunette. The topless photo I once found in her panty drawer flashed to mind. I shook it off and went back for the groceries.

My job here was to set up a home alert system, organize caregivers, and take her to chemo on Monday. I also needed to suggest she update her will; but first, we needed some fun. We spent rest of the weekend watching classic movies on cable—or rather, talking through them, which would have annoyed my husband to no end. We lucked into catching *Giant*, starring Elizabeth Taylor, who played the character I was named after. A love of movies is the only interest my parents had in common. That, maybe, and a love of breasts.

We also caught the end of *Gentlemen Prefer Blondes*, when Marilyn sings "Diamonds Are a Girl's Best Friend." When I played the DVD for my daughters, I made sure they watched until the end. Monroe, the "gold digger," tells her fiancé's wealthy father that beauty is for women just as money is for men. He declares that she isn't as stupid as he thought. Now I wish they hadn't seen it at all. The film was based on a series of short sketches in *Harper's Bazaar* written by Anita Loos, who published the bestseller in 1926, six years after the Nineteenth Amendment granted women the right to vote. Once the series was combined and published as *Gentlemen Prefer Blondes*, Edith Wharton called it the "Great American Novel."[2] This was the flapper era, when women bobbed their hair and bound their breasts, all the better to resemble young men, so they could work and drink and smoke. Loos wrote the novel as satire, but with Monroe filling out that strapless pink gown, the message was no joke.

"You know, my mother grew up in vaudeville," Mom said, pointing to her bedroom where the portrait of her mother, the voluptuous beauty in a strapless gown, now hung. "And she married millionaires. I married for love. Stupid."

"Romantic," I said.

"I've decided what I want for my birthday," Mom said. "If I live that long."

"You will," I said, to convince us both. "April is only a few months away."

"My mother died at sixty-five," she said. "I'll be eighty. I want a diamond bracelet."

I laughed, partly because she echoed the sentiment of Marilyn's song and partly because it would be tough for my sister and I to swing it. For the last decade, diamond sellers had advertised that women didn't need men to buy jewelry, but they never lowered the prices to match our paychecks.

"And I want a party with all my family. It can be my funeral if . . ."

"Mom, stop it. A party is a great idea." I panicked, wondering how to distract her from the reason I would now be visiting more often. This was Mom's second round of non-Hodgkin's lymphoma, and the dose of chemicals was as dangerous as the disease. Then it hit me.

"I need your help," I said. "I can't decide if I should get my boobs done again."

"I think my mother had a boob job," Mom said. "I remember seeing her get dressed about ten years before she died. They were very perky."

"Wow. That was before they were a thing."

"Breasts were always a thing. My cousin had an inflatable bra in the fifties. In the sixties, we looked for the scars on showgirls at the Tropicana in Vegas."

I lifted up my long-sleeved black T-shirt, the one I'd been wearing since dawn, to show her mine.

"They look good." She nodded. I slipped off my bra and she shrugged. "Do what you want."

I rose to go shower. "That's the problem. I don't know. And it's expensive."

"If I die, you'll have the money to do it."

"Mom! I can use my credit card."

"You only live once."

I'd heard that before. I got in the shower and considered my own bucket list. Were perfect boobs on it? If I were going to die—and I remember that feeling of surrender—I would do something with my girls. The real ones. My husband was working in Paris, a place I'd love to take them. We'd never been abroad together. Chloe had never been abroad at all. But I was nearing the end of my five-year treatment plan and I wasn't going to die. Neither was my mother, if I could help it. I averted my eyes from the mirror as I stepped out of the shower.

• • •

On the table at the chemo clinic we found a newspaper showing pictures of the Women's March. A side article described how disaffected black women were planning an alternate protest. I hoped next year would be better and, for the first time, I realized there would be a next year. We hadn't solved anything. The fourth wave of feminism had barely begun.

My mother picked up a magazine, so dog-eared that I passed her my purse-sized bottle of hand sanitizer. A former San Francisco 49ers cheerleader sued the NFL for fixing salaries. Even the Dallas Cowboys cheerleaders only made $150 per game. I knew because I looked it up during a troubling addiction to their reality show, *Making of the Team.* The men earned millions while the women were told their full-time commitment to the macho male action heroes was an honor. But where else could they dance for an audience of millions every week? And they were truly talented.

My mom traded me the sanitizer for the magazine. "I always wanted to be a cheerleader," she said.

"So did I," I admitted. I didn't watch the show to root for favorites— I imagined I was one of them. Shoot me now.

The nurse wouldn't allow me in the chemo room once Mom was hooked up. I returned to her condo to organize a home care schedule and start planning her party. Organizing flights and hotel rooms and twenty-somethings' vacation days was tricky. I called Juliette, who was just starting to look for a new job, then decided to mail her my Women's March sweatshirt. Hard to believe the march had only been two days earlier. I packaged souvenir pins for Chloe in Colorado, and called about coordinating pain blocks and surgery to remove steel rods from her arm.

At the end of the week, I drove home and unpacked the Women's March poster from the trunk of my car.

I was counting down days until my next drive to the desert, when Los Angeles shut down for the Academy Awards. Mom called to tell me about an E! fashion special that explained ways to get more cleavage. That evening, we put the phone on speaker and rated Oscar dresses. Taraji P. Henson wore my favorite, an off-the-shoulder, midnight blue velvet, custom Alberta Feretti gown that evoked images of Old Hollywood. Her décolletage would have been daring if not for the plunging necklines of Amy Adams and Viola Davis and, oh my goodness, Mandi Gosling,[3] Ryan Gosling's sister.

Plans for my mother's eightieth birthday party began to coalesce. Marie Claire requested photos for a slideshow, so I scoured old scrapbooks. I searched for the Polaroid of Mom posing as a *Playboy* pinup. Could I have imagined it?

Meanwhile, the docuseries *American Playboy: The Hugh Hefner Story* was released on Amazon and I asked my mom if she'd be interested in watching it. Was she ever.

"Hefner liberated women and made it OK to enjoy sex," she told me, long-distance on the phone. "The Playmates chose to be in the magazine. It was an honor."

I stared at the phone, glad she couldn't figure out FaceTime to see me wince. My mother was the biggest feminist I knew. She had gotten her PhD and worked full-time while I was in elementary school. Her own father had refused to help her financially because he thought she'd divorced to be a women's libber. She'd followed me to California, got her MFCC license, and trained other therapists. How could she justify a culture that worked against her?

"Mom. If showing your breasts is the way to feel honored, it isn't much of a choice, is it?"

"You tried out."

Shit, I think. Did I tell her that? Now I wished I could see her. Was she smiling or serious? "I didn't think I'd have to take my top off," I said. "I just wanted—"

"Validation," she said, finishing my thought. "As a woman. Why do you think Caitlyn Jenner is talking about doing *Playboy*? It's not just to show off her plastic surgery."

Jenner wouldn't be the first trans woman to pose in a men's magazine. That was model Caroline Cossey, also known as Tula, a Bond girl back in the eighties.

"Mom, did you ever think of posing?"

"No, I was nice girl. I got validation from being married. That's why divorce was so hard."

That also explained the topless Polaroid. Validation from pleasing her man.

"Hefner wasn't perfect," my mother continued, "but his mother withheld love and his fiancé cheated on him."

"Yes, but his reaction helped define our entire culture! This isn't nature or nurture, it's both. Don't you see how Dad was influenced?"

"Your father didn't have good parenting either."

I avoided that rabbit hole for a safer one. "Did you ever go to a Playboy Club?"

"Yes," she said. "In Chicago. We dressed up and waited in line. It was exciting!"

I didn't know what to say.

A few days later, my father called. I asked if he still had all those leatherbound *Playboys*. He said no, he gave them away. He didn't want to talk about how valuable they would be now. He was more interested in telling me that he was on his way to Washington, DC. He was invited by President Trump's team to discuss the "bad science" of global warming.

I hung up and considered changing my name again. But, to what? To my husband's name? My mother's father's name?

Mom made it through the long slog of chemo rounds, but on a lower than ideal dose. Soon she started daily radiation, which required a custom-made cage for her face that was then bolted to a plank before they aimed the nuclear beam at her neck. It was horrific, and she hated it. Naturally, we went shopping to cheer her up. We sipped smoothies, then tried on lipstick until we went home and she surrendered to sleep.

During my next visit, I spoke with Mom's financial advisor from Hightower, who had founded a program called FEW, Financially Empowering Women. I was asking about it when his father-in-law and business partner said hello. A good-looking man who brought his entire family to my last local book signing, he asked if I was working on a new project. I told him I was considering a book about breasts.

He smiled, delighted. "Do they get bigger as the book goes on?"

"As a matter of fact," I said, "they do."

I excused myself to go laugh about it with my mother. We flipped through her new *Vanity Fair* and studied the photos of Emma Watson, the Harry Potter actress who started the HeForShe organization for gender equality at the United Nations. Her underboob was getting flak from a London radio host, whose viral tweet read, "Watson: Feminism, feminism . . . gender wage gap . . . why oh why am I not taken seriously . . . feminism . . . oh, and here are my tits!"[4] Every woman draws her own line between empowerment and exploitation. Why did we have to be *either/or*? Why not *and*? As for the fashionable underboob, it just looked chilly.

Back in Los Angeles, I emailed my mom a link to the video of former *Sports Illustrated* swimsuit model Chrissy Teigen making her "boobs talk."[5] It was impossible not to laugh. With swimsuit season ahead, magazines declared a new focus on the décolletage, one of women's "most beautiful" areas. There was even a quote from the dermatologist I'd seen about my chemo-ravaged nails, Dr. Ava Shamban, a Harvard-educated research scientist who appeared on *The Doctors* and *Extreme Makeover*. Online, beauty bloggers were posting lists of "boob masks" meant not only to smooth and brighten the skin, but to lift, tone, and reduce the loss of perkiness. Sheet masks had names ranging from Beauty and the Breast to Calm My Tits. Oh, how I missed the days we only worried about tan lines.

The week before my mother's birthday, I headed back to the bra department at Nordstrom and learned that, like most women, I was wearing the wrong size. The saleswoman wrapped the measuring tape around my mismatched breasts and declared I was a 30DDDD. This bizarre combination of digits was more unsettling than any other size I'd been. Alas, there was far less selection as well. I settled on a 32DDD. I wanted something thick enough to hide my nipples but thin enough to feel soft against my scars. I wanted lace and lift and silky straps. As usual, I wanted it all.

Three hours and hundreds of dollars later, I got home and my husband asked what took me so long. I modeled my new brassiere and his eyes lit up.

"It must be fantastic to walk around with breasts all day," he said.

I laughed and gave him a kiss. Boys are stupid.

My mother made it through treatment and we all met for her birthday in April. Tracy and her family drove five hours from Oxnard. My girls and their boyfriends flew in from Colorado and San Francisco. I couldn't wait. To pass the hours, I swam laps and tried to stretch out the shoulder that was now permanently tight on the bad boob side. The water felt good, but the chlorine peeled my organic nail polish right off. The fingernails that never reattached after chemo were hideous, but oh well. I pulled on a high-necked dress that covered my port scar, then paced the driveway. By the time my daughters arrived, my heart was so full that my chest ached. When we hugged, it was hard to let go.

At last, it was party time. My mother's door was open, so we walked in together. A surprise waited inside. Mom had taken down Marilyn and made her own commemorative show. We crowded around to admire the photographs taped to the wall.

Right smack in the middle was the original Polaroid picture of my mother in her white bikini posing on the bed. Not topless, but close enough. My nieces giggled, my daughters pointed, and my sister and I exchanged knowing smiles. The boys hung back politely. Mom, stunning that night in a St. John suit and a blond wig, squeezed past to point at the words she wrote on the white border. The cursive spelled out her full name, followed by "PhD."

On the moonlit patio of Arnold Palmer's Restaurant in La Quinta, we sang "Happy Birthday" around a long, linen-covered table. Tracy and I stood by our mother and presented a delicate bracelet of tiny diamonds. My husband began an impromptu speech and everyone turned to him in surprise. His eyes met mine, and I realized there was nothing impromptu about it. He eased into a story about my mother and how her legacy of beauty and brains was evident in the seven women around the table.

As my husband's charming tribute came to an end, waiters filled our goblets with sparkling liquids. I dinged a spoon against my glass. The air felt cooler as I stood, so I automatically rubbed my arms against my dress to keep my nipples at bay. I hoped the guys didn't notice, but polite coughing told me otherwise. I ignored it. We loved our husbands and cherished our boyfriends, but let's be honest, men came and went. The women around this table would understand.

When was the next time I would see my daughters, who lived farthest away? I wanted to hold onto this feeling, this family I fought for, the love for these young women who had nursed at my breast. I took a sip of water to calm my nerves and noticed the yellowed nail of my unpolished ring finger. I hoped it would grow back when I finished taking meds in a few months. That was it! We could celebrate my five-year anniversary. For the price of another breast surgery, I could fly my girls to Paris. We could admire true works of art, naked women on canvas, even a real Monet. I raised my glass to make a toast. As heir to the matriarchy, I felt the power to pass on a better world.

But with every sweet sip of champagne, more bubbles burst.

We planned the trip for October. During the summer, *Time* featured a cover story on female "Firsts," as if that was a good thing. How could it not point out the lack of seconds and thirds? In September, the Emmys celebrated female-centric shows like *The Handmaid's Tale* and *Big Little Lies*.

There were so many plunging necklines that headlines claimed "breasts rule the red carpet."[6] Julia Louis-Dreyfus won her sixth Emmy for playing a female president and was diagnosed with breast cancer the next day, as if in punishment. Hugh Hefner died, accompanied by spirited debate about his questionable legacy, but was then laid to rest in his prepaid crypt next to Marilyn Monroe, who probably rolled over in hers.

The day we boarded the plane to Paris, David Letterman, whose boob joke on *The Late Show* started this journey, was awarded the Mark Twain Prize for American Humor. When we arrived in France, the taxi driver saw we were American and asked us about President Trump. So did the hotel *concierge* and the *garçon* at the corner café. All we could do was shrug and apologize in our limited French vocabulary. The women there were treated with such reverence, no matter their age or cup size, that we bought scarves and tried to blend in.

While we climbed the stairs of Montmartre, Harvey Weinstein fell from a casting couch with a crash heard 'round the world. There had been rumblings about him and Bill O'Reilly and Bill Cosby for years, but nothing had ever changed. This felt different. The *New York Times* exposé and Ashley Judd's rape accusations were reprinted in headlines so bold that even I could translate it. Alyssa Milano publicized #MeToo founder Tarana Burke's call to action, and expanded a movement for survivors to expose sexual violence. It started to feel good to be American. A week later, when the wheels of our plane hit the tarmac back home, I truly believed we were returning to a changed country.

After the long flight to Los Angeles, we were exhausted but happy. We claimed our luggage, piled it high on a cart, and juggled purses and bags and carry-ons while collecting documents for various customs checkpoints. The crowded area was chaotic as travelers rolled carts across the tile floor and looked around for the appropriate exits. The girls had long layovers before their connecting flights.

Chloe, a twenty-five-year-old blond in skinny jeans, was excited to be in her hometown and had freshened up in the hopes of seeing some old friends before her flight to Denver. The two of us were chatting away when her carry-on tipped and she paused to grab the handle. I approached the gauntlet of uniformed customs officers and handed my second slip of paper to the man on the right while his gun-toting partner looked on from the left. They were both tall and muscular, so I ducked between them to catch up to my husband and Juliette a few yards ahead. When I turned back, Chloe was no longer behind me. The customs officers had stopped her. This was her first time going through customs, so I figured there was minor confusion. Then they stood up and started arguing with her. The exit guard with a gun in his holster ordered me to keep moving.

"That's my daughter," I said, stalling. My husband stopped a few feet up the ramp with our cart; Juliette retraced her steps to join us. Now we were an island in a stream of people rushing up the ramp that tunneled to the exit door. The guard demanded we keep moving. I could see from Chloe's stiff posture that she was in distress. I didn't know what to do. The guard advanced toward me and again insisted we leave her. The last thing we needed in our exhaustion was to be detained in customs with Trump's heightened security in place. I stepped slowly away.

The three of us hovered around the corner with our luggage cart. The guard forced us to move on. As people exited past us, we waited for Chloe. And waited. By now, I couldn't breathe, anxious about what could possibly be wrong.

She appeared, stone-faced, and said nothing as she marched past. We trailed her with the teetering cart along the narrow sidewalk past construction to the second terminal down for her next flight. Once inside, we corralled her in a small hallway by the restrooms, where she stood like a zombie.

"What happened?" Juliette asked.

Chloe dissolved into tears, sobbing as she tried to explain. Apparently, she had walked past the customs officers before realizing she needed to hand them her document. He'd pointed to his intimidating partner, then asked, "Which one of us do you want to take your pants off for?"

We stood, stunned, and took turns hugging her. How could this have happened right in front of our eyes? What kind of country would welcome her home like this?

When the tears subsided, I asked how she got away. She said she finally told them to fuck off. They had started laughing in response.

We spent the next two days on the phone trying to file a report. Or rather, John did—clearly, a man was needed. On the third day, the female supervisor called back saying they had completed their investigation. Cameras recording the incident made it clear that what Chloe said happened was true. John insisted the man be fired. The supervisor said disciplinary action was being taken. John asked whether the man was being fired, demoted, reprimanded—what? The woman said she understood how he felt, and she was upset, too, but she was prohibited from saying more. The law protected the man's privacy, not my daughter's.

Chloe didn't get home that night for another eight hours, well after midnight. I would have invited her to our condo, but we didn't have extra bedrooms. And she didn't want to be here. She texted about her arrival, but when I checked in on her, she didn't want to talk about it. She didn't want to call and issue a statement. She had been mugged in an airport before, though not by someone who worked there. She wanted the nightmare to end.

Had the man said, "Show me your tits," she would have laughed. Boobs were an easy target, and a woman's breasts were apparently public property. These predators had to go further to threaten a young woman for sport. At work. In public. In broad daylight.

Just when it seemed like the country was waking up to misogyny with the #MeToo movement, it became clear that was for celebrities. On the ground, without the power of the famous, it was all smoke and mirrors. After a few weeks, we shared photos of our trip to Paris and tried to put this behind us. The pain went unspoken, but it lingered like a mist.

First Females

1872 First Female Presidential Candidate (Equal Rights party): Victoria Claflin Woodhull

1932 First Female Senator: Hattie Wyatt Caraway

1969 First Female Black Congresswoman: Shirley Chisholm

1981 First Female Supreme Court Justice: Sandra Day O'Connor

1984 First Female Nominee for Vice President in Major Party: Geraldine Ferraro

1993 First Female Black Senator: Carol Moseley Braun

1997 First Female Secretary of State: Madeleine Albright

2005 First Female Black Secretary of State: Condoleezza Rice

2007 First Female Speaker of the House: Nancy Pelosi

2009 First Female Latinx Supreme Court Justice: Sonia Sotomayor

2016 First Female Nominee for President in Major Party: Hillary Clinton

2020 First Female, Black, Asian Nominee for Vice President in Major Party: Kamala Harris

2021 First Female Vice President: Kamala Harris

Nineteen

THE FOURTH WAVE

The first wave of feminism began with antislavery activists Susan B. Anthony and Elizabeth Cady Stanton, who launched the women's movement with a speech at the 1848 Seneca Falls Convention. Four years later, *Uncle Tom's Cabin*, an American novel with themes of social reform, attacked slavery and established the power of a woman to be an agent of change. Yet, during the Civil War, women were pressured to delay their fight for voting rights even though they, along with Sojourner Truth, pointed out that half of the slaves were women.[1] Together, these women helped pass the Fourteenth Amendment, which banned voting discrimination based on race . . . for men. It took fifty more years to pass the Nineteenth Amendment in 1920. And even then, it was not easy for all women to vote.

The second wave built up over the next forty years, cresting with the 1960s social rebellion against the Vietnam War, civil rights reforms, and the availability of the birth control pill. The third wave rose through the decades as health, education, and employment inequities became undeniable. It crashed in 2017 as a reaction to the election of the most aggressively misogynist president in history.

While "wave" is an imperfect metaphor, it is the one most widely used. And real waves don't crest out of nowhere. They build from a series of smaller, scattered waves, accumulating everything that came before and increasing with the winds. As the third wave of feminism began to curl, it pushed right into the next one. And just as that first wave grew from the combined winds of racial and gender issues, the exponential power of the fourth wave is defined by intersectional feminism.

In January of 2018, I flew to San Francisco to attend my second Women's March with my daughter, Juliette, who lived in nearby Alameda. Marie Claire, now a freshman at Berkeley, met us downtown. The three of us were the big sisters of our respective families, eager to lead. There was a party atmosphere in the crowd, knowing that women all over the country—men, too—were joining in. Juliette's friends who lived along the route hung banners and blasted Aretha Franklin's "Respect" from their windows until the police shut them down.

Over the past year, the protest had expanded from #MeToo to #TimesUp, creating a legal defense fund to fight for workplace equity that included sexual offenses as well as financial issues. Celebrities led the charge to collect $22 million by the end of the first year.[2] Leaked memos highlighted salary discrepancies all over Hollywood, like when Oscar winner Michelle Williams made a thousand dollars for a reshoot compared to her costar's $1.5 million. But corporate America was slow to change.

As we reached the end of the route, Juliette mentioned that the web company that had hired her as part of a push to employ more women, had been bought out by a company with over 4,500 stores in the United States. Their first move had been to replace her female bosses with men. She felt her job as copywriter was preserved since she was not only underpaid, but also the only one who could oversee the transfer of two million branded products.

When I called home to check in after the march, my husband countered with a report from his niece, also in her late twenties. She had just filed a complaint that her male co-worker at her hip international ad agency made 30 percent more than she did. It would take months for HR to make up for the disparity—and when they did, it was on the condition that she sign a Non-Disclosure agreement and vacate her office the same day. Feminism was no longer a dirty word. But how long would it take for #TimesUp to trickle down?

The Miss America Organization was showcasing Miss America 2018, Cara Mund, as their first Ivy League graduate. What they didn't mention was that 30 percent of her score had been based on crossing the stage in a bikini. In June, the new chair, Gretchen Carlson, the former Miss America and Fox news correspondent who sued Roger Ailes for sexual harassment in 2016, eliminated the swimsuit competition—and got death threats. Carlson also changed the evening gown portion to end the focus on "physical appearance."[3] In theory, I was delighted for all the little girls like me who dreamed of wearing the crown. But in reality, would I still call my mom to compare notes without the pretty dresses and perfect breasts? Sadly, no. I was raised in a world that valued beauty, and to this day, I'm still influenced by TV and advertising. I pore over fashion magazines every month, not just to look at the clothes, but to look at the women in them, aspirational ideals by their very name: *models*. When I watched Miss America, it wasn't to root for who best represents our nation. I wanted to identify with the beauty queens, to choose which gown I would wear, to imagine, just for a moment, that it was me. Without the visuals, it wasn't the same. My ambivalence remained.

Later that summer, John and I moved back to sea level in a house a mile away from our condo. After our trip to Paris the previous fall, I wanted extra bedrooms so my daughters could stay over. Of course, my dad wanted to visit, too, to see why we'd sacrificed our spectacular view. But I couldn't return his call after learning that seventeen different states had passed new restrictions on abortion, even in cases of rape and incest—and Ohio was one of them. The Buckeye State, where my father still lived, banned abortions after a heartbeat was audible, which can happen as early as five weeks. Had my breasts been less sensitive, I wouldn't have known I was pregnant that early. When I emailed my father about it, he brushed it off as no concern. But it was a huge concern for me and for every woman in his family. Dad felt that Trump was doing more good than harm, and then he sent me the dates for his visit.

"Not on my watch," John said. He refused to let my father in the house, let alone stay over. He felt that my father's politics were immoral and he wasn't going to enable the enabler with food or shelter.

This put me in an awkward position. This was my father, after all; I had his blood. I was supposed to love him even while I hated everything he stood for. He and his wife finally visited while John was out of town. We met for lunch, toured the house, and I drove them an hour north to my sister's neighborhood, where they checked into a hotel.

In September, we watched Brett Kavanaugh get confirmed for the Supreme Court without regard for Christine Blasey Ford's sobering account of sexual assault. The bro culture and tribe mentality of the Senate Judiciary Committee was so steeped in entitlement that nothing a Stanford professor could say would stop it. Like my father, these conservative white men bulldozed their way forward, never pausing to see the destruction they sowed. As long as they appreciated how women looked, and the ones they supported, supported them in return, they believed they were pro-women. The stereotype of emotionally weak females was reversed when steely-eyed Ford laid out her case against this hysterical man. As I watched Kavanaugh have a tantrum that any toddler's mother would put a stop to, another picture came to mind: a pubic hair on a Coke can.

The parallels of Anita Hill's testimony during Justice Clarence Thomas's confirmation hearings were unavoidable. I was pregnant with

Chloe in 1991, trying not to vomit while I watched the calm female lawyer be dismissed after describing her boss's abuse. I had been so sure that life would be different for my daughters. But there was no way to stop the good ole boys from winning.

I'd had my fill of frat parties during my year at UCLA; Ford's story was credible. Extreme examples of sexual abuse—from actresses who had been raped to Olympic athletes who were molested—earned the public's attention. But such violence occurred to women everywhere, and continued every day. There were only two sides to this battle and I could no longer separate myself from the conflict. I was on the side of the person with breasts.

For so long, I had normalized getting felt up by a chiropractor every week, because it was "only" my boobs. I had succumbed to unwanted sex on dates, because I thought I'd cultivated the attention. Now I favored female doctors, feared being alone in a room with a man, and gifted my daughters mace for their keychains. Even so, when Chloe was sexually harassed on the way home from our family trip to France, I hadn't understood I was part of the problem that led to that moment.

All my life, I had overlooked how this pattern of dividing women into *us* and *them* reduces our power to work together. It goes right back to judging women with large breasts as bimbos and small breasts as brains; women who are believed versus women who are ridiculed. Our bodies are the common denominator in the ways we are held back.

This revelation led me to the concept of comparative empathy. My father had taught me that if I still had my arms and legs, I wasn't really hurt. *Get over it* was the expression my first husband used. Like many, I internalized these rigid ideas to avoid playing victim. But therapists and neuroscientists explain that pain is relative. By ranking our suffering, we create a divide that weakens us all. Even if marching wasn't an immediate agent of change, it proved one thing: there is power in numbers. I added my name to #MeToo.

In November, my phone buzzed while I was out to dinner with my husband and some friends. I checked the number under the table in case it was an emergency. Chloe had changed my ex-husband Drew's name in my phone to "Don't Answer Father" due to the anxiety his calls provoked. He'd moved to Idaho a few months earlier and it had been peaceful since, so I clicked to read the text. *Dear Leslie,* he'd written, *I love you. I will never love anyone else. You are a fucking cunt you ruined my life you have to make Chloe call me fuck you fucking cunt.*

Shaken, I slipped my phone back in my purse and ran to the restroom to collect myself. I called Juliette to warn that her father was on the warpath again and also to ask if he knew my new address. Since our divorce, he had leaned on Juliette with constant calls that made her cry, but Chloe had cut off contact a few years earlier after he threatened to kill her dog. I let her know when he was in touch, but past efforts beyond that had only caused heartache. Our daughters were adults now; his relationship with them was not mine to fix. I was torn between keeping the text in case I needed evidence for another restraining order, or deleting it to dismiss the toxic energy. No longer hungry, I freshened my lipstick and returned to the table.

On Christmas Eve, Juliette called from her boyfriend's grandparent's home in Oregon to say her father had killed himself. The coroner's report described a gunshot wound to his head due to PTSD and depression. When the girls arrived at my house in Los Angeles a few days later, their rooms were ready. Instead, they shared a bed.

The very problems that had plagued my twenty-year marriage had come full circle to end Drew's life thirteen years later. I felt guilty, wondering how I could have helped him and given the girls a better father. At the same time, I wished I had left him earlier and could have protected them from this horror.

Over the next months, Juliette recovered from the emotional burden of his codependency, and rose from the ashes to get an exciting new job that doubled her pay. Chloe had moved back to the Valley where she grew up and moved in with a childhood friend, a man who was also a former Marine. In our minds, we all knew that their father's mental health was not our responsibility; in our hearts, we wanted to make it all better.

Drew was caught in the cycle of toxic masculinity. As a warrior, he was taught to be superior, to be strong, to be violent. His frustration at being unable to beat an unseen enemy caused insurmountable anger. When he couldn't fight the real enemy, I became an enemy, along with the other women in his life.

The struggle to escape the restrictions of society is part of what makes progress for both women and men so challenging. Some of that struggle is caused by underlying biology. While physical strength is no longer needed to govern, big, seemingly strong men typically do. That biological difference, coupled with centuries-old cultural precedent, still holds excessive influence. The father of my children could not possibly comprehend the forces that worked against him. This was a prison he could not escape.

This shadow hovered over 2019, and not only for me. American women rooted for the fourth wave of empowerment to make it to shore, but every time it got close, it receded. Instead of attending the Women's March, which felt more like a party than a protest as time went on, I donated money. E. Jean Carroll, a journalist whom I'd been following in *Elle* magazine for twenty-six years, publicly accused President Trump of rape—and was promptly fired. The US Women's Soccer players won the World Cup, but were still in court fighting for equal pay. NASA postponed the first spacewalk by female astronauts due to the dearth of spacesuits, designed thirty years earlier, that would fit them. Childcare and breastfeeding challenges kept us last on the list of family-friendly nations. Mothers were still separated from their children, who were housed in cages at the border.

Yet the backlash to Trump was building. In the two years since he was elected, so many more women ran for office that our representation in Congress rose 30 percent. We were still less than half of what we needed for equal representation, but it was real progress. Taylor Swift ignored the backlash the Chicks (then known as the Dixie Chicks) faced a decade earlier for an off-the-cuff political comment, and campaigned for the Equality Act to protect LGBTQ freedom. TV shows like *Shrill*, adapted from Lindy West's memoir, raised the voices of women who didn't fit in sample sizes. Victoria's Secret hired a plus-sized model and ended the fashion show amid allegations of sexual harassment.

But the tide swept out and Trump easily dodged impeachment. Who knew we needed rules against making up your own rules? It was the real live version of "The Emperor's New Clothes," but the powerful males still swore he was dressed. The *New York Times* reported a backlash against #MeToo and a rise in domestic violence. Men claimed they were the victims of the movement. Disgraced entertainers like Louis C. K. used it to make splashy comebacks.

All I could do to stay sane was say the Serenity Prayer every morning and focus on what I could control. I wasn't alone there, either. Self-care became an exploding market with stores and social media influencers. I bought tickets in advance to attend the ballet, concerts, weddings, and a month-long anniversary trip, with fingers crossed for 2020. Then the ball dropped.

By March, for the first time in history, every human being was on the same side, fighting a common enemy: the coronavirus. Not only was the threat of death all too real, but the *Atlantic* proclaimed that COVID-19 was a "disaster for feminism."[4] Quarantining families fell back into old-fashioned gender roles. While men claimed to be doing an equal share of childcare, housework, and home schooling, women disagreed.[5] Those women lucky enough to be able to earn money from home were under even more financial pressure amid the emotional upheaval. Many would opt out of the workplace entirely; the ones who hoped to return were destined to face an uphill climb back. The challenge of keeping everyone calm doubled the caregiving stress.

For those quarantined with abusive men, the stakes were even higher. Early figures following stay-at-home orders around the world showed a 30 percent increase[6] in reports of domestic violence. UN Women, the United Nations entity dedicated to gender equality, called it a "shadow pandemic."[7]

The fourth wave of feminism truly broke into the mainstream the moment that George Floyd, a Black American, was murdered by white policemen in plain view of the nation. This wave had been gaining speed and power for many years, following other unjust deaths and the work of women—especially women of color—striving for inclusion and intersectionality. White nationalist, armed men, who Trump considered "very fine people," entered government buildings without censure. It felt absurd to debate the patriotism of Colin Kaepernick taking a knee in front of the flag to highlight social justice and police brutality, especially in a sport that is overwhelmingly Black. Wealthy white pro football team owners who "blackballed" Kaepernick called it a financial decision. But the incidences of police violence had grown to include over 1,000 deaths per year, with a disproportionate number of attacks against people of color. So an entire nation stuck at home, frustrated by the lack of work and a justified fear of mortality, watched a white police officer take his time to suffocate a black man with his knee. Now we had all seen a human being die. Black Lives Matter became the most inclusive movement for equality that this nation has ever seen.

During the Miss America protests of 1968, while white women protested that the pageant reduced them to meat, the first Miss Black America contestants rehearsed a few blocks up the boardwalk. White women had the privilege to speak out against being prized for beauty, but Black women were still fighting just to be *seen* as beautiful, and to be allowed to be proud of it. The Miss Black America pageant waited to begin after midnight, a few hours after the mainstream pageant had ended, so that reporters would be available to cover it. The strategy worked. The next day, a photograph of Miss Black America was printed on the same page as a photograph of white Miss America.[8] This was proof that Black women were beautiful, too.

But who can gauge the damage that had already been done? Being systematically considered "not beautiful" is an insidious form of oppression buried deep in the mind. In a culture that values the way a woman looks over most other factors, this contributes to inequality within the gender. And it holds all women back in fighting systematic injustice.

The year 2020 marked the centennial anniversary of women getting the vote. And yet, only *white* women were guaranteed the vote that day. It wasn't until 1965—forty-five years later—that the Voting Rights Act prohibited voting discrimination based on sex or color. I was already in kindergarten. My mother was twenty-eight, teaching at Ohio State. The racial infighting of the women's liberation movement of the 1960s and '70s made it easy for the status quo—and Phyllis Schlafly—to divide and conquer the ERA.

Chrissy Teigen, an early donor to provide bail for jailed Black Lives Matter protestors, announced on social media that she was having her breast implants removed. My initial reaction was fury. How dare she influence millions of women as a role model, making us believe that her inflated breasts were what we needed to be beautiful? Halfway through typing an angry Instagram post, I realized I was still responding with judgment about other women's breasts. Teigen had been just as influenced as we all were. Men had paid her money year after year to present her enhanced breasts on the cover of sports magazines. And now she was taking her body back. I continued typing, but with a note of support. This was her body, and I applauded her right to do whatever she wanted with it.

The same goes for Dolly Parton, who announced her interest in posing for *Playboy* for her 75th birthday. Parton joked about wearing the same bunny costume as when she was on the cover at age 32, because her "boobs are the same." *Playboy* suspended publishing during the Covid-19 pandemic, but if her goal is public validation of her beauty, so be it. The voluptuous country star has always refused to be limited to *either/or*, pretty or smart, in favor of *and*. Which is why, soon after the global lockdown, Parton made a million-dollar donation to coronavirus research that helped fund critical early stages of the Moderna vaccine. Next, she broke her life-long political silence to publicly support Black Lives Matter. Parton leveraged our obsession with boobs, not only for her own career, but to fight for social justice.

How wonderful to see that women can be powerful at every age. Yet Parton's category of women represents the most discriminated of all. While she escapes gendered ageism with big boobs and savvy star power, the reality for the majority of American woman is quite different. Our youthful definition of beauty puts those with saggy boobs at risk. Even younger women discriminate against older women. They don't recognize how this contributes to the very problems that will hurt them later. Namely, older women are far more likely to be poor than older men.

This is one of the great failures of a social contract that provides security only as a vested reward for paid service. When the work you perform does not pay, you cease to matter when the job is done. Women lose retirement benefits due to unpaid decades of caregiving, earn less income when they do work, and therefore are less able to save and invest over their lifetime. And most are single. After a lifetime devoted to families and contributing to the workforce, older women are still judged by forces that begin with their bodies. Either they fight the natural aging process with the billion-dollar beauty industry or withdraw to a supporting role of grandmother where looks don't matter. Regardless of what path they choose, they become all but invisible. Shame on us. The power of older women is evident in the progress we have made so far and the momentum that moves us forward. The fourth wave of feminism needs to carry everyone to shore.

• • •

A first-grade photo of my thirty-one-year-old daughter, Juliette, is laminated in a paper frame that reads: President 2030. At the time, I believed we'd have a female president long before that date. In 2016, we had the first major-party nominee in Hilary Clinton. But there was no way white men were going to allow the first woman to follow the first black man into the highest office in the land.

It took a failure of leadership during the most devastating universal plague in recent history to put a woman in the Vice President's chair. And it's no coincidence that she rode in on the tails of an old white man. A heartbeat away from the presidency by default, Kamala Harris visually downplayed her sex. She accepted her role as the first woman elected to the White House in a suffragette-white suit loose enough to hide her figure, with an elegant version of the "pussy bow" designed to mimic a man's tie. In fact, she is known for her preference for men's fashion: blazers with pants instead of skirts; Chuck Taylor sneakers instead of high heels.

As the first female, Black, Asian-American to take that office, Harris embodies a trifecta of firsts. This is the part that gives me pause. While being first is a ceiling-breaking standard, it is also the exception that may prove the rule. This rule could create a tendency to check off all three boxes as one and done. Why have another woman, another Black, and another Asian-American if we've already proved it was possible in one fell swoop? We need to normalize representation by women who put on their bras one strap at a time every morning, just like the majority of Americans.

In spite of the outcome, the 2020 election reinforced the surprising statistics of white women voting once again for a pussy-grabbing misogynist. It's not just a boys-will-be-boys attitude or a willingness to follow their men into the fire. Women voting against women is a deeper example of how gender inequity has made women dependent on men. There is a longstanding belief that working men support their wives so they can stay home and raise the family. Yet it is the women who support the men, with free childcare, meal prep, cleaning, and home management. Without equal pay, childcare, and parental leave, structures readily available in most other countries, American women are dependent long after their beauty and their childbearing value has faded.

White middle-class housewives have a very real fear of financial insecurity. Certainly, their quality of life would not be matched without men. The danger of rebellion creates a Catch-22: they cannot risk supporting the very structures that would free them. In America, money is power. And despite the increasing minority of white men in our population, they continue to control our financial institutions. The Republican creed of individualism expresses the belief that if I can do it, so can you. And if you can't, it's your fault. The Constitution confirms and perpetuates a nation based on a hierarchy of race and gender that blocks the trajectory of a woman's independence.

Until we join together, not just women of all ages, color, and sexual orientation, but people of all genders, physical and mental abilities, and religion, women will be unable to rise to their proper place. From the first wave of fighting for the vote, to the second wave of personal liberation, to the third wave of financial empowerment, we have arrived at the fourth wave of inclusionary equality. The waves are coming faster now.

But equality starts with us. Our obsession with breasts, the part of our bodies that men look at when we first enter a room, is real. It is a fact of life that breasts have the power to feed the next generation as well as to kill us. The question is, how do we respond to that power?

When I get out of the shower, I look at my boobs that still don't match. I began with an obsession to fix them. But now they are both beautiful to me. I can dress them up or down, display them or hide them, make them talk or be silent. I love them.

Responding to the power of the breast also means becoming more aware of how others view my breasts—and breasts in general. This lets me see not only when others peg me based on my gender, but also my tendency to go along with it. That's real power. The more women feel it, the better we'll all be, women and men alike.

It's a boob's life.

Acknowledgments

Thanks to my husband, John Truby, for believing in this book, and for loving me and my boobs in sickness and health. Big hugs for my mother, Dr. Claire Lehr, and my beloved daughters, Juliette and Catherine, for understanding that baring my breasts reveals a bit of their cleavage, too. More hugs for my sister, Tracy, and her daughters, Marie Claire and Josilynn. My love and respect for this family of women inspires me to explore how we live in our world and how we can make the world we live in better.

Thanks to my agent Lisa Leshne, who not only understood what I was trying to say from the start, but fought for me to say it. Thanks to her intrepid assistants, Karisa Chappell Koontz and Samantha Morrice, for all of their help. Thanks to my dad for teaching me to never give up.

I will be forever in debt to my brilliant editors, Jessica Case and Katie McGuire, along with Claiborne Hancock at Pegasus Books. They took a chance on a book that was, like women, neither *either/or*, but *and*. Thanks to the rest of the Pegasus team, including Victoria Wenzel, Andrea Cordova, Kyle Daileda, and to Meaghan O'Brian for her sharp red pencil. Liza Anderson, Caitlin Green, and Whitney Peterson are the PR dream team and I rest better at night knowing Susie Stangland, Arianna Sadlikov and Fauzia Burke have my back in the jungle of social media. Also, I could not focus on the big picture without the fine-print help of Olivia Duell and Cheryl Callighan.

Melissa Oman championed this project from the moment I mentioned it, and it's a blast working with her and Julie Snyder to bring my words to life. Never in a million years could I have imagined being on the phone with the brilliant and beautiful Salma Hayek, let alone hear her say she's 'obsessed' with this book. Her enthusiasm, along with that of Siobhan Flynn and Pepe Tamez, means the world. I'm also incredibly lucky to have Mary Pender and attorney Alan Sacks in my corner.

Everyday I'm grateful for Doctors Janice Spinner, Armando Giuliano, Daniel Leiber, and Jay Calvert, plus Nurse Maggie Perrone, Karen Rinehart, Ann Behringer, and all the others who kept me alive. Much love to all the women out there fighting the good fight and to the families of those we lost, including my sister in pink, Darryle Pollack.

Thanks to all the writers who inspire me and the readers who laugh and cry along. Last but not least, kisses for the women whose friendship keeps me going in writing and life, especially Lisa Vaughan, Cathy Kazan, Janet Orloff, Sheryl Braunstein, Hope Edelman, Lisa Doctor, Debra Smallman, Tamara McDonald, Lynn Valverde, and Hollie Rice. Love your boobs!

Endnotes

One: Obsession

1   Archives of Sexual Behavior, per *Breasts: A Natural and Unnatural History* by Florence Williams.

2   https://www.airplanenoseart.com/

3   http://www.adweek.com/brand-marketing/breast-advertising-140889/

4   http://curioushistorian.comvintage-ads-that-would-never-be-allowed-today/13/Sabrina

Three: Live Nude Women, 1966

1   http://comicsalliance.com/betty-veronica-art-book-dan-decarlo-bruce-timm-review/

2   http://ngscollectors.ning.com/group/outside-looking-in-how-the-world-views-the-yellow-/forum/topics/the-dark-side-of-breasts?commentId=1029239%3AComment%3A99677&groupId=1029239%3AGroup%3A95671

3   John S. Weeren, "Fitful Sleep for Magazine Readers," *Princeton Alumni Weekly*, February 22, 2017, p. 56.

4   http://www.latimes.com/local/california/la-me-hugh-hefner-snap-story.html

5   https://en.wikipedia.org/wiki/Playboy

6   Joan Acocella, "The Girls Next Door: Life in the Centerfold," Book review of *The Playmate Book: Six Decades of Centerfolds* in *The New Yorker*, March 20, 2006.

Four: History According to Breasts, 1967–1970

1   https://www.nytimes.com/2017/08/15/opinion/vietnam-san-francisco-1967-summer.

2   https://www.rogerebert.com/reviews/the-graduate-1967

3   Sister Suffragette, Songwriters: Richard M. Sherman / Robert B. Sherman Sister Suffragette lyrics © Walt Disney Music Company (sung by Glynis Johns)

> *"We're clearly soldiers in petticoats*
> *And dauntless crusaders for woman's votes*
> *Though we adore men individually*
> *We agree that as a group they're rather stupid!*
> *Cast off the shackles of yesterday!*
> *Shoulder to shoulder into the fray!*
> *Our daughters' daughters will adore us*
> *And they'll sign in grateful chorus*
> *"Well done, Sister Suffragette!"*

ENDNOTES

4   http://www.redstockings.org/index.php?option=com_content&view =article&id=65&Itemid=103

5   http://alternativerhetoric.web.unc.edu/photography/miss-america-protest/

6   http://www.nj.gov/state/historical/it-happened-here/ihhnj-er-miss -america.pdf

7   https://deeperconsciousness.wordpress.com/2015/08/06/the-feminism -of-that-girl-and-marlo-thomas-a-brief-history-lesson/

8   Gail Collins, *America's Women* (New York: HarperCollins, 2003), 438.

9   http://plunderbund.com/2014/04/30/the-1970-ohio-state-riots-bigger -and-more-violent-than-Kent-state/

10 "What if you knew her/and found her dead on the ground/how can you run when you know," Neil Young, "Ohio." 45 rpm single by Crosby, Stills, Nash & Young originally recorded May 21, 1970.

11 https://en.wikipedia.org/wiki/Allison_Krause

12 http://www.rogerebert.com/reviews/great-movie-woodstock-1970

13 http://www.missamerica.org

14 http://time.com/3418349/john-oliver-miss-america-pageant -scholarships/

15 Hilary Friedman-Levy, *Here She Is* (Boston: Beacon Press, 2020), 213.

16 Dawn Keetly, *Public Women, Public Words*, vol. 2 (New York: Rowman & Littlefield, 2005), 172.

Beauty Pagents
1   Friedman-Levy, 92.

Five: Smart vs. Pretty, 1972
1   Nora Ephron, "A Few Words About My Breasts," *Esquire*, May 1972.

2   https://www.rogerebert.com/interviews/jayne-mansfield-1933-1967-the-girl -couldnt-help-it

3   June 6, 2016, Womens Leadership Council meeting, Spago's L.A. Also quoted in book, *Fierce Optimism* by Leeza Gibbons.

4   http://www.vanityfair.com/style/2015/08/farrah-fawcett-red-swimsuit-bruce -mcbroom-history-of-fashion or http://www.cnn.com/2009/SHOWBIZ /06/30/farrah.fawcett.poster/index.html?eref=ew

5   http://www.cnn.com/2009/SHOWBIZ/TV/06/25/obit.fawcett/

6   http://snltranscripts.jt.org/77/77amono.phtml

7   *TV Guide*, May 1977 interview with Aaron Spelling, p. 110.

8   http://www.sfgate.com/movies/article/Fawcett-Strips-Dignity-for-Playboy -New-video-2830083.php

ENDNOTES

Cheerleaders: Sis Boom Breasts!

1   https://www.nytimes.com/2018/06/01/sports/nfl-cheerleaders-lawsuit-.html
2   https://www.cnn.com/2020/07/16/us/washington-redskins-sexual
    -harassment-allegations/index.html

Six: California Girls, 1978

1   https://www.youtube.com/watch?v=aBFrYGCU460
2   http://www.thesmokinggun.com/documents/crime/so-you-wanna-be
    -hooters-girl
3   http://www.latimes.com/business/hollywood/la-fi-ct-himi-holland-20170423
    -story.html
4   http://youtube.com/watch?v=YSr5gQAHwBA
5   http://content.time.com/time/magazine/article/0,9171,159040,00.html

Seven: From Ms. To Mom, 1983

1   https://jezebel.com/the-feminist-history-behind-your-floppy-bow-blouse
    -whi-452560822
2   https://www.youtube.com/watch?v=XMKDouP2xeI
3   https://www.asherfergusson.com/raising-a-family-index/
4   http://www.aafp.org/about/policies/all/breastfeeding.html
5   Katie Hinde, "What We Don't Know About Breast Milk," Ted Talks: Society
    and Culture, March 28, 2017, video podcast.
6   http://100photos.time.com/photos/annie-leibovitz-demi-moore
7   http://www.nytimes.com/2005/01/09/magazine/toxic-breast-milk.html
8   http://time.com/3450144/behind-the-cover-are-you-mom-enough/
9   https://www.forbes.com/sites/tarahaelle/2015/08/21/how-toxic-is-your
    -breastmilk/#386f7c3ba1ae
10 https://normalizebreastfeeding.org
11 http://madamenoire.com/612233/smart-women-do-not-breastfeed-in-america/
12 https://www.cdc.gov/breastfeeding/pdf/2014breastfeedingreportcard.pdf
13 https://en.wikipedia.org/wiki/List_of_countries_by_infant_and_under-five
    _mortality_rates
14 https://cdc.gov/reproductivehealht/maternalinfanthealth/infantmortality

Emotional Abuse

1   https://www.liveabout.com/are-you-a-victim-of-emotional-abuse-1102421
2   https://www.unicef-irc.org/publications/pdf/digest6e.pdf
3   http://www.thehotline.org/resources/statistics/
4   https://www.loveisrespect.org/resources/dating-violence-statistics/

ENDNOTES

Ten: Boob Job, 2005

1   https://d2wirczt3b6wjm.cloudfront.net/News/Statistics/2006/plastic-surgery
    -gender-quick-facts-2006.pdf

Breast Augmentation by the Numbers

1   https://www.plasticsurgery.org/documents/News/Statistics/2019/plastic
    -surgery-statistics-full-report-2019.pdf
2   https://www.plasticsurgery.org/reconstructive-procedures/transfeminine-top
    -surgery

Eleven: Peek-a-Boob: Dating, 2006

1   https://www.youtube.com/watch?v=aQNkeugaAMc
2   http://www.washingtonpost.com/wp-dyn/content/article/2007/07/19
    /AR2007071902668.html

Twelve: Dressing for Sex, 2008

1   https://seejane.org/research-informs-empowers/data/
2   https://www.glamour.com/story/fans-apparently-had-a-lot-of-o
3   https://www.cnet.com/news/tomb-raider-alicia-vikander-lara-croft-bust
    -size-under-fire/
4   http://www.celebritynetworth.com/richest-/models/heidi-klum-net-worth/
5   Keziah Weir, "Super Magnate," *Elle*, May 2017, p 50.
6   http://thedreamstress.com/2011/04/queen-victoria's--dress-the-one-that
    -started-it-all/
7   https://fashionista.com/2012/07/the-history-and-future-of-the-couture-bride
8   Gerri Freid Kramer, *The Truth about Eating Disorders*. (New York: Book
    Builders LLC, 2005).
9   Naomi Wolf, "Brideland," in *To Be Real*, edited by Rebecca Walker (New
    York: Anchor Books, 1995), 40.
10 http://www.hollywoodreporter.com/news/e-orders-plastic-surgery-bridal-27905
11 https://www.theatlantic.com/entertainment/archive/2016/06/more
    -likely-to-be-killed-by-a-terrorist-than-to-get-married/485171/
12 https://www.reportlinker.com/p03449654/Global-Bridal-Wear-Industry
    .html?utm_source=GNW

Secrets of Victoria's Secret

1   https://www.businessinsider.com/ed-razek-cmo-victorias-secret-steps-down
    -report-2019-8
2   https://www.statista.com/topics/4819/victoria-s-secret/

Thirteen: Killer Boobs, 2012

1   https://ww5.komen.org/uploadedFiles/_Komen/Content/About_Us/Media
    _Center/Newsroom/breast-cancer-fact-sheet.pdf
2   https://www.ncbi.nlm.nih.gov/pmc/articles/PMC3298674/#__ffn_sectitle
3   Fred Harding, *Breast Cancer: Causes, Prevention, and Cure* (Devon, UK:
    Tekline Publishing, 2006), p. 110.
4   https://ww5.komen.org/AboutUs/AboutUs.html

US Breast Cancer Statistics

1   https://www.breastcancer.org/symptoms/understand_bc/statistics

Fourteen: Chemo Chick, 2013

1   https://sickofpink.com/2015/01/30/chemo-round-3-return-to-chemo-canyon
    -but-1st-a-detour-via-the-bachelor/
2   http://www.dailymail.co.uk/.../Oscars-2013- -Theron-says
    -shaving-head-freeing.html
3   http://www.mirror.co.uk/3am/celebrity-news/charlize-theron-upset-over
    -shaving-2680736
4   https://www.breastcancer.org/research-news/more-women-having
    -reconstruction-after-mx; https://www.ncbi.nlm.nih.gov/pmc/articles
    /PMC5722225/
5   Elsevier Health Sciences: "Significant increase in number of women tested
    for BRCA gene, but many high-risk patients still missing out: Detection of
    mutation carriers is still not being maximized, despite more and more women
    being tested, according to a new study." http://www.sciencedaily.com
    /releases/2017/03/170322092131.htm
6   Lucy Danziger, "Everyday People," *Elle*, August 2017, p. 123.
7   https://premierhealth.com/yourhealhh/women-wisdom-wellness/beware
    -high-levels-of-cortisol-the-sress-hormone
8   https://www.sciencedaily.com/releases/2013/08/130822194143.htm
9   Dr. Kristi Funk, Foreword in *The Pink Moon Lovelies: Empowering Stories of
    Survival* by Nicki Boscia Durlester (CreateSpace, 2013), 2–13.
10 https://www.cancer.org/cancer/breast-cancer/about/how-common-is-breast
    -cancer
11 https://familydoctor.org/caregiver-health-and-wellness/
12 Sophie Bickman, "The Squeeze: Silicon Valley reinvents the Breast
    Pump," *The California Sunday Magazine/Technologies, Los Angeles Times.*
    August 7, 2017, p. 18.
13 https://www.cancercenter.com/cancer-types/breast-cancer/about

14   https://www.nytimes.com//2020/05/20/us/women-economy-jobs-coronavirus
     -gender.html
15   https://www.vox.com/policy-and-politics/2020/5/18/21260209/facebook
     -sheryl-sandburg-interview-lean-in-women-coronavirus
16   Angela Saini, *Inferior: How Science Got Women Wrong—and the New Research
     that's Rewriting the Story*, (Boston: Beacon Press, 2017).
17   https://www.latimes.com/local/lanow/la-me-ln-maryam-mirzakhani-obit
     -20170715-story.html
18   https://www.breastcancer.org/symptoms/understand_bc/statistics

Fifteen: How *Not* to be a Role Model, 2013

1   http://www.eonline.com/news/36072/keeping-you-abreast-of-the-miss
     -usa-pageant
2   https://www.usmagazine.com/stylish/news/carrie-prejean-not-wrong-to-get
     -breast-implants-as-a-christian-20091611/
3   http://freethenipple.com/
4   https://www.elle.com/culture/books/a12119575/nicole-krauss-profile-october
     -2017/
5   https://fashionista.com/2012/01/ever-heard-of-the-brazilian-b-a-firsthand
     -look-into-the-popularity-of-boob-jobs-in-brazil
6   http://www.teen.com/2016/01/22/celebrities/celebrities-who-got-breast
     -surgery-boob-jobs-as-teens/#2
7   http://www.huffingtonpost.com/entry/naya-rivera-says-she-told-all-of-her
     -teachers-about-getting-a-boob-job-in-high-school_us
     _57c6f633e4b078581f106e4d

Breast Myths and Facts

1   https://www.healthline.com/health/third-nipple

Sixteen: Picasso Boobs, 2014

1   https://www.instyle.com/news/Emily-ratajkowski-boobs
2   http://www.nydailynews.com/entertainment/gossip/emily-ratajkowski
     -proves-magazine-photoshopped-lips-breasts-article-1.3500280
3   https://www.looktothestars.org/news/1954-katy-perry-gets-busted-for-charity.
4   http://slate.com/news-and-politics/2013/08/i-heartt-boobies-the-case-that
     -could-decide-the-fate-of-free-soeech-for-students
5   https://www.wired.com/2010/10/ff_futureofbreasts/
6   http://ascopubs.org/doi/abs/10.1200/JCO.2013.52.2284
7   https://www.wired.com/2010/10/ff_futureofbreasts/

8   http://www.foxnews.com/health/2015/02/26/more-butt-lifts-fewer-breast
     -implants-in-2014-says-us-plastic-surgery-report.html
9   http://www.smithsonianmag.com/history/amazon-women-there-any-truth
     -behind-myth-180950188/
10   https://www.youtube.com/watch?v=K5PEJP-wt0k
11   http://melanietesta.com/2014/02/the-grace-to-be-flat-and-fabulous/
12   www.flatandfabulous.org
13   https://hyperallergic.com/253588/too-nude-for-the-news-colbert-on-the
     -arbitrary-censorship-of-art/
14   https://www.theguardian.com/commentisfree/2014/nov/10/topless-keira
     -knightley-2014-breasts
15   http://www.huffingtonpost.com/2014/11/21/temporary-breast-enhancements
     _n_6199390.html
16   http://www.thedailybeast.com/exclusive-sony-hack-reveals-jennifer-lawrence
     -is-paid-less-than-her-male-co-stars
17   https://www.plasticsurgery.org/news/plastic-surgery-statistics
18   Richard Francis Mould, *A century of x-rays and radioactivity in medicine: with
     emphasis on photographic records of the early years* (Bristol: Routledge, 1993).

Seventeen: The Death of Daddy's Girl, 2016

1   http://www.dailywire.com/news/4157/7-quotes-show-donald-trump-doesnt
     -women-amanda-prestigiacomo#
2   http://www.dailywire.com/news/5322/trump-says-nobody-has-more-respect
     -women-me-here-amanda-prestigiacomo
3   https://www.independent.co.uk/news/world/americas/us-elections/donald
     -trump-ivanka-trump-creepiest-most-unsettling-comments-a-roundup
     -a7353876.html
4   http://www.salon.com/2017/09/14/ivanka-trump-has-no-power-as-a-white
     -house-adviser/
5   Saini, *Inferior: How Science Got it Wrong*.
6   http://www.lamag.com/mag-features/female-animators/

Women's Legal Rights

1   https://www.statista.com/statistics/737923/us-population-by-gender/
2   https://cawp.rutgers.edu/election2020-results-tracker

Eighteen: Boobs"R"Us, 2017

1   http://www.thewrap.com/snl-hot-robot-boob-mountain-felicity-jones
     -election-trump/

2   https://en.wikipedia.org/wiki/Gentlemen_Prefer_Blondes_(novel)

3   https://www.standard.co.uk/showbiz/celebrity-news/ryan-gosling-s-sister
     -mandi-sends-twitter-into-meltdown-at-oscars-a3477596.html

4   https://jezebel.com/emma-watsons-feminist-card-is-now-invalid
     -because-she-p-1792995010

5   https://www.youtube.com/watch?v=PPLaQD8TCcg

6   http://www.mercurynews.com/2017/09/17/emmys-offer-more-proof-that
     -womens-breasts-have-taken-over-red-carpet/, https://www.census.gov
     /quickfacts/fact/table/US/PST045217

Nineteen: The Fourth Wave

1   https://www.govinfo.gov/features/susan-b-anthony

2   https://www.hollywoodreporter.com/news/times-up-legal-defense-fund
     -celebrates-one-year-anniversary-1170467

3   https://deadline.com/2018/06/miss-america-cancels-swimsuit-competition
     -wont-judge-appearance-1202403617/

4   https://www.theatlantic.com/international/archive/2020/03/feminism
     -womens-rights-coronavirus-covid19/608302/

5   https://www.nytimes.com/2020/05/06/upshot/pandemic-chores
     -homeschooling-gender.html

6   https://www.ncbi.nlm.nih.go.nlm.v/pmc/articles/PMC7195322

7   https://forbes.com/sites/jackieabramian/2020/7/22/the-covid-pandemic-has
     -escalated-global-domestic-violence/#23d68820173e

8   https://www.nytimes.com/1968/09/09/archives/theres-now-miss-black
     -america.html